"Filled with examples from the careers of successful athletes, plus exercises, which may help readers apply the book's principles to their daily and business lives. Murphy's slant on self-help distinguishes his book from the derivative pack of such guides."

—Publishers Weekly

"Having been involved in top-level international sports for more than twenty years, I have had my share of contact with several members of Shane Murphy's profession. His approach far outshines that of anyone else I have worked with. You would be cheating yourself by not listening to his message."

—Jack Mortell,
Olympic team leader, short-track speed skating, 1994
Olympic head coach, short-track speed skating, 1992
World short-track relay champion, speed skating, 1976

"Shane deals with many elite athletes of varying backgrounds and temperaments, creating for them an atmosphere to achieve optimal performance. He gives direction with a purpose."

—Val Belmonte,
Director, coaching program, U.S. Olympic Hockey

"Shane Murphy is one of the finest people I have ever met. His books and insights will help everyone."

—Charles Davis,
Assistant Athletic Director, Stanford University

The Achievement Zone

An 8-step Guide to Peak
Performance in All Arenas of Life

SHANE MURPHY, PH. D.

BERKLEY BOOKS, NEW YORK

THE ACHIEVEMENT ZONE

A Berkley Book / published by arrangement with
the author

PRINTING HISTORY
G. P. Putnam's Sons edition / June 1996
Berkley trade paperback edition / February 1997

The Putnam Berkley World Wide Web site address is
http://www.berkley.com/berkley

ISBN: 0-425-15622-2

For my brother,

Chris,

the best sport

I've ever known

Contents

Preface

This book is written for anyone who has an interest in answering the question "How can I achieve what I want?" The last decade has seen an explosion in our knowledge of the psychology of excellence. My goal is to share this knowledge with you.

I would like to extend my deepest thanks to the thousands of athletes I have worked with over the years at the United States Olympic Training Center in Colorado Springs. I am always conscious that I have two roles in my work as a sport psychologist, for I am both a teacher and a student of the Achievement Zone. My work owes much to the knowledge athletes have shared with me. Their thoughtful feedback often provides me with new insights that help me understand the process of achieving success. I can never thank them enough for all the wonderful lessons and the great experiences. I hope this book at least partially repays my debt of gratitude.

More than ten years of modern sport psychology research, my own and others', is presented in these pages. I could not have made the progress described in this book without the stimulation and encouragement of my colleagues, but I take sole responsibility for the ideas I present.

To give you a feel for the work involved in mind/body training, I provide many examples of my experiences with Olympic athletes. In all cases where I discuss a client, I have maintained confidentiality by disguising the details of the situation while preserving the accuracy of the events that occurred. I describe these clients using only a changed first name.

However, I also thought you would like to hear about the Achievement Zone from athletes themselves. To present their ideas, I interviewed a number of Olympians and world champions just for this book. I hope you will enjoy the insights they shared with me. When an athlete's full name is used in these pages, I have either interviewed the athlete for the explicit purpose of citing him or her in this book or I have drawn a published quote from a television or newspaper interview.

I have included notes on all the scientific studies of the Achievement Zone that I discuss. These notes are presented at the end of the book.

Introduction

What does it take to do your very best, even when the pressure is on? Have you ever watched Olympic athletes as they compete and wondered how they deal with the turmoil they experience?

I will show you how Olympians learn to deal with pressure. Let's look ahead, to the Winter Olympic Games in Salt Lake City in 2002. I want you to meet Kerry, a competitor in figure skating. The first time I met Kerry she was twelve, a young hopeful working out at the Olympic Training Center in Colorado Springs. Now, in 2002, she is competing for her country against the best in the world.

A slender figure steps onto the surface of the Olympic Ice Palace. Arms stretched out, leaning forward, her body carves through the brilliant light pouring down from above. Kerry looks serene, although inside she is brimming with emotion. For an instant she thinks about the pressures facing her. *This is it, the Olympics. I've been skating for twelve years for this moment. Mom and Dad have sacrificed so much for me to be here. Now I'm so close I can almost touch it. I'm nervous; I can feel my heart pounding in my chest—I wonder if people can see it?*

But Kerry has prepared for years for the pressures of this moment. She will not let her emotions get the better of her. Her skates trace intricate gossamer patterns on the ice as she glides toward the center of the rink. She takes three deep breaths, feeling the cold, dry air bite into her lungs. It's a familiar feeling, and it helps her become calm. During the briefest moment Kerry mentally rehearses the start of her program. She pauses, looks up with a delicate tilt of her chin, and is ready to begin.

The music starts, and the twenty-year-old flows into her program, displaying artistry and power. She thinks, *The next jump is my combination. Go in fast and explode on the takeoff.* Kerry hits the jump perfectly, and the crowd roars in approval. More than 20,000 spectators are at the Ice Palace watching the Ladies' Original Program. It's estimated that more than 500 million people are watching this performance on television worldwide, but Kerry never thinks about the audience. Her concentration is focused with unerring intensity on this moment in time. Nothing else exists except the performance. Her mind and body are working together in perfect harmony.

As Kerry's program enters the fourth minute, her body is challenged by the fatigue of aching muscles. Her heart rate has been at least 190 beats per minute during the entire performance. Still, she looks poised and confident, belying the pain she is feeling. She thinks, *Power it home, give it everything for a big finish,* and she feels new energy surging into her tired body. Her aching muscles cause a wobble as she begins a challenging sit-spin combination, but immediately she reacts. She corrects the error and thinks, *Keep focused; concentrate on my technique; I've done this spin hundreds of times.* It looks terrific.

Now the program concludes and the crowd is rising, standing to give her a thunderous ovation. On the night when she had to have everything together, the young skater has given the performance of her life. She will wait to see the conclusion of her competition and whether she will receive the medal she has dreamed about. No matter what the result, however, Kerry knows she has won the most important battle—the battle to be her best.

How can elite athletes give such amazing performances when they are under so much pressure? The answer is that top athletes not only perfect their physical skills, they also train to master the psychological skills that allow them to deliver their best in competition. Kerry, for example, is like many athletes who have worked with me over the years. She knows that she must learn the mental skills of competition now in order to achieve excellence in the future.

Working with her coach, Kerry and I have put together a training plan to help her learn the psychological skills necessary to compete at the highest level. Kerry believes her training will help her achieve the goal of competing in the 2002 Olympics. Then, she hopes to be able to give the perfect performance I just described, mind and body working together for success. When it all comes together, athletes call it being in the Zone.

For over a decade, I've been helping people reach their own Zones, the level of mind/body harmony that allows them to achieve their goals. In 1987, I became the first full-time sport psychologist at the United States Olympic Committee's Training Center in Colorado Springs. Since then, I have worked every day with America's best athletes. In this book, I will share what I have learned about reaching the Zone from my research and my everyday work with athletes.

I will also tell you about the exciting finding that people from all walks of life can reach their personal Zone. I will show you how you can reach your maximum level of productivity, your own Achievement Zone. For several years, I have been working with clients from businesses large and small, teaching them the skills of success that I use with Olympic athletes. My clients tell me that the skills I teach help them achieve their best under pressure, allow them to stay focused during difficult tasks, and enable them to enjoy even the most challenging assignments. Psychologically, the world of corporate competition is very similar to the world of athletic competition!

Clients from many walks of life have told me of Zone experiences very similar to those of the athletes I work with. The process of achieving excellence seems to be the same no matter what the field of endeavor. I've taught the skills described in this book to bankers, pilots, educators, nuclear engineers, artists and performers, computer programmers, saleswomen, and students. In an era of corporate reengineering, downsizing, rightsizing, takeovers, and constant change, these are the skills that guarantee personal success in the workplace. Everyone can benefit from learning how to maximize their performance and reach their Achievement Zone. I'll show you how.

In the Zone

Athletes recognize the Zone as a special place where their performance is exceptional and consistent, automatic and flowing. An athlete is able to ignore all the pressures and let his or her body deliver the performance that has been learned so well. Competition is fun and exciting.

Recently I asked athletes at the Olympic Training Center to describe the Zone for me. An Olympic figure skater described it as "the performance where everything clicks. It's very fun to be in. No worries are present."

A U.S.A. rowing team member explained: "The Zone is the level of concentration, emotion, and confidence that you know makes you do your best. I usually feel relaxed, yet I am psyched at the same time. Everything is in the right balance. I'm confident, but I know I have to make it happen. I don't worry about outside factors."

One of the members of the U.S.A. ski team at Lillehammer described it this way: "My performance is always good in the Zone. I go into my run knowing that I can do it well. Even if I make a mistake, I'm quick to recover, and I don't let it affect the rest of my performance."

And one gymnast commented simply: "In the Zone there are no parts—only one whole experience."

Other terms have been used to express the same idea—"in sync," "in the groove," "playing unconscious"—but the expression "the Zone" is the one that has stuck. Whenever your concentration is highest and you're doing your very best, at work or at play, you're in your Achievement Zone.

How often does this occur? For most of us the sad answer is, not often enough. The ability is there. You know that your very best is achievable. Standing in your way, however, are all sorts of barriers to success. Sometimes there just isn't enough time to do your best work. Other times, too many competing demands pull you in conflicting directions. More often than not, even when well-prepared, you succumb to the pressure of competition.

How Can You Reach the Achievement Zone?

Most people consider the experience of the Achievement Zone to be rare and beyond their control. It's been described as an unattainable, almost mystical level of consciousness. But this is a myth. Research by sport psychologists has demonstrated that performing in the Achievement Zone is an experience available to everyone. It's an ability we can *all learn*. Athletes don't know how to perform at their best in competitive situations instinctively. They spend as much time practicing their competitive mental skills as they do their physical ones. What's missing for most people is knowledge of these mind/body skills and how to use them. But the eight skills that yield consistent performance in the Achievement Zone can be learned and practiced by anyone with the desire to excel.

Psychologist Dorsey Edmundson, from the University of Georgia, examined whether athletes learning about the mind/body skills change their behavior after training. In a study he conducted with Dr. Sean McCann and me at the Olympic Training Center in Colorado Springs, he found that athletes show dramatic changes in their behavior after mind/body skills training.

He taught athletes four of the mind/body skills you will learn: Keeping Cool, Creative Thinking, Productive Analysis, and Action Focus. The athletes used these skills little before he worked with them. But when he introduced a new skill, they quickly learned it and continued to use it frequently, even twenty weeks after training. The athletes reported that the mind/body skills they learned greatly helped their sports performance. Remember, these were athletes training for the Olympics. This shows me that even high-level performers can improve when they learn about the skills that enable them to reach the Achievement Zone.

Fascinating studies such as this are taking place all over the country. Sport psychologists, neuroscientists, and other experts are learning more every day about the mind/body skills necessary for success. Already, these ideas are having an impact on fields such as education and medicine. Schools that are using the mind/body skills in their student training are finding that students can learn better and faster when they adopt such an approach. Today, we are moving toward a scientific understanding of success, of what it takes to fulfill human potential. We don't have to rely on "commonsense" approaches, on secondhand advice, or on the opinions of gurus. Join me, then, as I take you on a journey to your own Achievement Zone.

Sport Psychology:

The Science of Success

I remember my first encounter with the Achievement Zone as clearly as if it were yesterday. I was fourteen years old and playing with five teammates in a district championship tennis final. We had worked hard all season to be the top team going into the playoffs, and we were rewarded with the number-one seed in the postseason. The final began horribly as we lost our first two doubles sets, 6–2, 6–2. A sudden thunderstorm gave us a brief respite. As we sat waiting for the skies to clear, we heard our opponents discussing what the championship trophy would look like in their clubhouse. We were furious! We had sweated blood and tears all season to be the top team, and now our final rival was gloating over what we'd hoped would be our prize. My friend David, the most reserved member of our team, stood up, looked at the rest of us, and said, "Let's go out and show them."

What followed amazed me. As we played our set, everything seemed to happen in slow motion. I felt I had all the time in the world to plan what I was going to do.

Here comes the ball. One of them is at the net, but he's too close to the center. If I go down the line with my forehand we win the point . . . *and bang! The ball would fly off my racket and do just what I had envisioned.*

Our team went out and made an incredible comeback to win the next three sets, 6–0, 6–0, 6–1. Although the final was due to be played over nine sets, our match was all over after seven. I remember the emotions our team experienced as we shook hands at the match's conclusion. It was not so much triumph as a shared feeling of wonder at how well we had played. I walked away from the courts thinking, Why can't I play like that all the time?

My ongoing interest in the answer to that question was one of the reasons I became a sport psychologist. Others like me have also sought to understand the conditions that create excellent performance. The result of our efforts has been an increase in our knowledge of what it takes to achieve excellence.

Sport Psychology

In 1986, Ingrid Kristiansen smashed the old world record in the 10,000 meters on her home track in Oslo. Afterward, she gave credit for her win not only to her physical training but also to her mental preparation. "I train for conditioning, but I have worked on my head, too," she said. "A sport psychologist has taught me a lot about being positive, about how a record breaker is simply one who goes first. If one does, other runners soon follow. There's nothing special but the timing, so there's no need to be afraid."

After American speed skater Dan Jansen broke his medal drought at the 1994 Lillehammer Olympics by winning the 1,000 meters, he spoke openly about the role mental training had played in his victory. Jansen described how he had worked with sport psychologist Dr. Jim Loehr to help him think more confidently about the 1,000-meter race, which was not his strongest event. His extra preparation paid off when a slip in his best event, the 500 meters, cost him a medal. This made the 1,000-meter race his last-ditch chance for an Olympic medal in an otherwise splendid career. Jansen came through in the clutch.

In 1987, unheralded young Australian Pat Cash defeated favorite Ivan Lendl in straight sets in the Wimbledon final. By doing so he denied Lendl the grass-court crown that was to elude him throughout his career. When Cash climbed up into the stands to hug his father, the sport psychologist who had worked with Cash, Jeff Bond, was right next to him, applauding proudly.

When young athletes training to make the Olympic Games go to the splendid new facilities at the Olympic Training Center in Colorado Springs, they work not only with coaches, physiologists, and nutrition experts, but also with sport psychologists. These experts in the mental side of sport teach athletes how to harness the power of their minds for more effective performance. Since my first Olympics in Seoul, sport psychologists have traveled with every U.S.A. Olympic team, and they also work with most of the U.S.A.'s national teams in the varied Olympic sports.

What is sport psychology, and why has it emerged at the forefront of modern breakthroughs in our understanding of high-level performance?

The New Science of Success

In many ways, sport psychologists have been groundbreakers in the study of human performance excellence. Understanding how people perform at their very best is a critical undertaking. Surgeons, airline pilots, military staff, executives, equipment operators, and many other skilled personnel must perform at their best for the safety or the satisfaction of others. But only in the area of sport has the mind/body connection and its relationship to performance been researched seriously.

You might wonder what you can learn from athletes and their experience of the Zone. The answer is, plenty! Athletes know all about the pressures of competition. Their careers are determined by how well they do against others. They can't hide from evaluation—their performance is out in front for everyone to see. In this demanding environment they have developed the competitive skills necessary to survive and excel. These skills can be used by anyone who works in a competitive environment. Being able to do your best when the pressure's on is as important for businesspeople, salespeople, professionals, and students as it is for athletes.

How well do you perform in competitive situations? Do you look forward to public presentations and formal evaluations with excitement, or do you dread the thought of them? Are you known as a "pressure performer" or do you wish you could do better when the pressure is on? Developing the skills to reach your Achievement Zone in competitive situations is the key to successfully handling pressure. Consider the following situations.

I recently consulted with four people trying to establish their own company. They were frustrated by a run of failures in landing new contracts. In the most recent setback, the group had prepared thoroughly for their final presentation to a potential client. The team members knew their material forward and backward and were very keen to win the account. But despite the preparation and high stakes, the presentation was flat and mundane. The account went to a competitor.

Another client I saw was a young lawyer, Jeff, who came to me after failing the bar exam. Jeff is smart and cocky, and his friends believed he would pass easily. But he got nervous during the final week of preparation. *If I don't pass now, I'll never get another chance*, he thought. He studied overtime to regain his confidence. On exam day he was tired and confused. The exam was a nightmare, and Jeff failed.

These situations have something in common. The people involved had the technical skills and the training to get the job done. But they failed to reach their goal. When the pressure was on, the sales team and Jeff both performed below expectations. The reason? They had the technical skills but not the competitive skills they needed for success. Their desire for the result they wanted was excellent, but they didn't know how to achieve it.

I've worked with many people in similar situations, and I've found that these results occur when people perform outside their Achievement Zone. They allow the pressure to make them tense, and they do less than their best. I've discovered that they can succeed in pressure situations by learning the same skills used by elite athletes.

In Search of the Skills of Success

Why is it that sometimes we perform to the very best of our capabilities, but at other times we accomplish much less than possible? Sport psychologists have been studying elite athletes for years in order to understand the answer to this question. They have used several techniques to discover the methods that athletes use to reach the Achievement Zone.

One approach used by sport psychologists is to compare successful athletes with those who don't make it to the top. What sets the winner apart? A second approach is to scientifically study the methods used by successful athletes. Sport psychologists compare people who try a task using a new method with people who try the task with no help. If the new approach makes a positive difference, this is evidence that it is important to achieving success.

A third approach is to conduct psychological testing of successful athletes. Sport psychologists ask athletes how they behave under different conditions and how they prepare psychologically for performances. Then they examine the answers to see if there is a consistent pattern related to success. Finally, a very useful approach for understanding success is to ask the great athletes how they reached the top. Interviewing successful competitors has led to much fascinating information on what it takes to succeed.

Using these four methods of inquiry, sport psychologists have discovered that athletic success is determined by two sets of skills.

The first set of skills is **technical.** You must know how to do the job. A gymnast, for example, must thoroughly know all the difficult moves she will perform on the mat and on the balance beam. She must be technically proficient in the skills of jumping, balancing, and somersaulting.

The second set of skills, often ignored until now, allows you to cope with the pressures of competition and deliver your best when the pressure's on. These **mind/body** skills allow you to stay in your Achievement Zone. The gymnast must be able to stay poised and focused at the Olympics, ignoring the glare of television lights and the noise of the crowd. This requires mastery of a very different set of skills, including the ability to calm down, the ability to concentrate, and the skill of refocusing quickly after a mistake.

Identifying the Mind/Body Skills

In 1987, at the Olympic Training Center in Colorado Springs, I began a large-scale effort to synthesize the findings concerning the mind/body skills for success. I used all four of the approaches discussed above to identify what it is that makes top athletes successful. Next, my colleagues in the United Kingdom and Australia helped me put together a test of these abilities. It was a long process; over the years my colleagues and I have tested more than 4,000 elite athletes. I have personally interviewed many more. But the findings are clear: Successful athletes consistently use the same mind/body skills to help them succeed. These skills enable the mind and body to work smoothly together to achieve success. Most important, athletes learn these skills during their training.

Our research, and that of my colleagues, has provided solid evidence that top athletes use some or all of *eight* **mind/body** skills in order to succeed. I'll tell you about our findings in the pages ahead, and show you what they mean for achieving success. The eight skills we have identified, which will be described in detail in the following chapters, are:

1. Action Focus

2. Creative Thinking

3. Productive Analysis

4. Keeping Cool

5. Concentration

6. Emotional Power

7. Energizing

8. Consistency

I have discussed these skills with clients from many other areas besides sport, and they agree that these are the same skills they use for success. Before I describe the eight skills, I'd like you to take the following test to see how well-developed your mind/body skills are right now.

How Good Are Your Mind/Body Skills?

Every reader of this book has already learned some of the mind/body skills necessary for success. But most people haven't mastered all of the skills. You may be very good at using some techniques but weaker when it comes to others. This test will help you determine the mind/body skills you most need to develop.

YOUR MIND/BODY SKILLS

Listed below are sixteen statements describing different approaches to life. Think about each statement and answer true or false.

1. I spend time planning how I will reach my goals.
2. I regularly evaluate whether I have made progress in reaching my goals.
3. Before I perform a task, I imagine being successful.
4. I visualize successfully dealing with things that might go wrong on a project.
5. I keep my thoughts positive when I am performing or presenting in an important situation.
6. I talk positively to myself to get the most out of my performance.
7. I practice using relaxation techniques so I can stay calm under pressure.
8. I am able to relax if I get too nervous.
9. During important tasks, I use reminders to tell myself what I should be concentrating on.
10. I perform effortlessly in evaluative situations without consciously thinking about it.
11. I am able to refocus effectively if I get upset during a project.
12. During an important project I quickly clear emotions that interfere with my performance.
13. I can raise my energy level when necessary.
14. When I need to, I can psych myself up for important situations.
15. I have a specific method of preparing before important tasks.
16. If I encounter a setback, I can rebound and still perform effectively.

If you answered "false" to one or more of the questions in the groups listed below, you should pay particular attention to the corresponding skill. You will probably benefit greatly from learning how to use it successfully.

Scoring Key

Question	Mind/Body Skill
Questions 1 and 2	Action Focus
Questions 3 and 4	Creative Thinking
Questions 5 and 6	Productive Analysis
Questions 7 and 8	Keeping Cool
Questions 9 and 10	Concentration
Questions 11 and 12	Emotional Power
Questions 13 and 14	Energizing
Questions 15 and 16	Consistency

The Eight Mind/Body Skills for Success

Let's take a quick look at what each of these eight skills means, using the words of top athletes themselves.

ACTION FOCUS

This is the skill of knowing how to successfully reach your long-term goals. It requires focusing on the task you need to accomplish rather than on the desired result. It means setting achievable goals as a stepping-stone to ultimate success.

> I don't worry about the final results, but I just do the best I can do. Funny, but I always compete more successfully that way.

> I use a lot of goal-setting in my swimming. I tend to make one long-term goal and then make little steps along the way. As long as I keep moving toward that big goal I don't get flustered if

I miss some of the little ones. That approach helped me set the world record.

CREATIVE THINKING

This is the skill of using your imagination to achieve your goals and solve problems.

Visualization is a key part of sports. That was the reason why I won the bronze medal. I think that if you can't visualize, it's important to practice it. I used to have a tough time visualizing good performance. But I worked on it and got better and better at it.

I imagine success and the feeling of success. I use visualization in workouts, at home, before competitions—everywhere!

PRODUCTIVE ANALYSIS

We all have an inner voice, but if we talk to ourselves negatively we perform poorly. Productive Analysis helps us stay confident. It also helps us identify weaknesses and find ways to improve.

I try not to change things in a big competition. I might feel a little bit off, but I don't focus on that. I focus on the hard work I've done, my training, my coach, the confidence I have in myself. If I start thinking about all the things I can't do, that's when I mess up.

If I swim a bad heat, I say to myself, "Well, it's a morning swim. I'll do better this evening." Then I work on the mistakes I made. My coach tells me how to improve, and I work on those things. I say, "I'll be ready for them tonight."

KEEPING COOL

The Keeping Cool skill allows you to deal with anxiety and prevent panic. Top athletes recognize that they will be nervous before big competitions. They practice skills such as deep breathing and muscle relaxation so they can calm down when the pressure's on.

> *The more relaxed I am, the more often I enter the Zone. I have to take the pressure off myself—and just let things happen.*

> *When I'm in the Zone, I'm calm and relaxed. Confident, yet a little scared, as in "This isn't going to be easy, but I can do it."*

CONCENTRATION

Concentration is the skill of blocking out distractions and focusing on the present challenge. Elite athletes learn to focus their Concentration so that they pay attention only to the things that will help them succeed. As a result, their performance flows smoothly.

> *The Achievement Zone is where everything becomes clear and focused. Nothing bothers you—you know instinctively what to do. You know that whatever happens, your reaction will be the right one. Nothing rattles you.*

> *For me, the Zone is a feeling of absolute focus. It's ultimate concentration on the moment. I tune out everything else but what I'm doing.*

EMOTIONAL POWER

Strong emotions are a natural part of sports. The best performers use their emotions constructively. They learn to deal with the inevitable negative emotions such as disappointment, frustration, and sadness. It's important to be able to refocus after getting upset if you wish to be successful.

If I get upset during practice, I take a quick time-out. I leave the mat and walk around until I cool down. It's dangerous for me to be out there practicing if I'm feeling angry.

Sometimes mistakes happen. It makes a huge difference how you deal with them. I never give up during a practice session, because that's good training for the pressure I'll encounter in competition. Instead, I refocus and keep going until I get it right.

ENERGIZING

Doing your best on a consistent basis takes lots of energy. The skill of Energizing enables you to keep going when you feel like quitting. You need Energizing if you frequently feel tired and worn out.

It's almost as though an extra energy cell were attached to my body.

When I'm in the Zone I feel the adrenaline pulsing through my blood. I'm controlled, focused, and charged with energy. It's like the "flight or fight" sensation can be funneled into my rowing to give me more strength.

CONSISTENCY

Sport psychologists have found that the best athletes prepare very carefully for every performance. They often have a set routine that they follow exactly.

I've learned to prepare carefully before I walk on the court. I must be in the right frame of mind in order to succeed. I let go of distractions and focus on what I need to do to win.

I never take any shot for granted. I go through the same mo-
tions, try to think the same productive thoughts, on every shot.
That way, I'm fully prepared to deal with the pressure of a six-
footer at the eighteenth to win a major. For me, it's like every
other shot I play.

What does it take to reach the Achievement Zone? The eight
mind/body skills I've identified are crucial for successful performance. Some of these skills are used on a daily basis by successful
people. Other skills are used only when needed—for example,
when dealing with distractions. But all eight skills are needed at
some time to consistently reach the Achievement Zone.

Using This Book

Each skill is presented in its own chapter. You don't need to master
the first skill (Action Focus) before you begin the second (Creative
Thinking). Feel free to jump around. But the final skill, Consistency, makes the most sense if you study it last.

I've included lots of exercises for you to do. I know from working with thousands of clients that people learn best by doing. So
don't just read this book. Try out the skills for yourself! You don't
need to go into a deep trance in the lotus position to learn these
mind/body skills. You'll find that you can use them anywhere: at
the office, while working at the computer, at your desk, while jogging, or during a presentation. Put these skills to work for you in all
areas of life.

I've also borrowed an idea from the champion athletes I've
worked with. Most of them keep a diary or logbook where they
write down good ideas. In this way they store up a treasure trove of
useful pieces of advice. If something works well, they make a note
of it. I would like you to try this idea. I would like you to start an
Achievement Zone diary, today. Throughout the book, I will be asking you to write down your observations and thoughts in this diary.

You don't need anything special, just lots of blank pages for writing down your discoveries. Over time, your diary will help you chart your progress—your advances and occasional minor setbacks. It will become a very useful learning tool.

Have Fun in the Achievement Zone!

You are about to begin an exciting journey during which you will discover how you can perform at your maximum potential. It takes practice to learn the skills I describe in the following chapters, but once you have mastered them, I am sure you will use them in every aspect of your life. While I won't promise that they will turn you into an Olympic athlete, I think you will be astonished at how much they will help you accomplish, whether you are an athlete, an artist, a surgeon, or a business executive.

Action Focus:

Achieve Your Life Goals

When I came to the Olympic Training Center in 1987, one of the first athletes I worked with was Stephanie, a seventeen-year-old swimmer. Stephanie believed that she would be on the 1988 Olympic Team, and she was not shy about telling me that this was her objective. When I spoke to her coach and to others in the sport, however, I found that the odds were against her. Young Stephanie was only the sixth-highest-rated American going into the Olympic Trials. But Stephanie was adamant that she would be on the U.S.A. team.

I wondered whether I should tell Stephanie that her goal was unrealistic. Perhaps I could persuade her to lower her sights? But I soon realized that Stephanie had a plan to back up her dream. She began with her objective of making the 1988 Olympic team and worked backward from there. What parts of her stroke did she need to work on? What extra training did she need to do to increase her strength and endurance? How could she in-

crease her speed? What swimmers did she need to compete against to im-prove? Stephanie was very Action Focused, always setting daily and weekly goals and working hard to reach them.

Stephanie had lots of questions. She was unrelenting in her search to find people with the answers she needed. Her coach at the Olympic Training Center, a former Olympic champion himself, was a huge help. The coach helped her design a special training program that went well beyond the usual requirements of an athlete at the Training Center. In the evenings, after the other athletes had gone back to their dormitory, I would often find Stephanie in the gym by herself, doing extra weight work and circuit train-ing. She spent several hours with me every week honing her mental ap-proach to swimming. Her capacity for hard work was amazing.

With her coach's help, Stephanie set goals for every workout and team practice session. For example, in some sessions she worked on reaching a cer-tain pace for every lap. At other times, she focused on improving her tech-nique, asking her coaches for constant feedback about how she was doing.

As she improved, Stephanie kept setting her goals higher and higher. She would be at the pool early in the morning to do either speed work or long swims to build endurance. With the aid of a stopwatch she kept metic-ulous track of her times. She charted her progress on a graph in her room. Her times kept going down.

The Olympic Trials in any sport are grueling, mentally as well as phys-ically. The best athletes in the United States are present, each one vying for those precious spots on the U.S.A. team. A slight mistake and your opportu-nity is gone for another four years—perhaps forever. Stephanie was mag-nificent. Defying the odds, she won her race by inches to wrap up a spot on the Olympic team. She had fulfilled her dream mission.

Never again would I think of throwing cold water on the dreams and hopes of a young Olympic aspirant. I had seen what commitment and the ability to stay focused on action could do.

What Is Action Focus?

Action Focus means being able to concentrate effectively on what you want to accomplish. It means learning to organize yourself around personally meaningful goals and not wasting energy worrying about results. Action Focus means finding satisfaction in personal improvement. Because of our culture's emphasis on short-term victories it is not an easy skill to learn, but it is the most basic mind/body skill for success. Once you learn the skill, you will be amazed at your ability to accomplish your goals.

We set goals all the time. At New Year's we make a list and put it up on the refrigerator door. After reading an article in the paper we're inspired to set a new fitness goal. I see staff at the companies I consult with setting output goals, incentive goals, productivity goals, team goals—you name it.

How effective are we in reaching these goals? The honest answer is: often not as effective as we might hope. For example, how many of your New Year's resolutions are you still keeping four months into the year?

What goals would you like to achieve? Before we begin to explore how to make these dream goals happen, I'd like you to try a simple exercise.

Your Life Goals

Think about three goals you have for the coming year. Choose one goal in each of the following areas:

- Your personal relationships. What do you want to achieve with your spouse, lover, close friends, or family members?
- Your work or education. What career goals do you want to accomplish in the coming year?
- Your favorite activity or sport. What goals do you have in the area of personal fitness or recreation?

Write down these three goals:

My personal relationship goal for the next year is:

My work or education goal for the next year is:

My fitness or sport goal for the next year is:

Keep these goals in mind as you read on. We will return to them in a minute.

Two Approaches to Competition

My colleagues in sport psychology have found that there are two styles used by athletes in competition. My experience tells me that these two styles are found everywhere that competition and evaluation exist. Only one of the styles leads to long-term success.

One way to approach competition is with a **result focus.** Individuals with this orientation to competition are only happy when they are visibly successful. Hank, a marketing representative I met recently, is a good example of someone with a result orientation. Hank constantly worries about what his boss thinks of him. When he gets praise he's on top of the world, but when his boss criticizes him, he's down in the dumps. A good week for Hank is when he makes a lot of successful sales calls. When his success rate drops, his gloom increases. Management are always trying to help Hank focus on other issues, such as customer satisfaction and long-term client retention, but Hank tells them that he's "a bottom-line kind of guy."

The result-focus approach to competition has a number of drawbacks. While people with this focus are keen to win, they won't risk new learning experiences if they think they might fail. This sharply limits their long-term improvement. Also, result-oriented athletes do their best only when they are evenly matched against their opposition. Against weaker opponents they tend to be over-confident, and against stronger opponents they tend to lack confidence. In both cases, their level of performance is not as good as it should be.

Another drawback of this style is that people will sometimes break the rules to maintain their highly successful public image. I've seen this with athletes who take steroids to gain a spot on the Olympic team. The consequences of the widespread adoption of a result focus were evident on Wall Street in the 1980s. When "greed is good" is the motto, the focus is obviously on individual success. Unfortunately, the downside is rampant cheating and a lack of moral, ethical behavior.

The second approach you can take to competition is to adopt an **Action Focus.** With this focus, people concentrate their energies on getting the job done, not on worrying about the praise or rewards they will receive. Instead, their reward is great satisfaction from consistently achieving high goals. The late Sam Walton was a legend in the retailing business. He took his small company, Wal-Mart, from nowhere to become one of the biggest retailers in the country. How? By a focus on every staffer helping to make things happen. "It's terribly important for everyone to get involved," said Mr. Walton. "Our best ideas come from clerks and stockboys." The corporate slogan at Wal-Mart says nothing about profits. Instead, it simply states, "We Care About Our People." The results speak for themselves.

Our sport psychology research shows that athletes with an Action Focus choose new learning opportunities—even when they risk making mistakes—in order to improve their skills. In this way they keep improving. Action-Focused athletes give consistently high effort, and they persist even in the face of failure. This makes them winners, more so than those who focus just on winning.

Individuals can learn an Action Focus, even when they begin with a results focus toward life. Rick McKinney has been at the top of his sport for more than twenty years. A champion archer, his record of success is astonishing: three world championships, four Olympic teams, two silver medals in the Olympics, and five silver medals and one bronze at the world championships. Between 1973 and 1988, every U.S. national championship was won by either Rick McKinney or his archrival, Darryl Pace.

When I asked Rick to comment on his amazing success over such a long period, he told me that his attitude toward competition was the critical factor. "Up until 1977, I competed to beat others and to win competitions. Then, in 1977, I finally won the world championship. I thought I would be so happy. Instead, my experience was the opposite. I was twenty-four years old and had been shooting for thirteen years, and suddenly I thought, *My life is over.* I was depressed for some time after winning that world title. I didn't think there was anything left for me to accomplish. After all, I had proved I was the best in the world. What more could I do?"

What snapped Rick out of his melancholy was the realization that he could still compete against himself. "That was a turning point in my life. Before then I was always comparing myself to others, but I suddenly realized that archery was for me. It was to see how good I could be and how much I could improve. It became fun again." Rick McKinney believes that he became a really good archer only after that realization. He went on to capture the 1983 and 1985 world titles and the 1984 Olympic silver medal—and he's still competing. "I have nothing left to prove, but the challenge is personal," commented Rick. "I still love competition. The drive is still there. When it becomes just work, just winning medals—that's when the drive goes away."

Learn Action Focus

If you examine the "goals" you usually set for yourself, you will find that they are often based on *results*. Yet such a result focus ultimately leads to poor performance and constant unhappiness. To live in the Achievement Zone, you must learn to set a new type of goal for yourself: a goal that emphasizes an Action Focus. Here are the five simple steps of setting effective goals that keep you focused on action:

Action Focus

Step 1. Focus on Concrete, Specific Actions

Step 2. Set Daily and Weekly Goals as Stepping-stones to Your Long-Term Goals

Step 3. Set Hard Goals Rather Than Easy Ones

Step 4. Keep Your Goals Clear and Positive

Step 5. Get Regular Feedback on Your Progress

Step 1. Focus on Concrete, Specific Actions

Winners love to get good results. But they know that to reach the top, they must develop a plan for gaining the results they desire. When I work with an athlete who wants to win the gold medal, I sit down with the athlete and coach and find out what it takes to win the gold in that sport. What actions lead to success in that sport? Then we can develop a plan.

An effective goal is stated in terms of the specific actions you will carry out; it doesn't specify the results you desire. What's the difference between an action and a result, you may ask? Let me show you.

Let's compare a typical "result goal" with a good "action goal." A result goal I often hear is "I'm going to lose weight." The trouble with this goal is that it gives you no direction. What will you do to lose weight? You don't know!

When I tell clients to write down their goal again, describing specific actions, they often make the mistake of making their *results* more specific. For example, the weight watcher above might set a new goal: "I will lose five pounds in the next two weeks, and ten pounds at the end of three months." This is more specific, but it's still not an action goal.

An action goal tells you exactly what you need to do. When someone tells me they want to lose weight, I ask them, "Why?" The usual answers I get are to look good or to be healthy. *Now* we're getting somewhere. To look good, the client must understand how her diet impacts her body. She will learn the importance of trimming fat from her daily intake, and set goals to match. She will learn how to increase her physical activity. For example, the weight watcher might write down goals such as these:

"I'm going to limit myself to fifty grams of fat each day. That means I have to keep track of my fat intake, start buying leaner meat, add grilled fish to my diet, eat smaller portions of high-fat foods, and substitute yogurt for ice cream."

"I will ride my bike around the park for thirty minutes every morning. If I miss my ride, I will go for a brisk walk in the afternoon."

These are totally different types of goals from the first two. Notice that they say *nothing about losing weight.* Instead, they focus on the specific actions the person must carry out in order to achieve the result of looking good.

There are some big differences between action goals and result goals. They make us look at our world differently. Action goals energize us. Result goals worry us. Let's look at the differences, using the example of someone preparing for a business presentation.

Differences Between Action Goals and Result Goals

ACTION GOALS	RESULT GOALS
EXAMPLES:	EXAMPLES:
"Prepare outline."	*"Make a great presentation."*
"Research my facts."	*"Impress the boss."*
"Rehearse with colleagues."	
■ *Focus your attention on what you have to do*	■ *Focus your attention on irrelevant factors*
■ *Are under your control*	■ *Are outside your control*
■ *Produce confidence, concentration*	■ *Produce worry, tension*
■ *Are effective guides to action*	■ *Give you no direction*
■ *Lead to achievement*	■ *Lead to inconsistent performance*

Results are outside your control

Why is it better to focus on action goals rather than on result goals? Because results are outside your control. "But they're not," I can hear many of you arguing. "If I work hard and apply myself, I know I'll get the results I want."

Believe me, I've had this argument many times. The belief that results are under our control shows a fundamental lack of understanding about competition. In sports, for example, there are no guarantees. No matter how hard you train and how well you run the race, someone may be better than you on that day. What can you do if a Carl Lewis races past you and sets the world record?

I worked with a talented young long jumper, Tony, before the 1992 Olympics. He had a good chance of making the U.S. team based on his results in competition. Yet he constantly worried about making the team. All Tony talked about was being on the United States Olympic team and winning a medal. I tried to get him to focus on his workouts, on improving his technique, but all he thought about was how far he was jumping. Was it enough to make the team? At the Olympic Trials in New Orleans his performance was way below expectations. The more he tried to break into the top three, the worse his jumps became. Tony eventually finished sixth, missing his goal by a wide margin. I believe that if I had been able to help him focus on action goals, Tony would have been on the plane to Barcelona instead of watching on television.

I sometimes hear from business clients that their company emphasizes a focus on "the bottom line." Managers punish failures and focus only on successes. Often, this is a recipe for disaster. It leads to a short-term, result-focused way of thinking that stifles employee creativity and sabotages the growth and development of the company. If staff are rewarded only for winning, they will be scared to fail. Yet only by failing do most people learn the important lessons that enable them to ultimately succeed.

At one company I heard a story (perhaps mythical) that makes this point beautifully. When he was a rookie, one of the company's leading figures was placed in charge of a new project that totally failed. His mistakes cost the company a million dollars. After the disaster, the young man went to his boss and handed in his resignation. "What's this?" demanded his boss. "I'm resigning," said the man. "You surely don't want to keep me around after this mess."

"Get back to work," said his boss, tearing up the resignation. "Your training cost me a million dollars. I'll be darned if I'm going to lose you now. You're too valuable." And the young man went on to a very successful career with the company.

In order to break out of the habit of thinking in terms of results, pay attention to setting *action* goals. By doing this, you will have a plan of action you know you can implement. And thinking about executing it will keep you from worrying about results.

Go back to the goals you wrote down in "Your Life Goals." Read them again and mark which ones are action goals and which are result goals. Out of the three goals you wrote down, how many were true action goals? If the answer is:

> 3—Excellent! You have a good understanding of the difference between focusing on actions and focusing on results.

The rest of this chapter may help you learn how to improve your goal-setting skills even more.

2—Good. You tend to set action goals, which will help you reach your Achievement Zone consistently. What is holding you back from setting action goals in that third life area? Lack of knowledge? Too much pressure to reach this goal?

1—The Action Focus skill will help you. You already know how to set action goals (you set one in this exercise), but at the moment you are still focused too much on results.

0—You can definitely benefit from learning to apply Action Focus. Your focus on results is currently preventing you from achieving at the level you desire.

Before you rewrite your goals from "Your Life Goals," let's look at the other four steps to effective goal-setting.

Step 2. Set Daily and Weekly Goals as Stepping-stones to Your Long-term Goals

Setting daily and weekly goals helps increase your productivity and effectiveness. These short-term goals show you the way to reach your long-term objectives, and they serve as measures of the progress you are making toward them.

The best strategy when setting weekly and daily action goals is to *work backward* from your long-term goal. If you want to buy a used car in six months and you need to save $1,000, how much will you need to put away every week?

Some quick arithmetic tells you that you need to save $38.46 each week in order to have $1,000 in six months (not including the interest you would earn in a bank account). If you need to save $38.46 every week, then you must save $7.69 every day, Monday to Friday. Now we're getting somewhere!

How can you save nearly eight dollars a day? How about bringing your lunch to work and skipping eating out? Just empty your pockets of loose change every day and save that money instead of frittering it away on knickknacks. Do you go out for drinks with your friends on Friday evenings? Have one drink and then switch to water—that will save you a few more dollars. Can you carpool on your way to work? That will save on gas. Once you get started, the ideas start flowing.

Once you have a specific, concrete daily goal—**I need to save $7.69 today**—it becomes much easier to do. When you say "I need $1,000 in six months," it seems much more daunting, and you are less likely to even make the effort.

In a study to measure the effectiveness of short-term goals, sport psychologists asked people who were doing weight training to set different types of goals. They found that people who set long-range weight-training goals *plus* some intermediate, stepping-stone goals did much better than people who were just asked to do their best. However, people who set *only* long-range goals did *not* do better than the weight trainers who were asked to do their best.

Swimmer Nelson Diebel, 1992 gold medalist in the 100-meter breaststroke in Barcelona, commented, "I use a lot of goal-setting in my swimming. I tend to make one long-term goal and then make little steps along the way. But it's not vitally important that I make all of the goals along the way as long as I keep moving towards the big goal."

"For example," he continued, "in 1988 I was fifth in the 100-meters breaststroke at the Olympic Trials. But I had only been swimming for a year and a half, so I suddenly realized 'I can *do* this swimming thing!' And I said to myself, 'I want to go to the Olympics in 1992.' But just setting out in 1988 and making my goal the Olympics in 1992 was too far off, it was too nebulous a concept.

"So I had to constantly make little goals—what times I wanted and so on. I figured that if I kept moving forward, one day I would look up from all these little steps I was taking and all of a sudden my big goal would be there. And it was, easily within reach." Diebel concluded, "So having these little short-term goals, these intermediate goals, helps you mentally prepare and also breaks up the monotony of trying for one big goal for an extended period of time."

Start on your goal today. Try the stepping-stone strategy yourself now. Go back to your goals for this year (page 24) and pick one you've been meaning to tackle.

What's the first step toward achieving this goal? Write it down. If you don't know what the first step is, that's your first goal. Find out! Write that goal down!

Find the time to work on that goal *today.* Schedule an hour of your day for that goal right now. If you can't spare an hour, make sure you set aside thirty minutes. If you can't spare thirty minutes, that goal isn't important enough for you. Find a new goal you really want to work on.

Let's look at an example of how this strategy works:

You've just been told that you'll be making a presentation to your division on a new piece of software that you've been working with for a month. You have one week to prepare.

What's the first step? You decide that you need to work through the manual so that you can show others where they can get help. A whole manual in one week! But first you have to study Chapter 1, right? You have some free time at 4 P.M., so you find a quiet spot, take the book and a pen and some paper to take notes, and spend an hour working on Chapter 1. Make brief notes of the important points. You don't have to finish the whole chapter. Just make sure you spend that hour working single-mindedly on Chapter 1.

If you get more done, great. But stop after an hour. Schedule your next study time for later. You lose effectiveness if you spend too much time on something. Remember that great athletes are always careful not to overtrain. They work as hard as they can for a practice session, then they stop and rest.

Using this strategy, you'll find that by the end of the week you're very prepared for your presentation. By getting Action Focused, you'll accomplish a lot more than someone who keeps thinking about how hard it will be to understand the whole manual in just seven days. Your goal isn't to become an expert on the new software, but to show your colleagues how they can use the program effectively.

Don't be afraid to ask for help when setting your weekly and daily goals. The more complicated your long-term goal, the harder it will be to break down into small steps. If you don't know *how* to move forward in small steps toward your long-term goals, it means you need some help working on your plan for success.

All the great athletes depend heavily on good coaches to help them with their goals, so ask yourself who *your* coach can be. If a coach isn't available, think about working on your goals with some friends. Often, the solution to the plan will be easier to see when there are others helping you and telling you their ideas.

Step 3. Set Hard Goals Rather Than Easy Ones

Is it better to set a goal you know you can reach, or to set one that is just a little bit out of reach?

It's better to set the goal you know you can accomplish, right? You don't want to get discouraged by setting goals that are too hard. Best to start on the easy goals first.

Wrong! Athletes who keep improving and moving forward set hard goals for themselves. They set goals that they can reach only with a great deal of effort. An average figure skater working on improving his upper-body strength might set an easy goal of two weight-lifting workouts a week. But the top performer will set a difficult goal of five workouts a week, three with free weights and two on circuit-training equipment. The result? The average figure skater will get a little bit better, but the top performer will make dramatic gains.

Why are hard goals more effective? Because they tap into a basic principle of human nature. We work harder to get things that are out of reach. If you challenge yourself with hard goals, you'll work harder and achieve more. And you'll get much greater satisfaction from your efforts.

This principle is one of the most difficult to follow, because it runs counter to a lot of the messages we hear in our culture. Messages such as "Lose twenty pounds in three weeks without effort" and "Make money the easy way, from the comfort of your own home" are everywhere in our society. There is something seductive and appealing about the thought that we can get something we want quickly and without effort. Deep down we know this idea is wrong, but I know many clients who have spent years pursuing such dreams of the "easy" way to riches and happiness. Inevitably, they are disappointed by the results or they witness their schemes backfiring.

The most dramatic examples of this in the world of sport are athletes who chose to take steroids in an effort to win a medal. Instead, they ended up being caught by the drug-testing system. There are no shortcuts that don't come with a high price.

When I interviewed racewalker and four-time Olympian Carl Scheuler, he mentioned that one of his strengths as a businessman is his attitude toward goals, attitudes he learned in racewalking. "As an assistant director in the City Planning Department of Colorado Springs, I find that having high expectations of myself is important. I learned that in racewalking. You *know* that most of the athletes trying out for the Olympic team at Trials won't make it, so you have to think that you *can*. Your goal has to be that much higher. I find that if I limit myself, if I say 'I can't do that,' then that holds me back. You only go as far as your own expectations."

Industrial-organizational psychologists have also found that in work settings, difficult but realistic goals help workers increase the quality and quantity of work they produce. So set goals that are just out of reach but not out of sight. If you *do* reach your tough goal, you will be delighted and you'll have increased confidence. But if you come up short, you will still have accomplished as much as you would have by setting a nonchallenging goal. It's a no-lose position.

I also suggest that you be flexible in your goals. If you are failing to reach a lot of your goals, change them so that they are more within reach. Otherwise you'll get too frustrated. As one of my colleagues always says to the athletes he works with, "Write your goals with a pencil on paper, don't carve them in stone. That's what an eraser is for!"

Step 4. Keep Your Goals Clear and Positive

Sometimes I come across athletes who get the message that they shouldn't use result goals, such as "I'm going to win this competition." So instead they think they should use such goals as "Just do my best." Oops! They've replaced a result goal with a no-goal!

The coach or colleague who advises you to "do your best" gives you no direction and nothing on which to focus. Setting such goals yourself is similarly fruitless.

When you write down your action goals, make them as precise and clear as possible. State them in the first person whenever you can—for example, "I will . . ." This will help you feel like it's *your* goal. Say, "I will go to the city library on Saturday morning to research and write the accounting proposal," instead of "The accounting proposal will be finished on Saturday."

Don't say don't. It's also important to make your goals positive. It's human nature to concentrate on the last thing you're told. So if a coach tells a young running back, "Don't fumble," it's more likely to make the running back think about fumbling. In contrast, the suggestion "Keep the ball tucked into your chest" is helpful. It's good, specific advice that gives the running back something concrete on which to focus.

The manager who sets a goal such as "We won't lose any existing clients in the third quarter" is making the same mistake. Instead of providing an Action Focus, he's promoting a mistake focus. This typically causes high levels of anxiety and actually hurts performance levels. It's not helpful to focus attention on a problem without providing a solution.

Instead of using "Don't" goals or "We will *not* . . ." goals, think of a possible solution to the target problem. Base the goal on this solution. For example, if a company wants to keep from losing clients, a solution might be to increase client satisfaction. So the goal might be "We will cut our average service response time to customers by fifty percent in the third quarter by using our new computer tracking and paging system." This goal will result in increased customer loyalty.

Step 5. Get Regular Feedback on Your Progress

Feedback is critical for the success of your goal-setting program. I learned this the hard way several years ago when I was promoted from head of a small group of sport psychologists to leader of a department of more than thirty scientists working with all Olympic sports. One of our most pressing problems was a perception that our department was too heavily focused on research and not enough on meeting the needs of our clients. We decided that we could solve this problem if we showed how much work we were doing for our clients. So we began keeping meticulous records of our work, and every three months we produced a report detailing all the hard work we'd done for the various sport groups we worked with.

The effort was a dismal failure. A year later we were still being criticized for doing too much research, and now we also heard the complaint that we were wasting time producing useless reports! We were going backward fast! Fortunately, one of my staff had a bright idea. We solved the problem by asking our clients to *tell us* about the work we were doing. We asked the sports groups we served to report on our progress and to measure the quality of our service delivery. The frequent feedback from our clients not only helped us measure our progress, it also showed the clients (and my boss) exactly what we were doing to help them reach their goals. After another year, we had turned the situation around so dramatically that we had become a model program within the organization. The constant customer feedback made my life as a manager immeasurably easier.

Feedback serves three very important functions.

First, it tells you how well you are doing so that you can make any necessary changes. Second, feedback increases your confidence. Whenever we get positive feedback, we feel good about ourselves, and this makes us more confident for the future. Third, feedback is motivating. You can measure your progress toward your goals. The closer you get, the harder you'll work.

Measure your progress. You can get regular feedback in several ways. One way is to set goals that are measurable, such as how often you do something. Say your goal is to work out at the fitness club five days a week. You can easily keep track of your fitness-club visits in your Achievement Zone diary. At the end of the week you can rate how well you did by the number of visits you made.

Keep score. Another good measure is keeping score. Say your goal is to cut the percentage of calories from fat in your daily diet from 50 percent to 30 percent. Keep track of your daily calories and your daily fat calories and work out the percentage on a daily basis. Over time you can see what sort of progress you're making.

Or say your work goal today is to spend two hours of uninterrupted time in the morning on an important project. Keep track of the time you spent on the project. If you don't reach your two-hour goal, you know that you need to make some changes. Do you take more time in the afternoon to work on the project? Or do you plan how to stop those unwanted phone calls from interrupting you?

Ask others for feedback. Another way to get useful feedback is to ask others to watch you in certain situations. Ask them to tell you how well you're doing on your goal.

I'm often asked to help athletes develop more self-control in pressure situations. A tennis player, for example, might throw her racket, curse under her breath, and bang balls into the fence when she is playing poorly. So I ask her practice partners to keep track of how often she does one of these things in a workout. She asks a friend to watch some matches and keep track of the negative behaviors during a match. The feedback is very useful to the athlete, who is often surprised at how often she loses her cool.

Or let's say a businesswoman has set a goal of becoming more of a contributor on team projects. She asks two of her colleagues to give her feedback after team meetings. They tell her how often she spoke up and suggested an idea to the group. It is a good idea to ask the people you are working with to be very specific with their feedback. For example, a vague "Oh, you were good today" is not nearly as helpful as "I liked the fact that you offered those two ideas on the McKinley project. But did you notice that you didn't say anything while we were talking about the new marketing strategy?" The more specific the feedback, the easier it is to find ways to improve.

Get some coaching. Coaches must be experts in giving good feedback. At the Olympic and professional level, the most important factor in helping athletes improve is the quality of the coaching they get. Good coaches not only point mistakes out to the athlete, they also show how to correct the mistake in the future.

Who are the "coaches" in your life? Who can tell when you're on the wrong course, and is also good enough to suggest how you can get back on track? Athletes cannot survive without such coaching. How about you? Most successful people I work with depend on one or two people for quality feedback. They know it is often easier for another to spot your mistakes than it is for you to pick up mistakes on your own.

These are the five basic steps to achieving an Action Focus. Use these principles and you'll be able to change your natural tendency to worry about results into an effective ability to get the job accomplished.

To give you an idea of how it's done, I'll show you how I helped a group of elite cyclists reach their goals. At the outset they were immobilized by their result goals. But with the help of the five steps they became Action Focused.

FROM RESULTS TO ACTION:
A CYCLING EXAMPLE

When I work with athletes, I often begin by asking them to give me a list of their goals for the coming year. Here's the list I got from a group of young cyclists.

- Break the national record in the pursuit at this year's finals
- Make the Junior World team
- Win my event at Junior World Trials
- Beat John X at this year's Nationals
- Lose weight

This was an admirable list of result goals from a group of highly motivated young people. But they didn't tell the cyclists what they should be doing.

Look at the list of goals from the same group a week later, after they learned how to use the five steps of Action Focus:

- Do a pure speed workout every three days for the next month to help me develop better speed for chases and finishes.
- Work on overcoming my fear of riding with the pack at the end of the race. Practice Keeping Cool exercises every day for fifteen minutes. Next month, begin to use them in practices. In March, begin to use them in races.
- Sit down with my coach and decide the time I need to win at Junior Worlds this year. Set goals for how much I need to improve every month in order to reach this time. Develop a training program with Coach to help me reach these monthly goals, and stick to it.
- Find out some reasons why John X has beaten me the past two years. Talk to coaches and other riders. Make a list

of areas I need to improve and write out a training plan for each area. Start with just two main goals. Also, write down my existing strengths and remind myself of them every day.

- Have my diet checked by a nutritionist. Ask her to help me write out a diet. I need one that will meet my energy needs and my muscle-development needs but that will also help me decrease the percentage of fat in my body. Have Mom and Dad help me stick to my new eating plan.

Can you see how these athletes incorporated what they had learned about Action Focus into their goals? These action goals are much more helpful, and they say little about results.

In order to help you set effective action goals, I've developed the following checklist. You can use it with any goal to see if it's a true action goal.

ACTION FOCUS CHECKLIST

Now we can go back to the goals you wrote down at the beginning of this chapter under "Your Life Goals." Let's try to make them the most helpful goals possible.

Ask yourself the following questions about each goal. Your answer will be "yes" to each question if you have an action goal.

- Does your goal state an action you must carry out? (Step 1)
- Is there a time frame associated with your goal? (Step 2)
- Is your goal challenging? (Step 3)
- Is your goal stated positively? (Step 4)
- Can you get regular feedback on your progress? (Step 5)

If you answered "no" to any of these questions, go back and look at your goal again. Modify it so that you can say "yes" to that question. How close can you get to answering "yes" to all five questions?

Don't worry if you miss some. Even the most successful people have difficulty staying Action Focused all the time. If you're stuck, show your goal to a friend and ask him or her for suggestions.

Use this checklist whenever you take the time to set an important goal. With practice, using these principles will become natural.

It's OK to want results. Just make sure you know how to get them! Sometimes at the end of my workshops a participant wants to know if the Action Focus skill means we should forget about results completely. I get a good chuckle from this question. How could we change such a basic characteristic of human nature as the desire for results? Our dreams, desires, wants, and wishes—aren't these basic to the fabric of our lives? The difference between those who successfully achieve their dreams and those who remain frustrated is the ability to move from desire to action. The following is a story I hope you find both inspiring and instructive. It's a dramatic example of the power of Action Focus.

LYNN'S UNEXPECTED MEDAL

During the 1992 Summer Olympics in Barcelona I received a phone call from an athlete I had worked with several times. Lynn was a veteran in her sport. At the age of twenty-nine, she had realized a lifelong dream by making the 1992 Olympic team. Although Lynn was a wonderful athlete and one of the best in the U.S.A. in her event, she had never had great international success. In fact, her best finish at a major world-level competition had been tenth. When she qualified for the Olympic team, a reporter from one of the major sports magazines actually asked her why she had accepted a place on the team. He felt that she should have stepped aside to let a younger athlete gain the Olympic experience!

When Lynn called me, she was excited but confused. After the first day of competition, with just one day left, she was in third place. Her opening day had exceeded her wildest expectations, and now everyone around her was talking about the Olympic medal that would be such a fitting crown to her long career. But whenever she thought about an Olympic medal, Lynn felt panic-stricken. "What do I do?" she asked. "I can't block out the thought of winning a medal, but when I think about it, I get too nervous to concentrate on tomorrow's competition."

Have you ever felt that way about something you really wanted? The more you wanted it, the more nervous you became? And the more nervous you became, the less likely you were to get what you wanted. Lynn was in that predicament. As we talked I realized that it would do no good for Lynn to practice relaxation exercises and try to forget about the medal. Her desire to achieve her ambition was so strong, she couldn't think about anything else. Instead, I asked Lynn to take some deep breaths and to calmly tell me what an Olympic medal would mean to her.

I asked her to imagine that she really had won a medal, to imagine how it would change her life. At first Lynn was too nervous to even contemplate the reality. But gradually she spoke of the vindication she would feel if she were recognized as one of the world's best. An Olympic medal would bring her fame and recognition, and would be a tremendous help in her career. She would earn more in endorsements and from appearing in competitions.

Lynn had always wanted to work as a commentator in televised sport, and an Olympic medal would give her the visibility she needed to get that opportunity. Perhaps most of all, Lynn felt that a medal would be a wonderful reward for all her work and sacrifices. It would be something she could share with her family, who had given her so much support.

As she spoke about the medal, Lynn's attitude changed. She had been thinking, This can't be happening. I'm so close to winning a medal, I don't believe it. I better not think about it, or it won't happen. Now *she started thinking,* I've worked long and hard for this medal. I deserve it, and it would lead to lots of good things if I won it.

When she tried not *to think about winning a medal, Lynn was really saying to herself that the success wasn't real, that it wouldn't happen. That attitude wouldn't help Lynn during the next day's competition, so I helped her think about the medal in a very real way. I did this by asking her to imagine that she had already won the medal. The next question I asked Lynn was "How are you going to go out there and win that medal tomorrow?"*

As Lynn thought about that, she realized what she had to do. She really did *want that medal. It was time for her to get down to business. Lynn needed to adopt an Action Focus, to concentrate on what* she *needed to do to be successful.*

From past experience she knew that she performed poorly when she got too psyched up, so she would use some skills she had learned to keep her heart rate down and her breathing steady. Fortunately, Lynn had worked with me and with a sport psychologist in her hometown to develop her mind/body skills, and she was confident she could use them successfully under pressure. She imagined she was back home, just practicing with her own coach. This helped her feel comfortable and at ease. We talked about sticking to that game plan, doing it just the way she had planned. We spent only a half hour on the phone, but when we ended Lynn expressed great confidence and optimism about the final day.

The next day I was extra nervous watching, but Lynn performed wonderfully, without even a sign of panic. She was the standout competitor on the second day, and missed a gold medal only because the leader was too far ahead to catch. I had tears in my eyes as they placed the silver medal around her neck, knowing how much that moment meant to her.

To me Lynn's story demonstrates that a desire for results is entirely natural. But when it comes time to perform, you have to put that desire aside and calmly focus on what action steps you need to take to get the job done. It's OK to think about results; just remember what you have to do to get them.

Action Focus Tips

I'll conclude by answering some of the objections I most frequently hear concerning the skill of Action Focus.

■ *It takes too much time. I don't have the time to set goals.* Actually, setting daily action goals will *save* you lots of time. Because action goals guide you so effectively, you will know exactly what you need to do every day. Instead of wasting time wondering "How am I going to do that?" you can get right to work.

■ *I've tried to stick to goals before and failed. I'll probably fail this time, too.* Now that you know how to set daily action goals, you can see that you will never fail to reach your goals. Because they are under your control, if you put in the time and effort you are *certain* to achieve them. If you don't, you need to take a look at the goals again and see where you made a mistake. Perhaps the goal was too vague, or too difficult for a beginner. Modify it and try again.

■ *If I set a goal that everyone can see, then I'm a public failure if I don't reach that goal.* It *does* take guts to set important goals for yourself in life. But there is no other path to achievement. And once you have learned to set personal action goals for yourself, you will find that your worries about failure will greatly decrease. Your action goals will give you positive rewards every day, and you will know you are making steady progress toward your long-term objectives.

Even if some of your long-term goals don't turn out the way you hoped, your record of success and achievement will speak for itself. Once you learn the Action Focus skill, you will be able to stop comparing yourself to others. Instead, you'll judge yourself on how well you are doing in achieving your personal action goals.

■ *I'm not a structured person like that. I prefer to be spontaneous.* Many athletes I work with believe that they have to be highly organized to use goals effectively. Because they don't see themselves as very organized, they don't use goals consistently. The truth is that I have seen all types of people, organized and very disorganized, learn to use goal-setting successfully.

Writing out a set of weekly goals doesn't mean that you have to follow a rigid schedule every day, with every minute planned. It takes just a few minutes every night to check on how well you did on today's goals and put down your goals for the next day. Then, once a week, it takes fifteen to thirty minutes to organize a plan for the next week. And if you don't like writing down goals, don't. Just think about what you want to accomplish, what problems you want to solve. Then do it.

▪ *Does Action Focus mean I shouldn't think about results?* Use your desire for results as a motivator. Why has one of my clients, Jeff, a judo athlete, dedicated the last ten years of life to such an obscure sport, putting his education and relationships on the back burner while training hard every day? In order to have the chance to win an Olympic gold medal. There are many times when Jeff must remind himself *why* he's working so hard and making so many sacrifices. But when he's feeling down, the thought of that Olympic gold keeps him going.

Put your desire for results to work for you in the same way. When you're feeling especially tired or discouraged, bring to mind a picture of the result you're striving for. Think about your child's education, or your new home, or the vacation you've dreamed about. That image will give you the strength to go on.

Understanding Action Focus will help you become much more effective in getting the results you want in life. Learn from the champions, who have discovered the secret of high-level achievement. Expect to succeed. Don't worry about the end result. Focus on your own actions. It's up to you.

How to Learn Action Focus

Step 1 ■
Focus on Concrete, Specific Actions

Step 2 ■
Set Daily and Weekly Goals as Stepping-stones
to Your Long-term Goals

Step 3 ■
Set Hard Goals Rather Than Easy Ones

Step 4 ■
Keep Your Goals Clear and Positive

Step 5 ■
Get Regular Feedback on Your Progress

Creative Thinking:

Use the Power of Your Imagination

In 1956 figure skater Tenley Albright was practicing for the Winter Olympics in Cortina, Italy, when she fell and hurt herself badly. Her left blade hit her right ankle and cut it all the way to the bone. Tenley's father, who was a surgeon, sewed her wound up. With the competition less than two weeks away, Tenley couldn't practice. She didn't know if she would recover in time to compete. And even if she were able to compete, she would have to do so without her usual training and preparation. In the time remaining before the Olympics, Tenley kept imagining her routine and rehearsing it mentally.

"It never occurred to me that I wouldn't compete," recalled Tenley. "Even though I couldn't actually walk on my ankle until just a few days before the event, somehow I was ready. Looking back, I realize it was visualization, the sort of thing that skaters train in now. We did it then by trial and error." By visualizing her program, she was able to retain her compe-

titive edge. With no practice, and on an injured ankle, Tenley Albright went on to win the gold medal in the women's figure skating competition at the 1956 Winter Olympics. She later entered Harvard Medical School and became a surgeon herself.

What Is Creative Thinking?

The essence of Creative Thinking is using your imagination to help you reach your goals. Many people I talk to believe they have little imagination, but I've learned that everyone can think with imagination and creativity. Unfortunately, most of us don't use our imaginations very often, especially on "important" tasks, such as school or work. But learning to use your imagination on a regular basis is a key to performing in your Achievement Zone.

Using Creative Thinking does not necessarily mean being creative in the usual sense of the word. It doesn't have to mean painting a masterpiece or inventing a new technology. Thinking creatively simply means using images and intuition instead of verbal processes and logic. Because education emphasizes analytical thinking, our creative powers are sometimes neglected. When you learn how to use them, you will be astonished to discover the difference your creative abilities can make in your performance. Visualization and the mental rehearsal of difficult situations can be much more beneficial to your performance than just practicing something over and over again!

Learn Creative Thinking

Athletes use Creative Thinking for a variety of purposes: rehearsing routines, planning competition strategies, staying calm under pressure, and dealing with problems and setbacks. My experience teaching thousands of athletes how to use Creative Thinking has shown me that anyone can learn to use imagination to enhance performance.

Over the next several pages I will explain how you can master the power of your imagination and develop your Creative Thinking skill by using the following three steps:

Creative Thinking

Step 1. Develop Your Imagination

Step 2. Imagine How You Will Reach Your Goals
- Plan Ahead
- Learn With Imagination
- Imagine Solutions to Problems

Step 3. Create a Successful Self-image

Once you learn these three steps you will have developed a tremendously powerful tool to help you achieve your full potential in life.

Step 1. Develop Your Imagination

The first step in successful visualization is learning how to make your imagination as vivid, realistic, and detailed as possible. The best way to do this is by involving all of your senses in the process. Let's begin by working to develop the sense that is most familiar to most of us: sight.

Sight. People I work with vary greatly in their ability to use visual imagery. Some people can see in vivid color, three-dimensionally, and with great detail. Others can imagine only the vaguest outlines, without color or detail. But wherever they start with this ability, they have been able to improve with practice—as you can.

Let's begin with an image that will help you move toward your life goals. I'd like you to spend some moments imagining what your dream home looks like. Close your eyes and imagine the home you would like to be in five years from now. Draw on your past experiences to create a vivid picture of your future home. Remember rooms and furnishings you've admired in the past, and see these things in your home.

Imagine how the house or apartment looks from outside. See the color and texture of the walls and roof as clearly as you can. Is it a brick home, or perhaps wood? A condo or a single unit? How many levels does it have? Notice details, such as the look of the doors and the windows. Next, view the home from different angles. Imagine moving inside the home. What does the front entranceway look like? How about the bedrooms, the living room and the kitchen? What features are you looking for in your dream home? An outdoor patio, a Jacuzzi, a large modern kitchen? Add your favorite features to your image and really focus on seeing them in your mind. How are you doing? Give yourself a pat on the back if you can imagine a house you'd really love to live in.

Next, I want you to practice putting yourself into your mental pictures as if you were really there. You may already have done this by instinct. If you haven't, let's practice that now by imagining that you are walking around in the house. What can you see as you look around you? What scenery are you seeing if you look out the window? Are you living in a quiet part of the country, or a bustling sector of the city? Does being in your house seem realistic? If you still need to work on it, pay more attention to details around you when you move around your own home. Later, close your eyes and try to remember these exactly. Keep practicing until you can imagine the experience in detail.

Hearing. The ability to "see" pictures in your mind is only part of the power of imagination. Elite athletes also make use of the other senses, and for some athletes, these are actually stronger and more vivid than the sense of sight.

Many people can hear sounds during an imagined experience. Try it now. Can you recall the voice of someone who is close to you? Can you hear what they are saying? Notice the voice pattern, the rise and fall of the person's speech.

Music can be a particularly powerful imagined experience. I worked with an archer who imagined listening to one of his favorite passages from a Beethoven symphony during breaks in the shooting. This music made him feel calm and strong. Many other athletes today listen to actual recordings of the music they like before or during a performance. They do this to calm down before a competition, or sometimes to psych themselves up for a big effort.

Smell. The sense of smell evokes strong memories. Can you remember a situation where the scents associated with that time or place were particularly vivid?

A professional baseball player I worked with always used images based on the sense of smell when he rehearsed pitching mechanics in his mind. The smell of newly cut grass, the tangy smell of tobacco juice, the leathery smell of the glove, all were used to make his mental picture particularly clear and vivid. "If I can't smell it," he used to say, "then I'm not really there."

Touch. This sense can trigger another rich source of memories. Try to bring to mind a memory that involves the sense of touch.

It might be the recollection of lying on a beach, the gritty feel of the sand beneath you, and the sensation of someone rubbing sunscreen oil on your back and shoulders. You may notice that related memories come with it, such as the smell of the sunscreen lotion or the tang of sea spray in the air.

One of the champion figure skaters I counseled relied primarily on the sense of touch in her visualizations before a competition. First she would imagine the feel of her new dress against her skin, often a novel sensation as she usually received her competition outfit only a week or two before the event. She would feel herself lacing her boots up tightly and walking stiffly on the covered blades. Then she would imagine the cold, dry air of the competition venue, and the crackly feel of the ice beneath her blades. She paid special attention to the feel of the ice, as this was one of the most important things she experienced during her performance. Imagining gliding over the ice with strong, smooth strokes helped her confidence as big competitions approached.

Taste. Many athletes use the sense of taste to create more powerful imagery. Swimmers make their mental rehearsals more real by remembering the taste of the chlorine in the water as they swim up and down the pool. A boxer I knew psyched himself up for fights by remembering the taste of blood in his mouth after a hard punch. Runners I have spoken with prepare for a tough race by recalling the taste of salt as they sweat through the tough process of staying on pace. As you explore the power of your imagination, try enhancing the situations you create in your mind by using taste.

Feel. The athletes I work with tell me that recollecting the feelings they experience as their body moves through its performance is *the* most important part of any image they rehearse. This is called the "kinesthetic" sensation by scientists. But the athletes I work with call it "getting the feel."

Chuck, a professional golfer who consulted with me, went through a little ritual every time he hit the ball. After he took his stance and settled on his grip, he would imagine the feel of a good shot with the club. It took only a few seconds, but he would recall the feel of a good swing. Next, he would concentrate on making the same good swing as he hit the real ball. It took extra effort to do this every time, especially when he was hitting practice balls, but it made Chuck a very consistent golfer and a very successful one.

Getting the feel of a race, or competition, or perhaps just a particular move, may involve actually moving around while imagining the event. When I interviewed gold medal–winning kayaker Norm Bellingham, he described sitting up and pretending he had a paddle in his hands as he rehearsed the strategy of an upcoming race. Elite athletes place a great deal of emphasis on mastering their sport by getting the right "feel" for the skills they practice. To perform a move such as a vault or a dive under the pressure of competition, the athlete must know what a perfect vault or dive feels like. The athlete then knows exactly what she must do. When she goes out in competition, she attempts to perform the move exactly as she felt it.

As you use Creative Thinking to perform at a higher level in your own life, it is important that you first learn what the experience of an excellent performance in your area really feels like, and that you rehearse the feeling in your mind until you have memorized it.

To show you how important adding the feel to an image is, I want you to try the following exercise.

PUT THE FEEL IN YOUR MENTAL PICTURES

First, imagine the following scene. Ideally, you should sit quietly with your eyes closed and have someone read it to you.

Imagine that you can see yourself jogging down a street close to your home on a beautiful autumn day. You are wearing a bright red tracksuit, and as you run, the wind blows the leaves from the street onto a neighbor's lawn. A girl on a bicycle passes you, and you see that she is delivering newspapers. She smiles and waves to you as she passes. There are potholes in the road, and another runner passes you in the opposite direction.

Now I want you to answer two questions about the scene you have just imagined:

1. How vivid was this scene in your imagination? (Give the scene a 1 to 5 rating. 1 is not at all vivid; 5 is very vivid.)

2. How strongly did you feel that you were really there? (A 1 would indicate that you weren't there at all; a 5 would indicate that the scene felt very real to you.)

OK, now I am going to ask you to imagine another situation. Again, the best way is to sit quietly with your eyes closed and have someone read it to you.

You are jogging down a street close to your home on a crisp autumn day. Imagine feeling the cold bite of the air in your nose and throat as you breathe in large gulps of air. Imagine you are jogging easily and smoothly, but you feel pleasantly tired. You notice your heart pounding in your chest. Your leg muscles are tired, especially the calf and thigh. Feel your feet slapping against the pavement. As you run, the warm sweat gathers on your body. Imagine the sensation of your tracksuit against your skin, warm and soft.

Now please answer the same two questions about the scene you have just imagined.

1. How vivid was this scene in your imagination? (Give the scene a 1 to 5 rating. 1 is not at all vivid; 5 is very vivid.)

2. How strongly did you feel that you were really there? (A 1 would indicate that you weren't there at all; a 5 would indicate that the scene felt very real to you.)

Which scene received a higher rating?

When I ask people to do this exercise, 80 percent of them tell me that the second scene was more vivid and that it made them feel as if they were actually there. The difference between the two scenes is that in the first I described it from a visual point of view only, whereas in the second scene I added suggestions to "get the feel" of the scene. By adding the feel to situations you imagine, they become clearer, more vivid, and more real. This is important as you learn to develop your Creative Thinking.

To practice adding feel to your imagination, let's return to your dream house. Spend some moments imagining yourself in the home of your dreams, and this time really get the feel of your ideal domicile. If you have stairs, imagine walking up them. Feel the muscles working as you climb the stairs. Imagine lying down on a bed. Relax and enjoy the feeling of your muscles unwinding, the softness of the bed beneath you. Take a bath and luxuriate in the warm water, surrounded by fragrant bubbles. Use the five senses plus the sense of feel to give this image of your dream home clarity and intensity.

When you open your eyes, you have a powerful feeling of the sort of home you'd love to live in. You can use this type of imagery to help you stay motivated. For example, if you're saving for a home, visualizing your goal can give you extra energy to put in more hours on a tough assignment at work. Adding different senses and feel to your imagination brings it alive.

Emotions. When you added the feel of your body into the mental pictures you created, you might have noticed that you remembered various emotions as well. This is very common. Once you start to get the hang of Creative Thinking, you will find that it's easy to recollect strong emotional experiences. Sometimes you might feel as if you were living them over again. Let's look at the role of emotion in enhancing our pictures in the mind, the last step in building your imagination.

Remember the happiest experience you have had recently. Use all five of your senses, as we practiced earlier, to re-create that picture in your mind as clearly as possible. Where were you? What was happening? Who was there? Are there any sounds you remember as part of that event? Don't forget to add the feel to the scene. How was your body feeling at that time? Were you moving around or were you still?

Now we can add the emotional memory to this picture. Remember how happy you felt. Focus in on the happiness and allow yourself to experience it again. Like taking a bath, step right into that happy feeling and allow it to wash over you. What sensations and changes do you notice in your body as you experience this happiness? Does your heart pound in your chest? Do you feel extra energy? Are there butterflies in your stomach, or is it a different feeling entirely? Do you feel like crying, you are so happy? Just allow yourself to experience those emotions for a moment or two more.

Before we continue, may I ask you a question? How do you

feel *right now?* If you are like most of my clients, this feeling of happiness will stay with you. You will notice that the physical sensations of the emotion remain, even after you stop imagining the situation. This ability to create real emotions via imagery is remarkable. It can be used to help you learn to handle emotional and stressful situations successfully.

Think of your imagination as you would a muscle, say your biceps. If you never give your biceps a workout, they'll end up flabby, out of shape. But if you use them often, they'll be in great condition. Your imagination works the same way. The more you use it, the stronger it will be for you when you really need it. In the next section I will show you how to put your imagination to work.

Step 2. Imagine How You Will Reach Your Goals

Now that you have learned how to use your imagination, let's look at the different applications for this ability. Creative Thinking can be extremely helpful in accomplishing the goals you have laid out with the Action Focus skill. Here are three ways you can use Creative Thinking to accomplish your goals:

- Plan Ahead
- Learn with Imagination
- Imagine Solutions to Problems

As you become more skilled you will discover many additional ways to use Creative Thinking to help you achieve success.

Plan Ahead

Gustav Weder, the great Swiss bobsled driver, talked about his use of the power of imagination at the Olympics in Lillehammer. He described how he used visualization to help him win a gold medal in the two-man event and a silver in the four-man. A year before the Games, Weder traveled to Lillehammer to preview the Olympic bobsled course. He took more than forty photos of the course, capturing every curve and straight on film. Weder paid particular attention to the entrances and exits of each curve.

When he returned home, he laid out the entire course, photo by photo, on his living-room floor. Each day he sat in front of the photos and practiced driving the course for an hour. He mentally rehearsed the course in his mind, practicing every turn and challenge on that icy, steep slope. Weder describes how he learned about each curve on the course. "In Curve One, I see I have to let him [the sled] go in and steer in the middle of the curve. Then in Curve Two I must hold my line at the entrance, let him go in very deep, and take him out up high." As he speaks, Weder's hands move as if he's steering the sled. With his eyes closed, his body leans one way and then the other as he navigates the course in his mind.

By the time Weder got to the Olympic Games, he was carefully prepared. His knowledge of the course, gained through imaginary rehearsal, helped him master all the challenges thrown at him. That's how you win a gold medal!

Sometimes you might hear it said that if you can visualize your goals clearly, they will happen. My work with Olympic champions indicates that this is not exactly true. Just because you visualize something does not make it happen. Gustav Weder did not simply dream about gold medals. He practiced—**in his imagination**—exactly how he was going to win Olympic competitions. This approach—planning every step of an event—allows you to rehearse situations that you can't reproduce. It's an important approach in business as well as in sport.

Corporate leaders I work with tell me how important it is for them to provide a **vision** of the future to their staff. This vision encapsulates the long-term goals of the company, and is often summarized in a mission statement. I believe that it is even more important for you, as an individual, to develop a vision of your career path. Where do you want to be five years from now? Use Creative Thinking to imagine several possibilities that appeal to you. The more real you can make your image, the easier it will be to see the concrete steps you must take to make that vision a reality. Use your imagination to picture the path to your goal. Really feel yourself moving down that path toward your goal. Keep practicing. The more you imagine the scenario, the better you will become at it.

At a recent camp I conducted for the national whitewater canoe/kayak team, I had the pleasure of discussing with world champions Davey and Cathy Hearn how they used Creative Thinking in their sport. In whitewater paddling, athletes must navigate a set course down a stretch of turbulent river. There are rocks and foaming white water in every direction, and the paddlers have to successfully navigate their craft down the river and through "gates," poles suspended above the river from wires stretching from bank to bank.

The athletes have to decide how they should paddle down the course once it is set. Should they try a safe, conservative move to get from Gate 17 to 18, or can they take a risk and go for it? They know that a mistake can cost them the race if they guess wrong. The challenge is that they do not get to take a test run on the course before the race starts. Their first run down the course is their first run in the race—it counts!

Cathy Hearn described how she deals with this problem. She walks along the banks of the river once the gates have been set up and visualizes that she is out paddling on the course. She looks carefully at the river, the waves, and the current. Based on experience, she decides on the best strategy for navigating that section of the course. Cathy closes her eyes and imagines doing it just that way, to see if it works.

If it doesn't, she tries another strategy. In this way, she paddles the whole course in her mind and plans out the race. This saves her many valuable seconds as she strives to be the fastest woman down the course. Cathy attributes much of her international success to this ability to use Creative Thinking.

Her brother, Davey Hearn, the 1995 world champion, described a similar use of mental imagery and added that he tries to give as much detail as possible to his vision of the river. That makes his imagery more realistic and gives him a better chance of planning a successful strategy.

You can adopt the same winning approach in your life. The power of imagination can be used very effectively to plan ahead and rehearse success. Remember when I showed you how to re-create your emotions through visualization earlier in the chapter? The next example will show you how to use this skill to prepare for pressure-filled situations.

SALLY'S OLYMPIC DILEMMA

Before the 1992 Olympics in Barcelona, I was working with a top woman athlete, Sally, who had a legitimate chance to win a gold medal. She was concerned because her event took place the first morning of the Games, immediately following Opening Ceremonies the night before. Because she had never been to an Olympic Games, she was worried that if she took part in Opening Ceremonies she would get so excited that she would have little energy left for her competition the next morning. On the other hand, she didn't know if she would ever make another Olympic team. She didn't want to finish her career without the experience of walking into the Olympic stadium behind the flag of her country.

When I met with Sally, I asked her to imagine the Opening Ceremonies experience. We watched some videos of previous Opening Ceremonies, and then I had Sally close her eyes, rest comfortably, and create a picture in her mind of walking into the Barcelona Olympic Stadium. She saw and felt herself marching with the other competitors, heard the cheer of the crowd, felt the heat of the summer's evening, and imagined how she would feel in that situation. To enhance the experience for her, I played some Olympic fanfare music in the background.

Sally told me that she imagined the situation so vividly, so realistically, that she actually felt the butterflies in her stomach. She was close to tears as she watched the flag of the United States and looked into the sea of faces around her in the stadium.

After this imaginary experience, Sally was convinced of two things.

First, she decided she didn't want to miss the Opening Ceremonies. Second, she realized that as long as she was well prepared, the positive emotional experience of being at Opening Ceremonies would not hurt her. Sally and her coach decided that she should rest in the early afternoon before the Opening Ceremonies in order to save up energy for the next day's competition. To become familiar with this afternoon rest, Sally built it into her daily schedule for a month before the Games. Also, she practiced imagining going straight back to her Olympic Village apartment after the Opening Ceremonies, calming down, and going immediately to sleep.

At Barcelona her plan worked just as she had imagined it would. She felt rested and ready for her competition and ended up with the gold medal she had always dreamed of winning. Sally's ability to re-create her emotions played an important role in her success.

As you can see from Sally's example, Creative Thinking allows you to plan for situations that are impossible to re-create in reality. But in your imagination you can place yourself in such a situation and decide how you will handle it. My business clients use Creative Thinking in this way to anticipate upcoming challenges and to envision potential opportunities. When opportunity knocks, they are prepared to take advantage.

Another way to utilize the power of your imagination is to harness it to help you learn new skills. Let's see how this approach works.

Learn with Imagination

Athletes and coaches recognize that one of the best ways to learn something is to rehearse it in your imagination. The National Team coach of the United States weight-lifting team, Dragomir Cioroslan, emphasizes this skill at every workout. If a young athlete is learning a lift at a new weight, Dragomir insists that the athlete concentrate on the feel of the lift before even holding the bar. When the lift is completed successfully, Dragomir immediately asks the athlete to remember exactly what it felt like. He wants the correct image of the lift stored away in memory so that the athlete can use it the next time. Often, Dragomir will suggest that a lifter close his eyes before trying a lift. He asks the athlete to visualize and feel the correct technique. If the lifter is having trouble learning the technique, Dragomir will use videotapes to show the athlete how he wants the lift completed.

In a study carried out at the Olympic Training Center in Colorado Springs, I found that more than 90 percent of elite athletes use imagination to learn their sports skills. Can using imagination increase the speed with which you learn new skills? Rob Woolfolk, Mark Parrish, and I studied this question by asking college students to practice putting a golf ball while using the Creative Thinking skill.

We took thirty students and divided them into three groups. They were all asked to practice putting for seven consecutive days. On the first day we measured their accuracy before they tried any learning strategy. For the next six days, one group was asked to imagine making a successful putt before every attempt. They were told to "imagine making a gentle backswing" and to visualize "stroking the putt smoothly down the target line." Then they were told to imagine the ball "rolling, rolling, right into the cup." A second group was also asked to imagine a putt before every attempt. After the same instructions regarding the stroke, they were told to imagine the golf ball "rolling, rolling toward the cup, but at the last second narrowly missing." The third and final group was told merely to sink each putt.

After six days, the group that used positive imagination before every putt had improved 30 percent when compared to the first day. The group that practiced every day, making no use of imagination, increased its accuracy by only 10 percent. This demonstrates how powerful Creative Thinking can be when used to learn a new task, even when people have not used the skill before.

Even more interesting, the group that visualized the ball missing the cup showed a *decrease* in accuracy of 21 percent after six days. Thinking about failure can actually hurt your performance.

You may have had a similar experience. Have you ever been about to do something when you have suddenly "seen" yourself mess up? Perhaps you were about to serve a tennis ball and had a picture of yourself hitting the ball into the net. Or you went into an exam with a clear picture in your mind of failing. What usually happens in such situations? Typically, you *do* hit the ball into the net or fail the exam. That is why it is very important in Creative Thinking to imagine carefully exactly the result you want to occur and how you will make it happen. Imagining a negative result will almost guarantee a negative outcome.

Other sport psychologists have shown that the greatest gains in performance occur when mental practice of a sports skill is combined with physical practice. When learning to play golf, for example, the greatest benefits occur when you physically practice at the driving range and also regularly rehearse the skills you are learning in your imagination. The great thing about learning with imagination is that you can do it anywhere. You can work on your golf game (or your big presentation) anytime—at home in the evening, during the lunch break, or while catching the train home.

The following example, drawn from my consulting experience, shows how the Creative Thinking skill can be used at work. People learn much more efficiently when they use Creative Thinking to gain new skills.

WHEN MISTAKES ARE UNACCEPTABLE

One of my more challenging assignments was helping with staff training at a large nuclear-energy company. Their reactor employees had to be ready to handle emergency situations without any hesitation. To remain in their critical jobs they had to pass a recertification exam every year. The company contacted me because they were looking for a way to help their employees with the tough exam.

The company was concerned because a small percentage of reactor operators usually failed the exam. The operators were experienced and knew their stuff. But they failed anyway. One major problem was that some of the complicated moves involved in handling emergencies were hard to remember, particularly when an operator had little time to give the right answer.

As I discussed the situation with the staff, it became clear that here was a perfect opportunity to apply Creative Thinking. Operators were studying for the exam in the same old manner. Staff were notified of the date of their exam and could study the protocols and procedures until exam time. Also, they could practice emergency techniques on simulation equipment. After that, they were on their own. When I suggested the technique of visualizing the complicated emergency moves during the study process, the staff immediately saw the potential benefits.

With the help of the staff, I put together a plan for a new way to study. The company made a video demonstrating exactly the right way of handling major emergency situations that might arise. As much as possible, this video showed the procedures from the operator's point of view. The video was made available to operators in a special viewing room at any time. Additionally, operators were taught how to visualize the emergency techniques as if they were actually working on the reactor.

The staff put together an audiotape to guide operators through the process of imagining the emergency procedures. Employees listened to this tape at regular intervals—not just when they were preparing for the exam, but also four and eight months after passing an exam.

The company took my ideas a step further and decided to compare the new learning methods they had devised, using Creative Thinking, with the old method of study. At some plants, operators continued to study using the old ways. At other plants, the company put the Creative Thinking methods into place. They found that the new learning method significantly improved the percentage of operators passing the recertification exam. Operators who used the Creative Thinking study method learned the material four times faster and retained three times as much information as those who did not. It also greatly reduced the stress level of employees during the exam process. This example demonstrates the tremendous benefits of adding imagination to the learning process.

A third way in which your imagination can help you reach your goals is by solving problems creatively. This has been a characteristic of inventors and problem solvers over the ages—they envision a new, creative approach to an old problem. Albert Einstein once said, "When I examine myself . . . I come to the conclusion that the gift of fantasy has meant more to me than my talent for absorbing positive knowledge." You don't need to develop a new theory of the universe to successfully employ your imagination in this way. You need only learn how to create vivid pictures in your mind of ways in which you might tackle the roadblock you are facing.

Imagine Solutions to Problems

No matter how well we plan ahead, surprises and roadblocks spring up that cause us to detour from our intended path. Athletes face such challenges on a daily basis. Successful athletes are remarkable because they not only anticipate problems, they seem to welcome the challenge of coming up with a creative solution.

Let me share an interesting story with you that Bill Tancred, a champion discus thrower, told me. Bill had an illustrious career—he was national champion of Great Britain, he competed in two Olympic Games, and he set a number of records. In the years that Bill competed, the acknowledged master of the discus was Al Oerter. Al, one of America's greatest athletes, won the discus gold medal at *four consecutive Olympics*—1956, 1960, 1964, and 1968!

With a smile, Bill told me about a time when he and Al met socially after they had both retired. They were having a great time swapping "secrets of the trade." Bill happened to mention the importance of mental preparation, and said that he strongly believed in the value of visualization. "Yes," said Al, "visualization is very important."

Bill told Al about his own visualization routine, how he would imagine that he was at the Olympics, marching in the Opening Ceremonies, that he was in competition and performing brilliantly, that he won the gold medal, and that the British national anthem was being played. Al shook his head and commented, "I never imagined winning the gold medal and hearing the national anthem." Bill was startled. "Well, if you used visualization and you didn't imagine winning the gold medal," Bill asked, "what did you imagine?"

Al considered for a moment before responding. "I used to imagine that it was the day of the Olympic finals, the day that I had spent the last four years preparing for, and that it was raining. *Pouring rain.* The throwing area was slippery, conditions were atrocious, and I had to go out and throw anyway. And I imagined myself throwing well. I visualized myself throwing strongly, with good technique, despite the rain. Or sometimes I would imagine that I was down to my last throw in the Olympic finals. The Russian was competing right ahead of me, and with his last throw he set a *world record!* So to win the gold medal, I now had to set a new world record. On my last throw of the Games, I would have to throw farther than anyone ever had. And I would imagine that I did just that; I would see myself setting a new world record. Those were the types of things I visualized. I thought about what might go wrong, and I imagined responding to the challenge."

"That answer," Bill told me, "really shook me up. I *never* imagined anything like that. Here I was, thinking I was preparing well mentally, and even in his mental preparation Al was always one step ahead of me!" Bill was genuinely astonished by Al Oerter's description of how he used visualization, but Bill realized that it made a lot of sense.

It should make a lot of sense to us, too. This story shows how you can reach your goals by visualizing how you will respond to potential obstacles.

When athletes lose their poise in competition, it's often when they're surprised by an unexpected occurrence. Creative Thinking can be used to prepare for setbacks ahead of time, thereby reducing their negative emotional impact. For example, a skater might visualize a fall in a routine but then imagine getting up quickly and performing a very strong finish. A tennis player might imagine a racket breaking in the middle of a point, and imagine how she will successfully deal with such a surprise.

I frequently use Creative Thinking in this way with my business clients. They learn that they need not wait for problem situations to occur before devising a solution to them. Indeed, companies that can respond fastest to challenges are usually those that gain the competitive edge in the marketplace. In business, a variation of this approach to problem solving is called **strategic planning.** This involves Creatively Thinking about business objectives and devising solutions to potential obstacles. You can utilize this same approach to problems at work or at home.

Try it now. Think about a problem you're facing today. Now imagine a solution to that problem. How does it feel? Imagine your approach as vividly as possible. Imagine what the results are. Do you think your approach has a chance of succeeding? If not, try another tactic. The great thing about your imagination is that you can try lots of options. Take some time and explore the situation from several angles. Get some advice from others and then imagine trying their solutions. Eventually one approach will seem the best to you. Your Creative Thinking has pointed out the path for you to follow. Remember that you do not have to do it alone. Creative solutions are often achieved by turning to others who have a different perspective on the problem.

One of my clients, Karla, a customer-service representative at a bank I work with, was agonizing over how to deal with a fellow employee. Her fellow staffer was very critical of other coworkers, often upsetting Karla with her sharp comments. Karla had tried pointing out the negative effects of the criticism to her colleague, but to no effect. Only when I asked Karla to close her eyes and imagine a solution to this problem did she see what to do. She imagined bringing up the issue while all the branch staff were in a monthly meeting, asking for input from her colleagues. When she tried this solution out for real, it worked like a charm. Many others felt just as she did, and their combined feedback brought about a behavior change in the critical colleague.

You can try the same approach in your life. If you're worried about failure, think about the situation realistically. Imagine what might happen if you fail. OK, so what? What are you going to do about it? The most important thing is not to worry about the failure, but to imagine how you will deal with it. Once you can imagine successfully dealing with failure, you can stop worrying about it.

I have suggested three ways in which you can use your imagination to help you achieve success: to help you plan ahead, to learn new skills, and to solve problems. But I suggest these approaches to help you think about possibilities, not to constrict your thinking. Of all the eight skills, Creative Thinking can be used in the greatest variety of ways. My clients continue to astonish me with new ways they have used imagination to help them reach their goals. Nourish your imagination, allow it to roam free every day, and you will also be surprised by the productive results of your Creative Thinking.

Step 3. Create a Successful Self-image

Creative Thinking is the mind/body skill most likely to change a setback into a victory. If you can find the strength to change your image of failure into a picture of success, you can find the hope to go on.

I cannot overemphasize how important your imagination is in shaping your reality. In a very real way, your imagination helps create the world you live in. You become the person you imagine you are. If you imagine you are successful, you'll be successful. If you imagine you are a failure, you'll probably be a failure.

Often, the way we do things flows from the way we see ourselves. A student believes he is poor at mathematics, so he avoids math wherever possible. Naturally, he does badly at solving math problems in exams. A young executive believes she knows her business but thinks she makes bad decisions. So she puts off decisions as long as possible, delegates them to others, and in general behaves in a way that confirms the self-image she has.

In order to change the way we act and behave, we must first change the way we look at ourselves. This begins in our minds, in our self-images. They can be changed through a conscious act of imagination, but it takes effort and practice. Let's see how it can be done.

I want to share Regina's story with you, a remarkable athlete who had the courage to change in a most tumultuous situation.

REGINA'S OLYMPIC DREAM BECOMES A NIGHTMARE

At the Summer Olympics in Seoul, in 1988, an athlete came to me who was distraught because she thought she was about to be kicked off the team. Regina was a sprinter, one of the best in the world. She had qualified for the Olympics by finishing fourth in the 100-meter final at the U.S.A. Track and Field Championships just months before. Although she did not qualify for a spot as an individual contestant, she gained an automatic berth as a member of the U.S.A. relay team.

Her problems began soon after the U.S.A. track and field team arrived at training camp. Regina had always had a reputation as a poor passer of the relay baton, and her problems soon resurfaced. On several occasions she dropped the baton on the handoff during practice. The more she focused on her poor handling, the worse the problem seemed to get. One of the coaches took her aside and told her "not to worry, keep working at it and you'll get it," but Regina was unable to hide her misgivings.

The situation became more tense when the athletes and coaches arrived in Seoul. One of the other sprinters, a famous athlete and a favorite in her events, began complaining about Regina's dropped passes. This athlete suggested that another runner, her teammate at a track club in North Carolina, replace Regina on the relay team. Regina was distressed to find that this athlete had not only gone to the coaches to complain, but to the press as well. The story was now in the newspapers (politics occur even at the Olympics). With less than a week to go before the race, Regina was unsure whether she would even get the chance to compete in the Olympics. Her dream of the past six years was threatened. It was at this point that one of the coaches suggested that Regina talk with me.

In working with Regina, I learned that her worry about her baton

handoffs started in high school. She had dropped a pass at the state cham-
pionships and cost her school a chance to win the state title. As so often hap-
pens, she became cautious and overly careful in relay races after that, which
only made her performance worse. But now, in Seoul, Regina had only a
few days to improve her relay passing performance.

I realized that Creative Thinking offered the best hope for Regina to
break her bad habit. Instead of imagining herself as a bad passer in the
relay, she needed to transform her thinking. I decided that my role was to
help Regina see herself as an excellent relay performer, able to execute
smooth, clean handoffs.

My first goal was to help Regina stop worrying so much about a bad
performance. I asked her why she thought dropping the baton would be so
terrible. She replied, "It would mean that I let everyone down, my family,
my friends, and my teammates. They are all depending on me."

I asked Regina to imagine that the Olympics were over and that she
was returning home. She had dropped the baton in the relay, just as she had
feared. What would the reactions of her family and friends be? After spend-
ing some minutes imagining such a situation, Regina responded with sur-
prise that they were very supportive. Nobody criticized her; instead they told
her how much they loved her and how proud they were of her achieving her
Olympic dream.

Next, I asked Regina to imagine the reaction of her teammates and
coaches if she dropped the baton in the Olympic final. This was even more
difficult for her to face, but after a while Regina told me that she saw her
teammates being very supportive as well. "Most of them are my friends,"
Regina told me. "They know how much I'm hurting, so I can see them
putting their arms around me, giving me a hug, and telling me to forget
about it." Regina realized, with the help of her Creative Thinking, that
dropping the baton would not be the end of the world. She would still have
her support network of family and friends. This realization helped Regina
relax and stop worrying, and we were then ready to move on to the next
step: changing the way Regina saw herself as a relay performer.

Now, I know that some of you are saying, "This is crazy. He asked her
to imagine dropping the baton in the Olympic final, and he expected
that to help her performance? I would never imagine doing the very thing

I am afraid of—that would only make it more likely to happen." But in fact, I have found that confronting *our fears is essential if we are to break bad habits. One of the reasons we keep doing things that are not good for us is that we fear the bad habit so much we avoid dealing with it. We don't even think about it. And we hope that it will go quietly away.*

Let me assure you that bad habits don't go away by themselves. My experience with hundreds of individuals confirms that. You have to do something about them, make the effort to change. But that means starting with a realistic view of your bad habit. Because we spend so much time avoiding the things that worry us, we often build up a set of illogical and unrealistic beliefs concerning them. That is what I needed Regina to reexamine—her unrealistic belief that if she dropped the baton in the Olympic relay her world would come to an end. Deep down she thought that everyone around her would reject her and blame her. It's nearly impossible to perform well with that sort of anxiety and fear hanging over you.

Now that Regina was more relaxed, she was able to work on changing her self-image as a relay racer. I asked Regina to tell me the type of performer she wanted to be. She said she wanted to be known as a flawless performer, a runner so consistent that she was "a robot." I next asked Regina to visualize herself in a race and to imagine performing like a machine, executing the reception and the pass of the baton with precision. At first this was difficult for Regina. She had a tendency to imagine mistakes, to see the baton dropping to the ground. But whenever this happened we would stop and she would imagine the scene again, this time creating a perfect image of a baton pass.

Regina practiced this Creative Thinking repeatedly over the next two days. She rehearsed perfect passes in her mind in the morning, at lunchtime, and in the evening. Soon she began to improve during the relay practice sessions. After several consecutive practices with flawless passes, the coach came up and congratulated her. The next day she was officially announced as one of the starting members of the relay team. Naturally Regina was delighted, but she continued to use her Creative Thinking strategy. She imagined robotlike performances right up to the day of competition. In the race itself, Regina said to herself "I'm a robot" several times before beginning her leg of the relay.

I wish I could report a totally happy ending to Regina's story, but as is often the case in sport, the story had a bittersweet conclusion. The U.S.A. relay team breezed through to the semifinals. They won their semifinal by a large margin, with Regina turning in a wonderfully smooth performance. But one of the other teams protested that two of Regina's teammates had completed their baton exchange outside the official passing area. After a videotape review, the team was disqualified.

Regina was terribly disappointed, but she was proud of her personal performance. I saw her briefly back in the States some months later and she reported that she was doing very well. She had started work with a large company in a junior management position. She was delighted at the positive reception she had received from her friends and family—just as she had imagined in Seoul!

Regina's accomplishment illustrates how Creative Thinking can be used to create a successful self-image. What do *you* imagine about yourself and about the world around you? As the final step in mastering Creative Thinking, I urge you to explore the possibilities in your life. Don't focus on the limitations around you. If you trust in yourself, you can achieve great things. Being able to imagine what you want is the first step on the road to success.

Creative Thinking Tips

■ Many people believe that you must be deeply relaxed in order to use imagination effectively. Not so! Athletes use their imaginations all the time in competitive situations. They don't have time to relax, but they still imagine success clearly. The great thing about your imagination is that you can use it anytime, anywhere.

■ If you can't *imagine* what to do, you probably can't do it. So get a clear description to help your image. For example, if you're learning a new computer program and you don't understand what to do, ask your trainer for an example. Vivid descriptions and lots of examples help the learning process.

■ If you're learning something step-by-step, occasionally rehearse the whole process. This will give you a feel for the flow of the task. For example, a beginning golfer is learning about the take-away, the backswing, shoulder turn, hip turn, and arm extension. Occasionally he should imagine the smooth feel of the whole body making a swing. Otherwise his swing may become jerky and fragmented.

■ Before starting a task, always go over it in your mind. See and feel yourself accomplishing the task successfully. It will give you great confidence. An Olympic high jumper will always feel herself going over the bar successfully before she starts the runup for her jump.

■ Remember that Creative Thinking takes practice. Begin by rehearsing familiar situations in your mind until they are as real and lifelike as possible. Once you become good at this, you will find that you can prepare for all sorts of new situations, from planning for a difficult interview to rehearsing new dance steps to calming down before a major test. I will continue to refer to the Creative Thinking skill in later chapters, and you will see that it plays a vital role in learning the other seven skills. Your mastery of the power of your imagination is essential to reaching your Achievement Zone.

How to Learn Creative Thinking

Step 1 ■

Develop Your Imagination

Step 2 ■

Imagine How You Will Reach Your Goals
- Plan Ahead
- Learn with Imagination
- Imagine Solutions to Problems

Step 3 ■

Create a Successful Self-image

Productive Analysis:

Think
Like a Winner

One of the most memorable moments I've witnessed at the Olympics was the "Battle of the Brians" in 1988. Brian Orser, Canada's figure-skating champion, had won the silver medal in Sarajevo in 1984 and was the reigning world champion. Brian Boitano, U.S.A. champion, had won the world championship in 1986. They were clearly the top competitors at Calgary, and they proved it with wonderful performances. Rarely do we see the very best skating in the Olympics because of the enormous pressure, but both Orser and Boitano gave brilliant virtuoso exhibitions. In a heartbreakingly close decision, the judges awarded the gold medal to Boitano.

Interviewed after the event, Brian Boitano gave a fascinating account of the inner struggle that a performer undergoes under such conditions. "It was hard because there was a voice talking to me saying, This is it, this is the Olympics," *said Boitano.* "But the other voice said, Just treat it like another competition. You know how to do it, you've done it millions of times. *So it was kind of a fight, a tug-of-war. I said to myself,* Just take one thing at a time," *continued Boitano,* "and if you take one thing at a time you know how to do everything and it can't go wrong. *It was a fight, it was an exhausting fight. It was pressure at its ultimate. I'm more proud of myself for getting through it with the best all-around competition I've skated in my life than anything else I've done."*

What Is Productive Analysis?

Brian Boitano's success was no accident. That voice saying *This is the Olympics* could have distracted him, made him skate poorly. But his other voice prevailed. *You've done it a million times,* he said to himself. He was using the skill of Productive Analysis to take charge of his performance.

As you saw with the example of Regina in the previous chapter, a successful self-image can actually lead to success, while a poor self-image can lead to failure. In that chapter, I showed you how to use images to combat self-defeating perceptions and reach your goals. In this chapter I look at the ways successful people use verbal, logical thought to accomplish their objectives.

Productive Analysis is the skill of replacing negative thoughts that hurt your performance with productive ones that will help you perform in your Achievement Zone. Everyone has what I like to refer to as an "inner voice." It's that little conversation that takes place in your mind while you are in the middle of a task. Sometimes that inner voice helps, often it hurts performance. We often don't realize that the voice is even speaking to us. But high achievers have found that what they say to themselves, especially in important situations, makes the difference between success and failure.

Two athletes I worked with before the Barcelona Olympics illustrate the influence of this inner voice on our performance. Both were dealing with the same physical obstacle—they had been badly injured in the year before the Games. One was a gymnast, Eric, who came to the Olympic Training Center in Colorado Springs to rehabilitate an injured shoulder. The other, Alan, was a cyclist who had badly injured his knee in a fall. They had a severe injury in common, but their reactions to that situation were very different.

Eric took advantage of every opportunity the Training Center presented. Even though he couldn't train for six months, he attended all team practices and helped out his teammates whenever possible. He worked hard on his fitness and asked for a modern training program from the Center's strength coach. Eric improved in every way he could. He came to see me to work on his visualization. Each day he watched several hours of tape of the world's top gymnasts and imagined that he was performing the same routines.

When I asked Eric about his plans, he told me that he was still thinking of making the Olympic team. "I keep telling myself that I can do it," said Eric. "I tell myself that this is a golden opportunity to get stronger, fitter, and tougher—even though I can't get out on the mat. When the doctor tells me that I can train on the equipment again in a few months, I want to be as ready as possible." It came as no surprise to those of us who knew Eric when he accomplished his goal a year later. He earned a spot on the Olympic team and finished in the top ten in Barcelona—a remarkable achievement.

Alan, on the other hand, came to see me because he was depressed. He was bitter about the accident that had caused his injury, and complained about the coaches who had asked him to ride on the day of the accident. "It was supposed to be my rest day," said Alan. "But the coach wanted me to ride to help pace some of the young guys. If I hadn't gone out that day, this never would have happened. Now my big chance to make the Olympic team is ruined. I may never get another shot at it."

I tried to help Alan to think productively about what he might do to speed his rehabilitation, but he couldn't see past his misfortune. There was still more than sixteen months until the Olympic Games, but Alan could focus only on the time he was missing from training. Needless to say, he lived up to his own expectations. His rehabilitation was lengthy, and when he got back on the bike he wasn't the same rider he had once been. Alan did not make the United States Olympic team.

The big difference between Eric and Alan was what they were saying to themselves. Eric's "inner voice" was upbeat and optimistic—it was productive. Alan's voice was pessimistic and gloomy. Their performances were a reflection of their inner thoughts. Eric's performance was outstanding; Alan's was dismal. I have observed the same phenomenon countless times. Athletes live up to their own expectations. Indeed, we all do.

What you say to yourself makes all the difference! That is why verbal thinking, what we say to ourselves in performance situations, is so critical for optimal achievement. For example, many clients tell me that their jobs are very stressful. They feel they are under constant pressure. It's important to realize that your job or your career doesn't cause pressure. *You* are the one who says whether the situation is stressful or not!

We have a saying at the Olympic Training Center in Colorado Springs. It goes like this:

The only pressure that exists is the pressure you put on yourself.

How to Put Productive Analysis into Practice

There are three basic steps to learning the Productive Analysis skill.

First, you must become aware of your inner voice. Once you

Productive Analysis

Step 1. Be Aware of Your Inner Voice

Step 2. Use Your Critic Productively

Step 3. Replace Negativity with Productivity

---

are tuned in to your own style of thought, you will be able to recognize the typical pattern of negative thoughts that affect your performance (what I call your Critic).

The next step is to realistically identify areas of your life in which you wish to improve. The trick is to be honest about your weaknesses without being too hard on yourself. Only by overcoming weaknesses can you attain excellence. This will allow you to move ahead of others who are stuck in the same old place. Your internal Critic can actually help you identify potential areas of change.

Finally, you will reach your Achievement Zone if you come up with productive alternatives to the negative ways of thinking you have identified. Once you have become attuned to your self-limiting thought patterns, you can replace your negative thoughts with productive ones. Let's take a look at these three steps in detail.

Step 1. Be Aware of Your Inner Voice

The first step is to become aware of the impact your inner voice has on your daily life. Some people are naturally tuned in to their self-talk. When I ask them to describe their inner conversations, they are able to play them back for me word for word. But many others are not aware of when and how they talk to themselves. They draw a blank when I ask them to describe their thoughts in a particular situation. Whether you are very much in tune with your inner voice, or whether you tune it out, you can begin your mastery of Productive Analysis by refining awareness of your internal conversations.

If you pay attention to how you think, you'll notice that your thoughts often occur in the form of an internal dialogue, as if you were listening to two people having a conversation. Brian Boitano aptly described it as a tug-of-war.

The Critic

Have you noticed that one of your inner voices is often negative, guilty, and won't shut up? I call this inner voice the Critic. This voice is almost automatic. It will pop into your head without any warning, and it usually makes you miserable. This was the voice Brian Boitano heard when he said to himself, *This is it, this is the Olympics.*

If the Critic is in control of your inner voice in situations that demand good performance, you will always do poorly. Sport psychologist Judy Van Raalte and her colleagues at Springfield College proved this in a study of twenty-four elite junior tennis players. Observers watched the tennis players during two United States Tennis Association tournaments. They found that players who tended to talk out loud to themselves in a critical way were more likely to lose points during a match. These players said such things as "You are so slow!" and "Why can't I serve?" and "Oh God, that's horrible."

On the other hand, the best players were more in control of what they said to themselves and how they reacted. They spoke to themselves in an encouraging way—for example, saying "Come on!" and "Let's go!" and "Move your feet." Fascinatingly, the players who answered "yes" to the question "Did what you said to yourself during the match affect the outcome of the match?" won many more points than players who answered "no" to the question. The players who believed in the power of their inner voice were the winners!

How to Identify Negative Thoughts

Much of the skill of Productive Analysis comes from being able to identify the typical negative thoughts of your Critic, then replacing them with productive thoughts that will help you reach your Achievement Zone. We all have typical patterns of negative thinking, born out of our experiences in childhood and adolescence.

Here's a good way you can start to identify the thoughts that interfere with your performance. This method was used by sport psychology researchers Sue Jackson and Glyn Roberts of the University of Illinois to help collegiate athletes discover the impact of their inner voice. They asked two hundred college athletes what they were thinking about during their very best and their very worst performances.

Jackson and Roberts found that during their best performances ever, 66 percent of the athletes were thinking about the performance itself. They were concentrating on what they were doing. For example, one tennis player described her thoughts during her best match:

> *I wrote down some goals before the match. One was to really enjoy myself and the other was to be completely focused on the ball. I was going to try to achieve these goals and not worry about the outcome. I was trying to play one point at a time and focus on the ball, to really try to see the ball. I was confident but not really thinking about winning or losing—I was totally engrossed in the task at hand. Nothing else existed. Just me, the ball, and nothing else. So I played in total control.*

On the other hand, when they described their worst performances ever, an amazing 88 percent of the athletes said they were worrying about the *result* of their competition. They were so focused on the outcome of their event, they were not able to concentrate on what they were doing. For example, one runner described his thoughts during the race like this:

> *In the back of my mind, I was thinking,* I'm not that good. Do I really belong up here? *Running the race, I was not focused at all. I was looking everywhere. I remember at one point thinking that I should be up further. I thought,* Well, what does it matter, you're not going to qualify anyway. *Instead of concentrating on the task at hand, I let the fear of outcome paralyze me.*

Does this sound familiar? Even in their inner thoughts, successful athletes are Action Focused! I have used this method with many athletes to help them become aware of the impact of their thoughts on their sports performance. Try the following exercise yourself.

BEST AND WORST PERFORMANCE THOUGHTS

Think about one of the areas where you want to be more successful. What gives you problems in that area? For example, a golfer might be great from tee to green but have trouble on the putting surface. Or an executive may be very productive but have a hard time giving critical feedback to others. What situation gives you problems?

Now think back to the time when you handled this problem best. Remember a time when, for whatever reason, you did very well in that difficult situation. For example, I was working with a recreational golfer, Terri, who was having putting problems. I asked Terri to remember the very best round of putting she ever had. She wrote down in her Achievement Zone diary all the productive things she was thinking or saying to herself in that situation. Do the same yourself. To help yourself remember, use your Creative Thinking skill to imagine that day as clearly as possible.

Here are the thoughts Terri wrote down:

- Have fun. The round is already ruined, so just learn from today.
- Soak up information when you get on the green. Pay attention to the break, the wind, the speed, and what sort of putt you want to leave yourself.
- Decide what putt you want to hit, and then step up and do it. Go for it.

Next, think of one of the worst experiences you had in your problem situation. Think of a time when everything went wrong and you ended up frustrated or unhappy. Again, use your Creative Thinking skill to re-create the feelings of that day in your mind. Now write down all the thoughts you had in your diary.

The negative thoughts Terri came up with are listed below:

- You can break 100 today, but you have to putt really well.
- This is makable; I should make this putt.
- What's wrong with me? I was putting better than this last year.
- You're too nervous. Don't take so much time; just hit it.

By tuning in to your inner voice you will be able to identify patterns of thought that are effective for you and types of thought that hurt your performance. This knowledge will enable you to identify the type of thinking that will help you reach your personal Achievement Zone. For example, Terri learned that when she reminded herself to have fun and to study her putts, she performed well. When she thought about her score and began rushing, she putted poorly.

Think of a second type of problem you would like to solve. Pick an area of your life that is different from the first issue you considered. Go through the two steps I described for the first problem. Think of a time when you did well on that problem and write down all the thoughts you had on that occasion. Then think of a time when you did badly in that area and again write down all the things you said to yourself at that time.

Compare your productive thoughts and your negative thoughts for these two different problems. Some of the things you said were probably very different. Our Achievement Zone is always partly adapted to the specific situation we encounter. But some of your thoughts in the two situations were probably very similar. The similar productive thoughts may be generally useful to you across a wide variety of situations. The similar negative thoughts are probably typical hurtful things you say to yourself.

Begin making a list of productive thoughts, and another list of your most common negative thoughts. Carry around a notepad in which you can jot down your discoveries. You never know when you'll identify a powerful negative thought or discover a productive way of thinking about a problem.

Ask your spouse, or a close friend, for help in identifying your typical harmful thoughts. Tell them about the two problems you came up with in this exercise and ask, "You know me pretty well. What would I usually say to myself in that situation?" You will be surprised at how much of your inner voice people who know you well can identify. This is because the words of our Critic tend to come out in our conversations with others.

As you become more aware of your inner voice, you'll come to realize the impact of your thoughts on your behavior. You'll recognize that productive thinking leads to success, while negative thinking usually results in poor, or even disastrous, performance.

I'll share an experience I had with a very talented skier who was struggling on the World Cup circuit. She began to improve only after she realized how her inner voice was affecting her performance.

JANE'S STRUGGLE ON THE SLOPES

Jane was one of the top skiers in the United States, but when she competed in Europe, she usually turned in a disappointing and lackluster performance. Her coach asked her to work with me, because he knew that she had the ability to do well against the top European skiers.

After my first meeting with Jane, I had a hunch that her internal Critic was in control of her thoughts during competitions. I asked her to think back to her last World Cup race in Switzerland. As she described the race, I asked Jane to tell me what she was thinking about at the starting gate, as she skied down the course, and after the race was finished. The words she used told me a great deal about her:

What was my time? You're kidding; that's horrible. Jane, you blew it again. How could you be such a dummy? I knew exactly what line I wanted to hold down those last few curves, and I didn't do it. I screwed up. I'm hopeless; I'll never get it. What is the coach going to say to me now?

Jane was a perfect example of someone who thinks negatively instead of productively. She had correctly identified a major mistake she made—she skied the wrong line through the bottom turns. But instead of working to improve her technique, she relentlessly criticized herself for the mistake she made.

Unfortunately, many of us lead our lives exactly like Jane. We know we make mistakes, but instead of doing something about them, we waste time and energy feeling guilty and stupid about our areas of weakness. As a result, we never improve. We need to be productive with our self-criticism. We need to help ourselves succeed.

The effective approach is to use the Productive Analysis skill to analyze the negative thoughts of the Critic. Then you can replace them with productive thoughts. Jane's first step was to keep a diary of what she said to herself every day. She wrote in it after practices and before she went to bed. After two weeks we went over the diary together. Jane was surprised that her comments were nearly all negative. We talked about how such negative thinking can hurt performance, destroying confidence and sapping energy. Jane felt that this might be a reason for her race problems, and wondered what she could do to change.

Together we made a list of the common negative things that Jane said to herself. That was the easy part! She had quite a long list! In the next—and most important—step we came up with a productive replacement for *each of Jane's typical negative thoughts. Let's take a look at part of the list Jane and I developed:*

Negative Thoughts	Productive Thoughts
I'm such a dummy. I'll never learn.	*I made a mistake. I know what I did wrong. Now, let's correct it.*
What will my coach say? He thinks I'm an idiot.	*I need to tell Coach about this mistake. He can help me correct it.*
I'm wasting my time out here. I'm not as good as the others.	*My start was my best ever. I'm definitely improving. I'm going to beat those Europeans!*

Jane decided to practice her new, productive thoughts whenever possible. If she caught herself thinking negatively she immediately tried to say something productive to herself. It took several months of hard work, but gradually Jane learned that she could be critical without *being* negative. As her Productive Analysis skill grew, she began to use the productive statements she had come up with instead of her old negative thinking.

She soon began to see results from her new way of thinking. By getting rid of negative thoughts she increased her energy level and motivation. She began to look forward to competing instead of dreading it. Her relationship with her coach improved dramatically. Instead of worrying about his criticisms, she eagerly anticipated going over the race with him, looking for new ways to improve. Perhaps most important, skiing became fun again, just as it had been when she first started. In the next year, she placed in the top ten in the World Cup season and won a World Cup race in Europe.

Step 2. Use Your Critic Productively

After you have identified the negative thoughts of your Critic, it's important to be able to replace your automatic, negative thoughts with a productive approach toward performance. I call this approach productive thinking.

What is productive thinking? Surely it's just the opposite of negative thinking? Instead of worrying, you tell yourself that good things will happen. Isn't that the power of positive thinking? Think about success, and you'll automatically achieve it.

I wish it were that simple. But if it were, everyone would be a success story. We all want success! No, productive thinking means using your inner voice in a helpful way to move you toward your goals. At times, that means being critical, even tough, with yourself. Let me explain.

Why "Positive Thinking" Isn't Enough

One of the greatest myths of our time is that we can achieve greatness simply via the power of positive thinking. In my work with athletes I hear many motivational speeches. A common theme is that if you can just imagine yourself succeeding, you will succeed. "Imagine fulfilling your greatest dream," shouted one "motivational expert" I was listening to, "and if you really believe you can do it, the dream will come true."

The truth is that positive thinking by itself will do very little for us. We would all like to believe that if we want something to happen badly enough it will happen—but this just isn't true. Hard work is what allows us to reach our goals, and there is no substitute for effort and practice.

I heard the problem with positive thinking clearly summarized one day by shooter Bob Foth. I spoke with him after he'd attended a whole-day workshop conducted by an expert in motivation. Bob is one of our country's greatest shooters; he has won several World Cup events, and he won a silver medal at the 1992 Olympics in Barcelona. When I spoke to him, he was puzzled and confused.

"How can it be true that I am supposed to 'think positively' all the time?" he asked. "I spend hours practicing every day, and often I have to be very critical of myself. I have to catch my own mistakes, notice if my form is wrong. I have to be very hard on myself to keep improving my technique and focus. If I have any weaknesses, I have to spot and get rid of them. When I'm up there on the line, I need to know that I'm a stronger shooter, that I'm a better-prepared athlete, than the next guy. I can't afford weaknesses. What good would it do me to always think positively? What I need to learn is how to be more objectively critical of myself."

This honest athlete pinpointed the problem with the myth of positive thinking. If we want to keep improving in life we need to identify our weaknesses and deficiencies. Only then can we figure out how to improve. Instead of "positive thinking," this requires the type of thinking I have identified in successful people as Productive Analysis—the ability to be critical without also being negative.

Put Your Critic to Work

It might surprise you to learn that you can use your Critic in a very helpful way. How? By using your Critic to identify weaknesses so that you can figure out ways to improve.

This is how Jane the skier changed her negative thinking into productive thinking. The Critic is so persuasive because it is often half right. *Don't mess up this speech like you did last time,* it shouts.

It's *true* that the last time you gave a speech in front of a group of people you were hesitant and unconvincing. But that doesn't mean you will give a bad speech this time. Your Critic doesn't realize that change is possible.

So use your Critic to help you improve. Look realistically at your negative thoughts. Is there a problem here? Could you improve this area? Then go ahead and do so.

The answer to your poor speech-making is to learn the skills you need to speak better in front of groups. Once the problem is identified (thanks to the Critic), you are in a position to do something about it. Perhaps you can join a local Toastmasters group to enhance your public-speaking skills. Perhaps a colleague who is a wonderful presenter will agree to work with you to help your approach. There are lots of possible solutions. But you will only reach those solutions if you deal with the negative thoughts of the Critic.

Recognize that the Critic is based in your past, not your present. Once you've improved, your Critic will take a while to catch up with the new you. When you make mistakes, acknowledge them and recognize that you have identified an area where you have problems. Resolve to learn what you need to so that the problem doesn't happen again. Then stop worrying about it! If you realistically decide that you don't need to improve in an area, learn to ignore your Critic.

It's like a golfer who has always had problems playing a shot out of a bunker. After years of hitting terrible shots out of the sand, he gives in and goes for some lessons. With tuition and practice, he's soon hitting beautiful explosion shots out of bunkers. In his next competition, however, his first shot from a greenside bunker produces great anxiety. *Don't mess it up!* screams his Critic. His Critic is thinking about years of bad shots. It will take a while for it to catch up with the new golfer who can hit smooth sand shots.

How can you ignore your Critic while you're performing? Well, that's the next part of Productive Analysis. Once you've used your Critic to help you, it's still important to reduce your negative thinking. Especially in performance situations, thinking negatively doesn't help.

Step 3. Replace Negativity with Productivity

To reach the Achievement Zone you must replace negative thinking (which interferes with good performance) with productive thinking (which promotes excellence). You saw how effective this was for Jane in the example above. Successful people find that when they reduce their negative thoughts, they are more likely to achieve their goals. Now I'm going to show you how to do the same thing.

The best way to eliminate unwanted negative thoughts is to focus on desired productive thoughts. Train your mind to notice negative thoughts and to immediately replace them with productive ones. Let's see how it's done.

REPLACE NEGATIVITY WITH PRODUCTIVITY

Go back to the list of negative thoughts you collected in the exercise "Best and Worst Performance Thoughts." Select one performance area that is causing you problems.

Take a blank page. Draw a line down the middle. On the left-hand side, write down your negative thoughts in that situation.

On the other side, write down a helpful thought for each of those hurtful thoughts. Think about the best way to counteract each negative thought.

Here are some examples for someone afraid of public speaking.

Negative Thought	Productive Thought
This will be a disaster.	This is a great chance to practice my new speaking skills.
No one is interested in what I have to say.	I'm fascinated by this topic. I'll show others my enthusiasm.
My stomach is in knots. I feel awful.	I'm excited to be here. It's normal to have butterflies.

Take some time to come up with a list of productive thoughts that satisfy you. Experiment. If you come up with something better, use it. Ask others for advice. Carry that page around with you and keep working on it for a few days.

The next step is to become comfortable thinking productively. Repetition, or practice, is the best approach.

For example, someone afraid of public speaking might rehearse a speech in front of a mirror. Here's how to do it. First, use Creative Thinking to imagine being in front of an audience. Try to really feel the nerves you typically have before giving a speech. If your image of the scene is strong, you'll probably start hearing those negative thoughts. As soon as you think negatively, say your replacement productive thought in a firm, loud voice. You might feel silly, but that's OK. You're practicing, just as an athlete must practice in order to improve.

The next time you rehearse your speech, begin by saying your productive thoughts out loud. If you need to say them a couple of times to build up your confidence, do it. Proceed at your own pace.

Finally, imagine giving the speech, and as you do, say your productive thoughts silently to yourself. Never utter a negative thought without replacing it with a productive one.

You can use this method to prepare for any performance or evaluation. Whenever you catch yourself thinking negatively (and you will), start thinking productively instead. Don't get upset if you're still thinking negatively even after practice. Remember, it took years for you to get where you are today. Calmly stop the negative thought and start a productive thought. You'll be amazed at how much better you can do in any situation when you master this approach.

At times it's hard to battle your negative thoughts and come up with good alternatives. To help you out, I thought I'd offer some suggestions about learning to think productively.

Suggestions for Productive Thinking

The goal of productive thinking is to create a suitable climate for you to reach your Achievement Zone. This will give you the greatest chance of success. As you change and grow, your productive thoughts will change with you. Here are some helpful suggestions based on the experiences of the Olympic and professional athletes with whom I've worked.

Focus on the present. Productive thoughts keep athletes focused on the task and on their own actions. They exclude thoughts about the past or the future. For example: *This next event is a whole new race. Forget the last race and focus on my game plan. I still know exactly what I must do to perform well. MOVE ON.*

Think about your action goals. To keep your thoughts productive, make sure you keep an Action Focus. Don't start worrying about the end result. For example: *I can't control how high I place. All I can control is my own performance. I'm going to think about my action goals for this competition and concentrate on those.*

Find ways to improve. This is the most consistent piece of advice I hear from top-level performers in all walks of life. Once they abandon the bad habit of always comparing themselves to others, they find that their path to success is guided by a constant search for personal improvement. This is a key skill of Productive Analysis.

Sport psychologist Bob Rotella and his colleagues from the University of Virginia provide a good example of this strategy. They studied competitive skiers in North America and found that the most successful skiers shared an interesting characteristic. After looking at the racecourse, they went back and made a picture of it in their minds. Then, in the time available between inspecting the course and reaching the starting gate, they planned effective strategies for skiing the course.

For example, a good skier might decide that a particular turn was icy and steep and would plan a conservative strategy for that portion of the course. Less successful skiers, on the other hand, simply tried to think positively prior to racing. Positive thinking doesn't hurt, but these athletes were wasting time they could have been using to prepare for the challenges ahead. As we saw in the chapter on Creative Thinking, it's not enough to visualize a positive result; it's much better to plan how you're going to get there.

Be honest with yourself in determining what areas *you* need to improve in to really accomplish your goals.

Look for the silver lining in dark clouds. The champion athletes I've seen at the Olympics can look at a difficult situation and see opportunity instead of disaster. This allows them to remain positive and enthusiastic in the face of adversity, rather than become worried and depressed. Such an attitude can keep them in the Achievement Zone and help them win despite setbacks.

I saw a wonderful example of this attitude when I was conducting a workshop for the U.S. national archery team before the Seoul Olympics. We were talking about the effects of shooting in a strong wind, and the experienced archers agreed that such conditions made shooting very difficult. But one of the archers, a thirteen-year-old girl who didn't look big or strong enough to draw back the giant bow used in Olympic archery, jumped into the conversation and said she liked shooting in the wind. The older athletes looked at her as if she were crazy.

"I think about it like this," she explained. "If the wind is strong, I figure that half the field has given up already, so I'm only shooting against fifty percent of the competitors I normally face. And I practice shooting in the wind a lot. Whenever the wind gusts up at home, I grab a bow and run outside to get some practice. So I know I'm a pretty good shooter in the wind. Overall, I like it when the wind blows." There was silence after her remarks as the others considered what she had to say. I was thinking, here is a young champion in the making. With such an ability to look on the bright side, how could she go wrong?

Sure enough, she made the Olympic team the next year. With her teammates, she won the bronze medal in team competition. She continued to dominate U.S. competitions in the coming years, and was again an Olympian in 1992.

I have found that people are not born with this kind of perspective. They learn these attitudes from others. When you're faced with a very difficult or daunting task, think carefully about the special strengths you may be able to use in this situation. What aspects of this challenge could possibly give you an advantage? If the problem facing you is a tough one, it may be hard for you to see any positives. So give yourself time and brainstorm the situation. Ask others for advice. Perhaps someone else can give you the key to see the problem in a whole new light, as the young archer did for all of us at that workshop.

Remember, once you've read this book, every difficult, disheartening, or depressing situation you face will be a chance to practice and get better at your mind/body skills! And you'll only improve with practice.

Reinforce your successes. When I watch practices at the Olympic Training Center I often hear the phrase "That's just like me!" said by an athlete who has done something well. Top athletes reinforce themselves with positive feedback for doing things well. This is the opposite of our natural tendency to focus on our mistakes (*You're so stupid. That was a typical dumb mistake*). Whenever you accomplish something that makes you proud, pause for a moment and replay the success in your mind. Then say to yourself, *That's the new me!*

Be honest with yourself. Just saying positive things to yourself often doesn't work because *you don't really believe what you're saying.* Great athletes can say to themselves, *Come on, you can do this. You've done it thousands of times in practice. Let's do it one more time,* because they *have* done it thousands of times in practice. They're not lying; they're being honest with themselves. This is a good, productive thought for them because it reminds them of all their hard work and brings back their confidence.

Imagine what the impact would be of saying to yourself, *Come on, you've done this five times before and you did OK twice and bombed the other three times.* It just doesn't cut it.

Focus on those areas where you have a right to be confident. If you identify areas that are still weak, make a note to work on those in future practice sessions. You must have done the hard work that will cause you to *believe* in your abilities. There are no shortcuts and gimmicks to productive thinking.

Concentrate on the things you can control. One of my favorite sayings, often attributed to baseball great Satchel Paige, sums up this suggestion perfectly. He once said: "If it's outside your control, ain't no use worrying, 'cause it's outside your control. And if it's under your control, ain't no use worrying, 'cause it's under your control."

Isn't that a wonderful philosophy to live by?

Great athletes face factors outside their control at all times— the weather, referees, the opposition, the playing conditions, the competition schedule, and so on. Less successful athletes let these factors bother them. The champions put these concerns aside and concentrate on the one crucial factor for excellence—themselves. Here's another example to show how you can use productive thinking to overcome worry about external factors. I was discussing the effects of corporate downsizing with a business colleague, Al, and he told me how he stays focused in the face of constant change. I thought his self-talk was terrific, and I'll share it with you.

With all this downsizing in the company, I wonder if they'll let me go. Hey, I can't worry about that. There are lots of changes going on, so that means lots of chances for me to show my abilities. The main thing is for me to do a great job. And if they do lay me off, the better work I do, the more marketable I'll be later on.

Look at mistakes as a chance to learn. People who are ineffective have a tendency to see every mistake as a huge disaster. Successful people, on the other hand, view mistakes as an opportunity to learn. When sport psychologists Ron Smith and Frank Smoll studied hundreds of Little League coaches to find out what set the best coaches apart, they found that the critical factor was an ability to catch mistakes and immediately offer a good solution.

Dragomir Cioroslan, national coach of the U.S. weight-lifting program, told me that the way a coach treats mistakes is a vital part of the training process. "You not only have to catch somebody doing the wrong movement," he explained, "you must also provide the solution to the mistake as quickly as possible. Even when I am correcting mistakes, I focus on positive feedback to the athlete. This helps them build confidence and strive for excellence."

To master the ability to think productively, acknowledge your mistakes honestly. Don't be defensive. Other people will respect you more for admitting you made a mistake than for trying to cover it up or pass the blame. Then ask yourself the question, "What did I learn from this mistake? What do I need to change next time to do it better?" This approach will always move you toward your Achievement Zone rather than away from it.

If you follow these suggestions, you will find that you can replace your negative thoughts with the valuable skill of thinking productively. Making a change in your thinking often means having to change the way in which you look at the world. For some people, this can be a frightening challenge. But if you are stuck, or unhappy with your current level of achievement, the benefits can be tremendous. I want to share with you a story of a man I worked with who had the courage to risk changing his inner voice. It's a great example of all the ideas we've been discussing.

FRANK'S BAD ATTITUDE

The vice president in charge of personnel for an engineering company asked me for advice on how to work with one of their engineers. Frank was one of the senior employees in the organization, and no one had more experience in product design and research. But he was so hard to work with that the company was thinking about firing him. He was very critical of anyone else's ideas, but rarely offered new ideas of his own. The vice president had come to me in a last-ditch effort to develop a new approach to working with Frank.

I asked if I could have one meeting with Frank. He agreed, and we met in his office a week later. I took an immediate liking to him. Far from being the grouchy tyrant I had pictured from the stories about him, I found Frank to be a very quiet, sensitive man. But he was extremely worried. He had heard rumors of his imminent dismissal, and at age fifty-five he wasn't sure he could find a job at an equivalent seniority level elsewhere. As we discussed Frank's role in the firm, I realized that his internal Critic was so firmly in control that he could hardly imagine a different way of interacting with people. I asked him if he would like to meet with me for a month or two to see if I could help him, and he agreed.

At the next meeting, Frank told me his view of the company. He felt that it had grown too much in recent years, and that the "suits and ties" had too great an influence. Frank thought that while such issues as marketing and profitability had become a priority, the basic function of the engineering departments, research and product design, were being ignored. He was particularly incensed by the fact that he had been overlooked for promotion three times. Instead his boss had advanced younger engineers who Frank felt were less competent.

As a result, Frank had withdrawn into a shell. Because his unpopular opinions were always criticized, he stopped offering them. He felt that the projects he was in charge of were not challenging, so he was unhappy in his work. The management noticed. He realized that sometimes he took out his frustrations on those who worked with him, but he didn't see how he could change his feelings.

Frank's basic problem was that he had developed a "bad attitude." I had seen similar problems many times before. Often, the problem involves competent, solid people who have been overtaken by change and who have failed to adapt. In Frank's case, he realized how negative he was becoming.

So why didn't he change? Perhaps partly out of fear of what change might bring. Perhaps because Frank believed that the quality of his work mattered more than his attitude. "How can they fire me when I'm the best damn engineer they have?" he complained.

How wrong this belief is! In a recent survey of American executives, 90 percent said the reason for firing an employee had to do with a bad attitude. It usually doesn't say this on the pink slip. The reason given might be low productivity, frequent work absences, or poor communication with management and employees. But the real reason can often be summed up as a bad attitude.

I knew that simply telling Frank to improve his attitude wouldn't help; his boss had already tried this approach. I needed to help him understand the impact of his negative thoughts on his work. During subsequent meetings with Frank, I introduced the notion of listening to his inner voice. Frank accepted this idea readily. He knew that his inner voice was a problem, because it kept him up at night. He was losing a lot of sleep worrying about the future.

I asked Frank to make a list of the things he said to himself when he got into conflicts at work. During one week, I asked Frank to write down a few of his thoughts every hour for two days. Here is a partial list of the thoughts that Frank came up with:

- *I know more about the project than this guy. Who is he to be telling me how to organize the project?*
- *I hate working with this guy. He got the promotion that I should have received. Just looking at him reminds me of that.*
- *Work is terrible. My projects have a low priority, nobody listens to me, and I might get fired any day.*
- *I work harder than anyone else here. I should get more credit for my work.*
- *I'm not sucking up to the "suits and ties" to get ahead. I refuse to play that game. I'll do it my way.*

Frank's complete list was a lot longer, and it gave him lots of opportunities for change. I asked Frank to give me an honest rating of how each of these thoughts probably affected his productivity. At first he claimed that what he thought about had no impact on the quality of his work. But I asked him to imagine that a younger engineer was coming to him for advice. "What would your reaction be," I questioned Frank, "if he told you that these were his typical thoughts?"

Frank realized that he would try to convince the younger engineer to be more positive. "It couldn't be as bad as he thinks," said Frank. "If it were, he should quit." This realization was an important turning point in our work. As soon as Frank realized that he might be happier if he left the company, he felt more in control of his future.

Now I challenged Frank to come up with thoughts that would be more helpful to him at work. Notice that I didn't get caught up in an argument with Frank about which opinions were right and which were wrong. His boss had fallen into that trap many times. Frank could not be convinced to change his mind, because he felt he was right.

Instead, I worked with Frank's basic human desire to have his work appreciated. I knew that Frank wanted to accomplish more at his company, and he was willing to work with me to reach that goal.

We refined Frank's productivity ideas in a give-and-take process over the next several meetings. Here are some of the ideas that Frank came up with for more productive ways of talking to himself:

- *My experience will help on this project, but I don't know all the answers. I will listen to his ideas and not criticize them. Then I will offer my own suggestions in a positive manner.*
- *I can't blame him for being promoted. Anyone would accept such an offer. I'll take my grievance to management, which is where it belongs.*
- *Work is not going well, but I have lots of other positives in my life. I love my wife, I have a great home, I'm very well respected in this field. Instead of worrying, I will dedicate myself to making work better.*
- *It would be nice to get more credit for my work, but if I'm satisfied with my effort, that's the most important thing. I only work hard because I want to.*
- *I don't have to be like the "suits and ties" in order to work well with them. They want me to be more enthusiastic. I want to do really important work. We can find some common ground.*

Once Frank had come up with a strong list of productive thoughts, he began going into his office first thing in the morning to think about them for five minutes. Then he opened his door and started work. He did the same thing after lunch, for just five minutes. Frank also wrote a short computer program, which put one of these productive thoughts on his screen every hour. He would read the thought and then dismiss it from the screen. Gradually, Frank began to replace his negative thoughts with productive ones.

I met with Frank only occasionally over the next six months. But the feedback I got from others was impressive. The personnel vice president called me to say that Frank was "a new man." He couldn't believe the changes. Others were also impressed by Frank's manner, and he was asked to head up several new projects. When he did well on these projects, he was given even greater responsibility. Within twelve months he received the promotion he wanted. Now, three years later, he is division chief of the entire research program for the company.

I know how much courage it took for Frank to make those changes. He was very comfortable in his old way of looking at the world, and there was no guarantee that the new way we talked about would bring any improvements. But the risks he took in abandoning his Critic-oriented style of thinking were repaid many times over.

You have a big advantage over Frank. You already recognize the importance of being in your personal Achievement Zone in order to be successful. With your head start, imagine what you can accomplish with Productive Analysis. Find the negative thinking habits that are holding you back from reaching your goals at work, at play, and in your relationships. Replace them with a productive approach, and you will experience greater success than you thought possible. I've seen the transformation in so many people—I know you can do it too.

Productive Analysis Tips

▪ Many of the athletes I work with have favorite sayings that they use to motivate themselves. Just reading these sayings can increase your determination to reach your goals.

For example, Olympic archer Jay Barrs offered these two sayings as his favorites: "If you're not out in front of the pack, the scenery never changes" and "If you're not making dust, you're eating dust."

▪ When I interviewed Norm Bellingham, he shared some of his favorite thoughts collected from his competitors. "Richard Fox, the Englishman, is one of the greatest paddlers ever in our sport," explained Norm. "Two things he said always stuck with me. They are: 'Never make the same mistake twice' and 'I want to train so that my ninety percent is as good as other people's hundred percent.'"

▪ One of my own favorites comes from a movie by Penny Marshall called *A League of Their Own.* In it, Tom Hanks plays a broken-down major leaguer who makes a comeback as a manager of a professional women's baseball team during World War II. At one point, one of the players tells Hanks's character that she is quitting the team, because "it's just too hard." Hanks stares at her and says: "It's supposed to be hard. If it wasn't hard, everyone would do it. The hard is what makes it great."

Hanks's character was talking about baseball, but that attitude can be applied to everything we do.

Here is a list of some affirmative sayings that I have gathered over the years. See which ones appeal to you. Whenever you find yourself thinking negatively, think about one of these sayings, or one of your own, instead:

I will always give 100 percent effort.

Once I set goals for myself I will always strive to reach them.

I am proud of always giving my best, even if I don't achieve my goal.

When faced with a challenge, I will always try to be in my Achievement Zone.

I have the skills to cope with any problem.

I love to win, but my goal is to achieve to the full extent of my capabilities.

I don't like the present situation, but I can cope with it.

I don't have to be perfect to achieve my goals. I need to focus on my best effort.

Things didn't go my way, but it's not the end of the world. I look forward to next time.

I can't change other people. I can change how I react to other people.

Life is too short to get upset over this.

I'll enjoy my successes in life. I know that no success is permanent, so the time to enjoy it is now.

I know how to keep cool under pressure. It's not such a big thing.

I know I can stay in control in any situation. I know how to be in my Achievement Zone.

I lead a balanced life.

I never stop learning. I can always improve.

My mistakes give me feedback, showing me where I can become stronger.

The only pressure that exists is the pressure I put on myself.

What other favorite sayings inspire and motivate you? Make a special page of them in your Achievement Zone diary. Write down your favorites on cards and put them up somewhere you can see them every day.

Read them and think about them on a regular basis. You will find that such beliefs can shape your life for the better. Remember, you have the ability to choose the beliefs that will guide you in life. Choose productively!

SUMMARY

How to Learn Productive Analysis

Step 1 ■
Be Aware of Your Inner Voice

Step 2 ■
Use Your Critic Productively

Step 3 ■
Replace Negativity with Productivity

Keeping Cool:

Stay Calm in Pressure Situations

I interviewed Olympic archery champion Jay Barrs during a practice session with the U.S. team. I asked Jay how he felt at the end of an Olympic final, with the gold medal on the line. "I was really scared, really nervous," he told me. "But because I had practiced so much to be ready for that moment, it was a good feeling. With three arrows to go I knew I was very close to the lead. I walked up to the line and I remember bending down over the TV mike and saying, 'Check, mike, one, two, three.' I was feeling cool. But then my first shot was too soft and was a seven. I always get most nervous over the second shot, so I concentrated on making a strong shot, and it was. It was a nine.

"I can't describe what it felt like on that last shot. I couldn't feel my body below the waist, I was so nervous. It felt like I was floating. I knew the arrow was a ten the moment it left my bow. We have two and a half minutes to shoot those three arrows, but mine were gone in thirty-one seconds. Later I found out that the Korean champion, Park Sung-soo, had shot only

one arrow when I finished, and it was a seven, so he needed two tens to tie me. He shot two nines."

Jay is now preparing for another Olympics, this time in the United States. When I spoke with him, I wanted to know what helped him win that gold medal in 1988. "I was able to perform so well in that situation because I had prepared so often for it. At home in Arizona I would try to re-create the butterflies and the goose bumps of an Olympic final while I was practicing. I would say to myself, These last three arrows are for the gold medal, *and I would feel the nerves, despite the 115-degree heat and the lonely surroundings. In my mind I would hear the whistle to go to the line and I would hear the roar of the crowd. I could feel the pressure very strongly. And I would tell myself,* Execute three good arrows. Don't worry about the score, get off three good shots. *And that's exactly what I told myself when I went to the line in Seoul. All that preparation paid off."*

Jay Barrs's preparation did indeed pay off. He won the gold medal in archery in Seoul, Korea, at the age of twenty-six. He shot 338 points out of a possible 360 in the last round.

What Is Keeping Cool?

Have you ever watched the Olympics on television and wondered how the athletes feel as they compete with millions of people watching? If you're like me, you probably marvel at how calm they seem under such pressure-filled circumstances. How do athletes remain anxiety-free under such conditions? I'll let you in on a secret. They don't.

If you could come with me backstage at the Olympics you would see a great number of very, very nervous people. Athletes pacing and fidgeting, complaining about some delay in the start of their event; people looking tense and uptight, cracking a smile but with clenched teeth; and people running off to the bathroom, sometimes several times in a short period. Often, the tension in the air is so thick that you swear you can feel it.

This is a truth about champions and elite competitors that

many people don't know—they're just like you and me in their reactions to stressful situations. They get just as nervous when they have to go out and be evaluated. I have never worked with a great athlete, be it a world champion or an Olympic gold medalist, who never got nervous before a big match or event. They all do.

The big difference between these champions and most of us is that *they have learned how to stay cool and focused when the pressure is on.* They don't panic when they get nervous, and they use specific strategies to keep their nerves under control. Despite the stress they're under, they know how to achieve at a very high level. I call the skill they use Keeping Cool.

The Keeping Cool skill is extremely important in reaching your Achievement Zone. By mastering Keeping Cool, you can:

- Learn how to stay calm and look confident when giving a performance or making a speech.
- Handle stressful situations in a productive and professional way.
- Perform at your best, even when the pressure is greatest and others are evaluating your performance.

Gold medals are not won by chance, and Olympic athletes are fully prepared for the pressure they'll encounter at the Olympics. In fact, many of them use their anxiety in a constructive way to push themselves to even greater heights. Let me share a story with you that shows how two gold medal winners dealt successfully with the stress of the Olympic experience.

JOE AND SCOTT'S SPECTACULAR TRIUMPH IN BARCELONA

One of the surprise gold medals for the United States team in Barcelona was won by the whitewater canoe pair of Scott Strasbaugh and Joe Jacobi. The veteran (Strasbaugh, twenty-nine) and the youngster (Jacobi, twenty-two) were not given much chance after racing poorly in Europe the previous year. In addition, both were coming off injuries that kept them out of the water for a long period at the end of 1990.

Their Olympic competitors, especially the French and Czechoslovakian pairs, were battle-hardened with a string of successes in big races. Surprisingly, though, the two Americans found themselves with the fastest run on the board after the first trip down the roiling waters of La Seu d'Urgeill. Now the challenge was to stay there. In whitewater, each pair has two runs to establish their fastest time. The two times are not added together. So any pair could come down the course the second time and beat them.

When I spoke to Joe Jacobi about their great performance on the first run, he attributed it to their ability to relax before they started. "The pressure of the Olympics makes you think about all the wrong things. For two weeks we had been in a poor frame of mind. You think about the medals, you worry about the course, you get bothered by the media, and I admit that we let it get to us. But just five minutes before the race we managed to change it all around. Scott turned to me and said, 'Let's have fun.' That did it. From then on we just wanted to see how well we could do."

I asked Joe if their first run was close to perfect. "Far from it," Joe replied. "We made several mistakes; in fact, we nearly tipped the boat over on Gate 20. But the test of slalom is to see who can make the least mistakes and bounce back quickest from the ones you make. Our concentration was excellent. But our coach, Fritz Haller, didn't let us sit around and feel pleased with ourselves. He took out his clipboard and showed us all the mistakes we had made. Fritz was adamant that we would have to improve our time in the second run if we wanted to medal. 'There were a lot of uncharacteristic mistakes out there,' said Fritz. 'You can't expect to be fortunate like that again.' And he was right. Two boats beat our first-run time on the second run."

Joe and Scott had about two and a half hours to wait for their next run. Lots of time to get nervous! I wanted to know how Joe coped with it. "I did a lot of belly breathing," he said. "I held each breath for several seconds, and I said the words 'relax, recharge, ready' to myself on each breath. I did that dozens of times in the trailer between the two runs. Then we went out and warmed up and visualized ourselves going down the course. We knew we didn't need to do a lot differently, just have better lines between gates and hit the up gates tighter."

The second run was even better than the first. But on the very last gate they seemed sure to hit and incur a penalty. Then Joe suddenly twisted his body into an impossible position and swept under the pole with inches to spare. At the end the cameras showed Joe throwing his fist in the air. But there were still ten boats to come, and any of them could have bumped the two Americans out of first. They didn't. "When I crossed the finish line, I didn't know we had won the race, but I was so glad that we had done our best at the Olympics," said Joe. "That's what really mattered to us, and we achieved our goal. So many people looked out for us—it was a team effort. I'll always remember the media people coming out of their trailers and applauding us—that was amazing. The reporters asked us afterwards if we said anything to each other before our second run. The only thing Scott said was 'Do you want to get in the boat now?'"

Joe and Scott's story shows how important it is to Keep Cool when the pressure's on. The difference between success and disappointment at the Olympics is a combination of the right training and being able to stay cool on the big day. Successful athletes take the staying cool part of the success formula very seriously. Take a page out of their book, and learn how to Keep Cool when you really need to.

Learn Keeping Cool

There are three steps to mastering Keeping Cool. They are:

Keeping Cool

Step 1. It's OK to Be Nervous

Step 2. Learn How to Relax the Mind/Body

Step 3. Calm Down in Pressure Situations

In this chapter I'll guide you through exercises to learn these Keeping Cool skills. If you follow the guidelines I present, you'll become skilled at dealing with pressure situations.

Step 1. It's OK to Be Nervous

Almost all of us have experienced performance anxiety, or nervousness, at one time or another. It may have been before a big exam, an important interview, or a presentation to the CEO of your company. Suddenly, your mind fills with unwanted thoughts, making it difficult for you to concentrate on anything else. *I'm a nervous wreck. I'm afraid I'll blow it. What if I forget what I'm supposed to say? I know this is going to be a disaster.* These thoughts are typically accompanied by unpleasant physical symptoms. You may experience nausea or discomfort in the stomach, difficulty breathing, a rapid heartbeat, muscle tension, or dizziness and numbness.

Not surprisingly, these thoughts and sensations can interfere with your performance. You might get flustered in the middle of the interview and lose your poise in front of the very people you wanted to impress. Or perhaps you panic when you can't answer a test question and don't finish the exam because of this.

Most of us don't like the sensation of being nervous, and even more important, we don't know how to handle it. Many clients have come to me because their anxiety *interferes with effective performance.* The two big problems I see time and time again are **avoidance** of the stressful situation, and **panic** when the pressure is on. Both these problems are the result of ineffective coping with performance anxiety. I'll describe these two problems, and then I'll show you how to prevent them by learning Keeping Cool.

Avoidance

Many people deal with performance anxiety by avoiding the stressful task as much as possible. If there is no deadline or urgency about the goal, we tend to come up with ways to avoid it.

For example, the student who knows he must study for a big

exam keeps putting it off. He might even go so far as to sit down with his books, but even then he finds ways to avoid studying. He might go and get another book from the library or discover that he needs a new pen and paper. Perhaps he remembers that he hasn't done his household chores. Something "more immediate" keeps popping up.

This pattern of avoidance is called *procrastination,* and it's very common. It's a dangerous habit, because the procrastinator typically leaves everything to the last minute and then completes the job in a mad, frantic rush. Procrastinators minimize their anxiety by cramming it into the shortest possible time. Although the work might get done, it is usually of poor quality and doesn't show the procrastinator's true capabilities. In the long run, this poor-quality work catches up to the procrastinator and holds him or her back from promotion and achievement.

Panic

A second characteristic response to performance anxiety is panic. Panic occurs when you don't know how to handle the nerves you feel in the pressure situation. Success becomes impossible in this stage. Characteristics of a state of panic include:

- *You "freeze" and can't remember what you're supposed to do or how to do it.*
- *Your mind begins to race.* There are too many thoughts competing for attention, and you can't focus or concentrate.
- *You feel out of control.* Skills and knowledge that you thought you had excellent control over now seem unreliable and weak.
- *You make bad choices.* Distracted and confused by your feelings, you forget to pay attention to important details. An example is the Michigan basketball player Chris Webber, who called a time-out in the closing seconds of the 1993 NCAA Championship Game. His team, however, had no time-outs left, so North Carolina got the ball and won the game.
- *You rush.* Because the feelings of panic are so unpleasant, you rush to get the performance over quickly so you can escape from the situation as soon as possible.

None of these characteristics help performance. Indeed, the Olympic athletes I work with tell me that these are the same characteristics they experience when they perform badly. If you recognize yourself in any of these descriptions, you will benefit from learning the Keeping Cool skills practiced by athletes.

How Top Athletes Handle Performance Anxiety

The big myth is that if you get nervous, you'll perform poorly. It's not true! My study of elite athletes has shown that they routinely get nervous before big competitions. Yet many of them go on to perform extremely well despite their nervousness. If you care about your performance, it's normal to worry. Top coaches know from experience that nervousness is a natural part of sport and competition. In fact, coaches worry if their athletes *don't* get nervous! A leading football coach always asked his players if they were nervous. "The ones that said no were the ones that *I'd* get nervous about," said the coach. "The ones who admitted they were fearful always seemed to do better."

That's because being nervous can actually help you do your best. Have you ever wondered why world records are so often set at world championships and Olympics? It's because athletes use their nerves to push themselves to excellent performance. The nervousness you experience before a performance is your body's way of preparing you for the challenge ahead. The heart rate speeds up, blood pressure rises, the rate of breathing increases, and the muscles of the body tense as the body gets ready for "battle."

Early man was without weapons in his battle against predators, enemies, and a hostile environment, so he survived by using his superior intelligence and by anticipating danger. The body's reaction to danger (which we call nervousness today) gave him extra strength in battle or extra energy to flee.

Today, that rush of adrenaline can be very useful to elite athletes. The extra energy can be harnessed to help them perform at a superior level. If you think about it, you will also likely recall times when you were very nervous and yet still went out and performed very well. What is important at this stage is not to lose your confidence, despite the nervousness.

Great athletes know this and expect to be nervous when they're ready to perform. Marjorie Jackson, the wonderful Australian sprinter who won both the 100 meters and 200 meters at the Olympic Games in Helsinki in 1952, was interviewed after her last race before retiring at age twenty-two. It was the Commonwealth Games in Vancouver in 1954. "I've never been so nervous in all my life," she said. Marjorie then reported that she told herself, *It's a good sign. You'll probably break the world record.* Which is precisely what she did, running the 220 yards in 24 seconds flat. She broke the old record of 24.2 seconds held by the great Dutch sprinter Fanny Blankers-Koen.

Jackson recognized her nervousness, but she did not give in to panic. Instead, she was remarkably confident ("You'll probably break the world record"). Her approach illustrates the first step in the Keeping Cool skill. Don't fight the butterflies you feel before competition. It's okay to be nervous!

What separates these athletes from the rest of us? They have learned how to use their nervousness to propel themselves to a new level of excellence. They don't avoid competitive situations, because they know that testing themselves against others will help them improve. And they use specific relaxation strategies to prevent panic.

I want you to learn these same skills. I'll show you how to recognize nervousness and *accept it as a natural part of the competitive process.* I'll also show you how to keep your cool when others around you are losing theirs. The trick is not to panic when the pressure is on. First, you must learn and practice some specific relaxation strategies, which you will later use in pressure situations.

Step 2: Learn How to Relax the Mind/Body

To be successful, your mind and body must work seamlessly together. Anxiety and panic interfere with mind/body integration. The mind can't enjoy the performance experience if it's thinking ahead, worrying about what's going to happen. If your body becomes too tense, smooth execution of a task becomes impossible. Athletes and sport psychologists have developed several useful strategies for dealing with competition anxiety. I'll now show you how to use these techniques.

The following is a list of the relaxation strategies I'll be talking about:

1. Deep breathing
2. Muscle relaxation
3. Centering
4. Visualization
5. Autogenic training
6. Coping affirmations

Let me say right at the beginning that there isn't any *one* correct way of staying calm in pressure situations. Athletes have found that many different methods help them stay calm and focused. In addition to the methods I describe in this chapter, approaches such as yoga, t'ai chi, and zen are popular. If you have had experience with relaxation strategies other than the ones I mention, that's great. Remember that the *method* you use to stay calm in performance situations isn't as important as the fact that you *have the skill* to Keep Cool under pressure.

Athletes sometimes ask me if it's better to relax the mind or the body. Some techniques, such as deep breathing, seem to be very physical. Others, such as visualization, appear to be much more mental. My answer is that it doesn't matter where you begin. What matters is where you end up. Whether you start with a physical or a mental approach, relaxation should end with the whole mind/body feeling calm and peaceful. Therefore, your choice of approach should be guided by your own preferences.

The best way to learn is by doing. So for each of these approaches I have provided a step-by-step learning exercise. This will help you master the skill of relaxing the mind/body.

I would suggest that you try all the exercises several times each to see which ones suit your style for reaching the Achievement Zone. You may be surprised when an exercise that seemed unappealing to you is actually very effective in helping you reach your personal Zone of optimal performance. Use that approach until you become really good at it. You might even learn several different methods and use them in different situations.

It's helpful to give yourself a "wake-up" suggestion just before you end any of these relaxation methods. Before you stop, say to yourself, "When I open my eyes I will feel alert and rested." Take a few deep breaths, open your eyes, and stretch. Before you begin an activity after any of these relaxation methods, make sure that you're wide awake and focused. You may not need to be deeply relaxed in order to perform at your best. Instead, you will use the relaxation control you learn to prevent stress and panic.

1. Deep breathing

Many of the problems athletes experience with tension and anxiety are related to breathing. It's very common for athletes to change the way they breathe when the competition reaches a critical point. Unconsciously, they breathe less often and hold their breath longer. This results in their muscles becoming tense and their heart rate speeding up, which hurts performance.

What you should do in pressure situations is the exact opposite. You should breathe more deeply and regularly. This helps the muscles stay loose and keeps the heart rate down. The result is a smooth performance.

Working with performers in other fields has taught me that poor breathing is a universal problem, one that afflicts actors, musicians, and public speakers. However, these problems can be overcome by learning good breathing habits.

It's counterproductive to worry about whether you're breathing well or not. When you think about something simple like breathing, you usually mess it up. So the best strategy is to practice breathing properly until it's so comfortable that it becomes automatic. In the next exercise I'll show you how to breathe effectively. Deep breathing, sometimes called abdominal breathing because of the muscles you use, is a very effective way to help yourself Keep Cool.

When you get in pressure situations, remind yourself to breathe deeply. For example, take a few deep breaths before beginning a speech or presentation. During pauses or breaks, say a cue word such as "deep" or "relax," which will remind you to keep breathing deeply.

Learn the skill of breathing effectively by trying the following exercise today.

LEARN DEEP BREATHING

For each relaxation exercise, choose a comfortable position in which to begin. You might lie on your back on a firm, supporting surface. Or sit in a chair with your knees comfortably apart, palms resting on thighs.

Have someone read the following instructions to you. Or record yourself and play the tape back as you rest comfortably.

Close your eyes. I want you first to become aware of your breathing. Notice the air flowing in and out of the lungs. Observe your breathing pattern for a few moments.

Now become aware of the air flowing into your lungs and as you breathe in, take the fresh air all the way to the bottom of your lungs. Feel your lungs filling with fresh air from the bottom up. Don't force it; allow it to happen. Take several breaths in this way.

Now take some deep breaths using your abdomen. It should feel as if your stomach is filling with air as you breathe in. Don't even use the chest muscles to breathe at this stage. Hold the breath for just a moment and then breathe out.

Return to your resting, quiet breathing pattern. Just be aware of the air flowing gently into and out of your lungs. Don't take deep breaths, just be aware of how you are breathing naturally. Breathe naturally for the next minute or so.

Take some more deep breaths from the abdomen, letting the fresh air flow all the way down to the bottom of your lungs, down toward the very core, the energy source for your body. Each time you breathe out, let tension and anxiety go with the breath. Just let it drain from your body.

Return to a natural pattern of breathing. Take a moment to become aware of the feeling of relaxation and to enjoy it. Notice how your body feels after you have blown out the tension and anxiety.

In a moment this exercise will come to an end. You can take these feelings of peace, calm, and relaxation with you. You are ready to meet whatever challenges you face.

Take three deep breaths now. Use your abdominal muscles to draw the air all the way to the bottom of the lungs, and as you do, feel energy and alertness flowing into you, spreading out from your center core to all parts of your body. You are ready for action! You feel terrific. Restored. Recharged. Open your eyes and enjoy your new energy.

FOR YOUR ACHIEVEMENT ZONE DIARY

Write down your thoughts about the exercise you have just completed.

- What did you notice about your typical breathing pattern?
- Was this pattern different at the end of the exercise than at the beginning?
- How did you feel when you were doing the deep breathing, taking the air all the way to the bottom of your lungs?
- How did you feel as you breathed in?
- How did you feel as you breathed out?
- What aspects of your breathing do you want to work on in order to be more effective in performance situations?
- How do you feel now that the exercise is finished?
- How useful will deep breathing be in helping you reach your Achievement Zone?

(You can adapt these questions to all the relaxation exercises that follow. Make notes on each relaxation method in your Achievement Zone diary.)

2. Muscle relaxation

With muscle relaxation, you can learn where all your muscle groups are located and how to relax them quickly. At first, the complete exercise takes up to half an hour to complete. With practice, you will be able to relax tension in major muscle groups in a matter of minutes. Athletes use this technique to help them loosen important muscles that they will use in their upcoming performance. For example, a swimmer may use the technique to relax the arms, shoulders, and legs before a race.

You will find that relaxing your muscles not only prepares your body for a performance or competition, it also relaxes your mind. For example, when you are speaking in front of a group, your greatest tension may be in the stomach and back. If you use muscle relaxation to keep these muscles loose, you will find that this will also eliminate some of your anxiety.

To learn how to use muscle relaxation effectively, you should expect to do the following exercise at least four days a week for several weeks until you feel comfortable with the entire procedure. Then you can try achieving the same effect in a shorter period of time. Finally, try using the muscle-relaxation technique in actual performance situations.

LEARN MUSCLE RELAXATION

1. Find a quiet place, free from distractions, where you can lie down with your eyes closed. Soft, relaxing music in the background may help, but it isn't necessary. Later, you can practice this skill sitting up, then with eyes open, and finally while engaging in other activities.

2. Focus on slowing your breathing down. Inhale a deep breath, hold it for three to five seconds, and SLOWLY EXHALE. Take as many of these deep breaths as necessary to begin to feel calm. Your breathing should be slow and rhythmic before you proceed to the muscle-relaxation process.

3. Beginning with the muscles in your neck, TIGHTEN the muscles by bringing your chin slowly down to your chest until you can clearly feel the tension. Hold for three seconds. Become very aware of where those muscles are and what the tension in them feels like. Then RELAX the muscles. Let all of the tension go. Feel it drain out of your muscles as they become loose and relaxed. Notice the DIFFERENCE between the feelings of tension and relaxation.

(The level of tension you decide to maintain is up to you. It should not be a level that is painful or uncomfortable. Be careful if you have a history of problems with a particular muscle group. You may want to skip the TENSE cycle and just focus on letting the muscles RELAX if you find it difficult or painful.)

Repeat this process (TENSE-HOLD-RELAX) with the muscles in your neck. Let the tension drain away; let it just flow out of the muscles, leaving them loose and relaxed. Enjoy this feeling.

Sit up and feel your neck muscles perfectly supporting your head, with your head and chin up. Now repeat the TENSE-HOLD-RELAX process by bringing your right ear slowly down to your right shoulder and stretching your neck muscles. HOLD the tension, then RELAX. Let the tension drain away.

Now repeat these steps on your left side. Repeat until the muscles in your neck feel very relaxed and comfortable.

4. Move on to the muscles in your shoulders. TIGHTEN the muscles by raising the shoulders toward the ears until you can clearly feel the tension. Hold for three seconds. Become very aware of where those muscles are and what tension in them feels like. Then RELAX the muscles.

Repeat this process (TENSE-HOLD-RELAX) with the same muscles in your shoulders. Let the tension drain away and enjoy this feeling in the muscles of your shoulders.

5. Now that you understand the basic muscle relaxation process (TENSE-HOLD-RELAX), move through all of the following muscle groups and repeat this process TWICE for each muscle group. (If the muscles still feel tense, you may repeat the TENSE-HOLD-RELAX cycle as many times as you like):

6. Tense-hold-relax the arm muscles, one arm at a time, by bringing the hand up to the shoulder, feeling the tension in the muscles and noticing the difference when you relax the muscles.

7. Tense-hold-relax the arm muscles, one arm at a time, by stretching the hand and arm out as far as they will go.

8. Tense-hold-relax the hand muscles, making a fist.

9. Tense-hold-relax the hand muscles, stretching the fingers as wide apart as they can go until you feel the tension.

10. Tense-hold-relax the chest muscles by pulling your shoulders and arms back, and bending your neck backward until you feel the tension in your chest muscles.

11. Tense-hold-relax the abdominal muscles by pulling your stomach in until you feel the tension. Really let go of the tension completely on this one.

12. Tense-hold-relax the muscles in your buttocks by clenching the muscles until you feel the tension.

13. Tense-hold-relax the muscles in your thighs by clenching the muscles until you feel the tension.

14. Tense-hold-relax the muscles in your legs by pressing your feet down firmly against the floor (if you are sitting).

15. Tense-hold-relax the muscles in your legs by straightening the knees and pressing the backs of your legs down into the floor (if you are lying down).

16. Tense-hold-relax the muscles in your leg by pointing the toes away from the body and bending your feet at the ankles.

17. Tense-hold-relax the muscles in your feet by curling up your toes and flexing your feet until you feel the tension.

18. Tense-hold-relax the muscles in your feet by spreading the toes as far apart as they will go until you feel the tension.

19. Let's move back to the head and eliminate any tension there. Tense-hold-relax the muscles in your forehead by squeezing the muscles as if you are frowning. Let go any tension in the forehead.

20. Tense-hold-relax the muscles in your face and jaw by grimacing. Show your teeth as you feel the tension. Then let it go.

21. Tense-hold-relax the muscles around your mouth by opening it as wide as you can. Feel the tension in your lower jaw especially. Then let it all go.

22. Mentally scan your body for any remaining tension. If there is an area that still feels tense, repeat the tense-hold-relax cycle one or two more times in that area. Also, if there are any

particular muscle groups you missed in the exercise, or that you want to pay special attention to, do them now.

23. It's time to rest and do nothing. Become aware of your breathing, the breath flowing into and out of your body. Just take several minutes to enjoy this delicious feeling.

24. Repeat a cue word or phrase that you can use to trigger this calm feeling in the future. You might use *calm, peaceful, deeply relaxed,* or your own personal favorite.

This entire procedure should last ten to twenty minutes; the goal is to evoke deep relaxation. With training and practice in this procedure, an athlete can learn to relax in a matter of seconds.

When you need to relax quickly in a performance situation, repeat your trigger words to yourself several times (for example, *deeply relaxed, deeply relaxed, deeply relaxed*). Concentrate on relaxing the most important muscle group. For example, a computer programmer might focus on her neck and shoulders. A speaker might focus on the chest and stomach. However, it is unrealistic to expect to achieve this type of muscle-tension control after only a few sessions. It may take a few months to perfect this skill. Remember, a commitment of time and effort is necessary to become good at using mind/body skills.

3. Centering

Centering is a technique that is extremely useful in performance situations because it is fast and effective. It is a quick relaxation technique developed by sport psychologists specifically for use in situations where time is limited. With practice, you can use centering to get rid of tension in a matter of seconds. Olympic medalist Bob Foth told me that he can now relax deeply by centering, whereas it used to take him some time using muscle relaxation.

You can use centering whenever you have a moment to pause during a performance situation. It is extremely useful for:

- refocusing
- recovering from a mistake, and
- calming down after experiencing a strong emotion.

Practice the following centering exercise until you feel comfortable doing it. Then try centering in performance situations. The more you use it, the easier it will be to center when you're in a real pressure situation.

Learn Centering

In order to use this technique effectively, you should learn the deep-breathing approach first.

1. Take a stance as if you were preparing to resist someone pushing you. Your feet should be roughly shoulder width apart. You should feel that you are standing straight, not slouching over or holding yourself overly erect with chest thrust out. Check the position of your chin—it should be level, not tucked in or sticking up. Feel your center of gravity. It should be low, giving you increased stability. Try to feel that your legs are growing into the floor. You should feel your weight distributed along the entire length of your foot—not on the front or the heel.

2. Take a deep breath using the deep-breathing technique. As you fill your lungs from the abdomen up (not the chest down), say the word "in" to yourself.

3. Exhale through your mouth. Allow your breath to come out with an audible gasp. Feel your body relax as you breathe out. Feel your center of gravity moving even lower in your body. Say the word "relax" to yourself as you breathe.

4. Repeat this procedure twice. Feel the tension leave your body as you breathe out.

5. As soon as you have finished centering, begin your performance. Go for it!

Centering can help you regain calm in a variety of situations. For example, a basketball player might use centering whenever he is reentering the game after being on the bench. He might also use it to stay loose every time he goes to the free-throw line. And he can use it to help focus his attention after a break in play.

---

4. Visualization

Your imagination is a powerful tool for helping you reach your goals. You can also use it to help you Keep Cool in stressful situations. A very popular strategy among athletes is to use the "peaceful scene" approach.

To use this approach, think of a scene that you find tranquil and calm. You might think of lying on a tropical beach, walking through a quiet forest, or sitting in a mountain meadow. Create the scene in your imagination as vividly as possible. Use your Creative Thinking skills to bring the scene to life with color, touch, smell, and feelings. Imagine that you are there. Then enjoy it. Imagine how peaceful and relaxed you feel in that situation.

Support the feelings of calm by repeating some positive affirmations. For example, you might tell yourself:

I feel very peaceful.

I am content.

I am warm and relaxed.

I feel refreshed, invigorated.

I feel calm and strong.

My spirit feels renewed.

When you first try imagining this scene, it might take some time. Give yourself ten to fifteen minutes when you are learning this visualization approach. With practice, you will be able to imagine the scene and feel relaxed in a minute or so. A useful strategy used by some of my clients is to carry a photo or a postcard of a favorite peaceful scene. Take the picture out and imagine that you are there when you need to calm down.

If you don't feel very creative about imagining your own peaceful scene, you're welcome to try the following visualization.

VISUALIZE A PEACEFUL SCENE

Imagine that you are out in the country. It's a sunny day and you enter a shady forest. The sky is a clear blue with some high clouds. You feel very peaceful. Imagine that you are really there, walking through the tall trees. Feel yourself in that scene as clearly as possible. What does the grass under your feet look like? Can you hear the sound of a mountain brook running somewhere nearby? Imagine smelling the fresh air of the forest. The natural fragrances are crisp and pleasant. Bend down and feel the coolness of the grass, the freshness of the earth.

Imagine that you throw down a rug to lie on. Feel yourself lying down, drinking in the beauty of the country around you. You are wonderfully at peace, with no worries or cares. Take the time to enjoy this moment. You don't have to answer any phones, go to any meetings. You can just relax. Feel that relaxation spreading through your body. It's so wonderful to be here and just unwind. Let go of any tension in your body. Imagine the muscles unwinding and loosening up, the tension flowing away.

As you enjoy the relaxation, scan your body and identify any area that is sore or tense. Turn your attention to this area and let the fatigue drain away. Replace it with the heaviness and warmth of relaxation. Draw in the golden peace of this country afternoon and let the soothing calm spread through your body. Let go of tension and fatigue. Take in peace and healing.

Take three deep breaths. Feel new energy and alertness flowing through your body with each breath. You feel great. Open your eyes and enjoy your refreshed attitude. You can take this peace and calm with you when you end your imaginary excursion in the forest. When you go back to work you will feel restored and renewed.

5. Autogenic training

This approach to relaxation was developed in Europe, and sport psychologists from behind the Iron Curtain discovered many applications for it. It was a very popular relaxation method for athletes from the Soviet Union and East Germany.

The technique of autogenic training is based on the idea that our bodies respond strongly to suggestions. You can provide these suggestions to yourself. Relaxation is achieved by choosing a comfortable position and repeating a series of verbal suggestions. I remember wondering how effective such a method could be when I first learned of it as an undergraduate. Seeing is believing! I tried out the autogenic suggestions in our psychology lab. As I sat comfortably repeating the suggestion *My arm is heavy and warm,* a sensor measuring the skin temperature of my hand showed a two-degree rise! It is remarkable how deeply you can learn to relax if you practice this technique.

LEARN AUTOGENIC TRAINING

Choose a comfortable position. Make sure you won't be distracted while you are doing this exercise. A good position is sitting upright, your back and neck supported and your arms resting on the arms of the chair.

Take some deep breaths and release the tension in your body. Check that you are in a comfortable position. Don't cross your legs or clench your fists.

Let your attitude become one of simple awareness. Let go of any thoughts about what is happening in your day or in your life. Don't *try* to think about anything. Don't even worry about whether you are doing the training properly or not. Allow your mind to become calm.

The arms are the initial focus of attention. Begin by concentrating on your dominant arm. Repeat the following to yourself:

My right (or left) arm is heavy.

Say this four times. Pause for a few seconds between each phrase. Then say the same about your *other* arm. Repeat four times. Now say:

Both my arms are heavy.

Say this four times.

That's it! Try doing this for one or two minutes about six times a day. If you're serious about autogenic training, you should expect that it will take about six months to become skilled at this method. After a week, add some new instructions to your practice. After repeating the suggestions that your arms are heavy, add the suggestions:

My right (or left) leg is heavy (four times).
My left leg is heavy (four times).
Both my legs are heavy (four times).

After another week, use the suggestion that your arms and then your legs feel "warm and heavy." This is repeated until the desired effects are achieved. As you add suggestions and become better at relaxing, you can gradually increase the length of your practice sessions to about a half hour, once or twice a day.

Other common suggestions in autogenic training include:

My heart is calm and steady.
My breathing is calm and regular.

My abdomen is warm.
My forehead is cool.

Add one of these suggestions at a time to your program. Don't rush it. Autogenic training takes time to master. I've found that many clients experience a variety of unusual, even uncomfortable sensations during autogenic training. These sensations include tingling, dizziness, increased warmth or cold, buzzing feelings, headaches, and even a feeling like a small shock. Experts call these "autogenic discharges." Don't be alarmed by such feelings. They are a natural part of the training. Remind yourself that they will pass. Indeed, they will probably become less frequent as your training progresses.

As you become skilled at this technique, you can devise your own suggestions to fit your own needs. A computer programmer who spends a lot of time typing might add the suggestion *My neck and shoulders are warm and heavy.* An asthmatic can try the suggestion *My chest is warm and my throat is cool.* Further suggestions can be found in the books I recommend in the Notes section on page 254.

6. Coping affirmations

The ability to "talk yourself through" a stressful situation is a valuable skill in Keeping Cool. You might be able to remember a time when you did the opposite, when you "talked yourself out of" doing well in a competition or exam. Olympic gold medalist archer Jay Barrs told me that he realized he talked himself out of a medal in 1992. He hadn't trained seriously for the Olympics and only barely made the U.S.A. team going to Barcelona. Watching the other competitors, Jay kept telling himself *I'm not shooting well enough to beat these guys.* Of course, with thoughts like that, he was eliminated from competition. Only then did Jay *really* take a good look at the other archers. Too late, he realized that no one was shooting any better than he was. With a better attitude, he might have repeated his 1988 triumph.

A useful tip in using coping affirmations is to recognize that you don't have to pretend you will be perfect on a task. Athletes realistically acknowledge that they will be nervous and tense at the Olympics. Then they build this knowledge into their preparation. They use affirmations that *help them cope* with the anxiety, rather than pretend it isn't there. Working with many champions, I have come to realize that you don't have to be supremely confident to be successful. As long as you know you can cope with your nerves, you'll do well. I've shown you how to master the skill of talking to yourself in a productive way in the skill of Productive Analysis. The affirmations we discussed on page 103 can be utilized to help you Keep Cool in stressful situations.

Other Keeping Cool techniques

Let me briefly mention two other techniques for relaxing the mind/body. One is **biofeedback.** The basic idea here is that the body is hooked up to equipment that shows you the level of various body functions, such as blood pressure and heart rate. Normally we aren't aware of these functions, so we pay no attention to them. But scientists have found that if you concentrate on these aspects of the body you can influence them. For example, you can learn to raise or lower body temperature, change your heart rate, and even alter the types of electrical activity (brain waves) produced by the brain.

I expect that new technologies will continue to lead to a variety of new relaxation methods. Already, there are many videotapes, audiotapes, and CD-ROM products that teach various relaxation skills. New approaches are sure to develop. Biofeedback (and related technologies) can be an excellent method for learning mind/body relaxation. However, because it requires sophisticated equipment, it is not a viable approach for many people.

Another approach to Keeping Cool I should mention is **prayer.** Prayer isn't a relaxation method, but many athletes have found that prayer helps them Keep Cool in pressure situations. Their faith in God helps them stay calm, and it gives them a larger perspective that keeps them from worrying about results. If you have a strong faith, consider using prayer to Keep Cool in pressure situations.

The third step to Keeping Cool is to apply the relaxation skills you have learned in real-life pressure situations. By doing this, you can stay in the Achievement Zone and remain stress-free.

Step 3: Calm Down in Pressure Situations

I've worked with many people who've had to battle performance fears in order to learn to do their best. Performance and evaluation anxiety can affect not only athletes, but also actors and actresses, musicians, reporters, pilots, lawyers, and many others. The good news is that by practicing one of the relaxation methods I've described in Step 2, the harmful problems of performance anxiety can be overcome. Once you have become confident that you know how to relax, you can apply the relaxation method in stressful situations. In this step, I'll show you how.

When I told you about performance anxiety, I exploded the myth that athletes don't get nervous in stressful situations. They do. But a top athlete doesn't let her nervousness stop her from competing successfully. Here are some ideas for dealing with nerves in pressure situations.

How to Handle Nervousness

The secret to dealing with nervousness is to expect it. Remember the story of Marjorie Jackson, who had never been so nervous at a race. She reminded herself that this was a good thing and that she would probably set a world record. She did. She used coping affirmations to change the way she looked at nervousness. Instead of seeing it as a bad thing, she saw it as a good thing.

You can take the same approach. Recognize that it is very *normal* to get nervous in competition or when you're being evaluated. Some people will tell you they don't get nervous before a big challenge, but these folks are the exception. If you're like the rest of us and get nervous before a big event, pay attention to your nervousness and welcome it as a good sign. It might seem silly at first, but with practice you will realize that your nervousness really can help you. It can help you concentrate more sharply, it can make you react faster, and it can give you more energy when you need it.

When I asked Jay Barrs, Olympic champion archer, how he stays so cool and calm before competition, he just laughed. Despite his reputation as "Mr. Ice," Jay says he gets as nervous as anyone when competing. "People often say to me that I 'look as cool as a cucumber' out there, but I'm not. I'm nervous if I'm in a big competition, but I tell myself that's exactly what I want to feel. I tell myself it's an *excited* nervousness, not a scared nervousness." You can successfully use this same strategy. Don't get nervous, get excited.

Successful athletes accept nervousness as a natural part of the competitive process, and you should, too. But what do you do if your nerves turn into anxiety, if those butterflies in the stomach become huge birds with flapping wings? That's the time when you need the relaxation strategy you practiced in Step 2. Top athletes use specific relaxation strategies to prevent panic, and you can achieve success with the same approach.

How to Prevent Panic

Sport psychology researchers Graham Jones and Lew Hardy found that when athletes panic in competition, their performance is ruined. It's like falling off a cliff—once panic sets in, there's no going back. To investigate whether panic can be prevented, sport psychologist Ian Maynard and his colleagues taught soccer players a combined muscle-relaxation and deep-breathing technique. After eight weeks of training, the athletes were able to decrease their performance anxiety in game situations by 30 percent and their performance increased.

I've taught many athletes this approach—using a specific relaxation strategy to calm down when the pressure starts to build. They find it very helpful, because the athlete can prevent panic, even when the stress level is great.

The state of panic is almost the opposite of being in the Achievement Zone. So it's essential to learn the mind/body skills to prevent panic situations. But what do you do if things go wrong during a performance? How can you calm down if you've suddenly forgotten the next point in an important presentation and your heart is racing and your chest feels tight?

You can get rid of these feelings by using a short version of your relaxation exercise. If you practice such relaxation exercises on a regular basis, you will be ready to use them when you really need them. Deep breathing, for example, slows the heart rate, loosens the muscles, and oxygenates the blood—just what you need to calm down. When those feelings of panic begin, immediately use your relaxation strategy. If you remember to use relaxation whenever your anxiety rises, you'll lower your stress and improve your performance.

During a performance, you don't have a lot of time to respond to the challenges that are thrown at you. In the middle of a sales presentation, a customer suddenly asks you a difficult question for which you are completely unprepared. During an interview for a new job, you are asked to comment on a possible scenario that you have never before encountered. In such situations, it is natural to become flustered and make a mistake. Instead, this is the moment when you most need to respond effectively.

Two strategies will help you master such unexpected challenges. One is to have a short, effective Keeping Cool strategy ready for such situations. One-breath relaxation and Centering are both good techniques to use at such times. The second helpful strategy is to practice this relaxation exercise as often as possible at work and at home during minor crises. If you can calm down effectively in minor situations (when someone cuts you off on the road, or when the new VCR you bought breaks down) you will be much more confident when you need to stay calm in an important situation.

The other big mistake I often see in pressure situations—avoiding the situation—can also be prevented by using the relaxation methods you've learned.

How to Beat Avoidance

Avoidance strategies bring us short-term relief from the pressures of competition. But in the long run, they often produce the very failure we were trying to avoid thinking about. The employee who puts off doing the report until the last minute will probably end up doing an inadequate job. We must change such behavior, but how can we?

The answer is to lower your stress level by applying your new Keeping Cool skills in order to relax and get going.

Use relaxation to get started. Any long-term or important project seems intimidating, so simply decide what you need to do *today*. To get started on that goal, take some deep breaths and let your anxiety go. Feel yourself relax and unwind. Your mind is clear. Let go of worries about the future and focus on today. Open your eyes, and put all your energy into today's goal. Even the best athletes often have to relax and refocus in this way before a workout or training session. It helps them get the most out of everything they do.

The most important part of Keeping Cool is to apply your skill in relaxing to the performance situations in your life. It's great to be able to relax when you're lying down on a comfortable bed with the lights turned down, but it won't help you achieve success unless you know how to relax in front of a big audience or when taking a difficult exam. *That's* when you need to relax! By applying Keeping Cool skills you will be able to consistently perform in your Achievement Zone. Think of how effective you can be if you can Keep Cool in pressure situations. So get started on applying these skills today!

To give you some final suggestions about how to stay calm and relaxed when the pressure's on, I'll share one of my consulting experiences with you. The greatest obstacle to success in this case turned out to be performance anxiety. And the solution was to teach the people involved how to relax when necessary.

TROUBLE IN THE COCKPIT

Several years ago I was contacted by a commercial airline company. They asked me to advise them on a problem they were having with their pilot-training program. When I visited one of their major training centers, they explained how time-consuming it is for a pilot to get a license to fly commercial airliners. The company recruited only seasoned and experienced pilots to begin with, often Air Force or military pilots with thousands of hours of flying experience. These veteran recruits were then trained intensively to fly the large airplanes of the company and were given hundreds of hours of experience in simulators and training programs.

In order to get a commercial airline pilot's license, the candidates were required to pass a final exam administered by federal officials. Although only the best trainees made it to the final exam, a small but significant number of these trainees were unexpectedly failing. The problems often began in the instrument-rating tests for the large jets. Those who failed often complained of unusual physical symptoms during the exam, such as dizziness, nausea, or light-headedness. Yet these people had been flying for years without these problems. What was going on?

The unexpected failures were of great concern to the airline company. These trainees had invested a year or more of their lives in getting a license, and they could not continue in their chosen career without one. Additionally, the company was spending a quarter of a million dollars on each trainee, and did not expect failures at the last stage of the training process. The training officials hoped that my experience helping prepare athletes for the pressure of the Olympics would help their program.

I interviewed several recent graduates of the training program. All of them described the great pressure they felt during the final flight-simulation tests. They knew they were being observed and graded by federal examiners, and that their performance would mean the difference between getting or losing a license. The simulations themselves were extremely difficult, and often contained situations that were unexpected or surprising for the trainee pilot. Those who passed felt they had dealt successfully with this increased pressure. Those who failed usually felt they handled the pressure poorly and let it distract them. It seemed that the strange physical sensations of nausea and dizziness were being brought on by the psychological pressure of the exam.

As I studied the training program further, I discovered that great attention was given to providing trainees with the best technical training possible. But little thought was given to psychological or emotional training.

The simulators used to mimic the experience of flying a commercial airliner were amazing! Trainees were learning all the technical skills they needed to handle any emergency situation thrown at them in the simulator. But no systematic training was offered in the psychological skills they would need during the exam. Some trainees developed effective strategies for getting through the exam, but others did not and paid a heavy price.

The training staff were very interested in my findings. The exam process was designed to be stressful, because flying a large jet is a very tough job. As one pilot commented to me, "The safest pilot is one who has sometimes been a little scared." But the staff now realized that they had neglected to teach trainees a systematic way to deal with this stress. They enthusiastically worked on a program to teach Keeping Cool skills to all trainees. The program they finally developed included the following components:

- *Education on the anxiety response to stressful situations*
- *Experience recognizing the symptoms of anxiety and stress*
- *Basic training in several relaxation exercises, including:*
  - *Deep breathing*
  - *Muscle relaxation*
  - *Centering*
  - *Coping affirmations*
- *Developing a set of reminders (cues) to trigger a sense of relaxation in stressful situations*
- *Daily practice using relaxation in training situations*
- *Awareness of environmental factors that might help decrease stress— e.g., cutting down on caffeinated coffee, getting enough sleep, regular meetings with a counselor*
- *A special workshop focused on psychological preparation for the federal exam. Past trainees were brought in to talk about their experiences.*

- *A dress rehearsal of the federal exam, using Keeping Cool strategies throughout*

The most immediate impact of this Keeping Cool teaching program was that the trainees reported increased confidence in dealing with all aspects of training. Knowing that they had the psychological skills to handle challenging and stressful situations made them more confident in general.

Training staff also liked the program because it gave them a way to talk about something that everyone had always feared but no one wanted to confront—the danger of "choking" in the federal exam. I regularly consulted with the company, and two years later their problem with trainees unexpectedly failing the federal exam had been all but eliminated.

Of all the human emotions, anxiety is the greatest enemy of achievement. Not only does anxiety prevent us from performing in our Achievement Zone, it's such an unpleasant experience that we go out of our way to avoid it. By avoiding things we're afraid of, we fail to challenge ourselves. All too often, we settle for the safe and easy way we know well. High achievers are not immune to anxiety. But they've mastered the skill of Keeping Cool, which allows them to confront their fears and pursue their goals. Like Olympian Jay Barrs, they accept nervousness, go out to meet challenges, and know how to prevent panic. They know this is the only road to success. There is no other way.

Keeping Cool Tips

- Try all the relaxation exercises in this chapter at least once. You will find that some exercises fit with your personal style while others seem uncomfortable. But don't judge the book by its cover. Reading the exercises will not help you decide which ones will fit your style. Try them out.
- To use Keeping Cool strategies effectively, you must be able to use them when it counts—in action. When you select a relax-

ation method, practice using it in your daily routine. Do some muscle relaxation at work. Do some deep breathing in the car. Use centering before making a presentation. Make Keeping Cool a part of your life.

▪ In sport, excessive tension hurts good performance. You can't hit a smooth 7-iron to a small green if your shoulders and arms are tense. Use Keeping Cool to get rid of undesired tension before you act. For example, when you step up to hit the ball, you should feel smooth and loose. Use muscle relaxation or autogenic training to attain this feeling. Try this approach for any sport or motor skill.

SUMMARY

How to Learn Keeping Cool

Step 1 ▪
It's OK to Be Nervous
Overcome
- Avoidance
- Panic

Step 2 ▪
Learn How to Relax the Mind/Body
1. Deep breathing
2. Muscle relaxation
3. Centering
4. Visualization
5. Autogenic training
6. Coping affirmations

Step 3 ▪
Calm Down in Pressure Situations

Concentration:

Focus on Performance

Race-walker Carl Scheuler's specialty is the 50-kilometer walk, a fiendish event which makes the marathon look like a Sunday stroll around the lake. Competing in the 1992 Olympic Trials, Carl is nearing the end of the race. He crests a hill and sees the two race leaders just ahead of him. Gradually he begins to narrow the gap. In his mind he throws out a strong fishing line and hooks the man in front. Carl starts to reel him in, closer and closer, until he is right behind his competitor. Now he's ready to pass. Suddenly, a searing pain strikes Carl's right side. Sharp needles of fire seem to spread from his ribs to his hip. The pain slows his progress and the gap between he and the leaders widens again. What can he do?

Carl has trained himself to think through such situations carefully. First, he must recognize the pain for what it is: a cramp. These are common in an event which lasts four hours and covers over thirty miles. Carl's natural tendency is to panic, to think that the pain is a signal that something has gone wrong. But he knows from experience that if he can keep his pace for another five minutes the pain will fade. He needs to survive the cramp and he will be back in the race. Instead of focusing on the pain, he must concentrate on his technique.

The keys to success in race-walking are rhythm and pace, so he repeats to himself "good turnover, good turnover." He has practiced doing this hundreds of times. The words "good turnover" remind him that he must keep up a fast pace, bringing one leg forward as soon as the other hits the ground. It is a simple concept, but it requires a great effort at this late point in the race. Just as he planned, the words help him concentrate on his technique, and the physical pain of the cramp begins to recede into the background. Now he can look up and focus once more on taking the lead—this time for good. Carl goes on to win the race and makes his fourth successive United States Olympic team.

What Is Concentration?

Concentration is the ability to focus all your attention on what you are doing. When you are fully Concentrating, you are wholly absorbed in the present. You are not even aware that you are performing. You pay attention only to those things that are important, and distractions don't affect you. Carl Scheuler was able to overcome his pain and win the Olympic Trials because he had taught himself how to Concentrate even under the worst conditions.

Allan Kramer is a computer programmer for a software development company in Colorado. When doing his best work, he ignores interruptions such as ringing phones and the conversations of others. When he's on a roll he works through lunch and stays after the office closes, oblivious to the passage of the hours. At such times, Allan produces his finest-quality work, and does so in much less time than usual. Allan wishes he could Concentrate like this all the time.

Perhaps more than any other mind/body skill, people typically regard Concentration as an ability you're born with. "He has no

Concentration," people say sadly, and shake their heads. But this view is *wrong*. I know from experience. I've helped hundreds of athletes Concentrate better, and I can help you, too. Now let's look at how you can improve your own Concentration.

Learn Concentration

I'll show you three steps to greater Concentration. By applying these steps to your work and play, you'll discover the benefits that come from having more mental energy to give to your pursuits. First, learn how to focus your mind on what you're doing. Researchers have found that when people are successfully concentrating, their minds are relaxed but alert. This attitude is essential for taking in all the information you need in order to make good decisions. Second, you must identify the important aspects of performance (your cues) so that you can focus on them without distraction. Great performance occurs when people maintain a very simple focus of attention. Third, you must continually seek out ways to keep improving your performance. Concentration suffers when you become bored or stale. These three steps are summarized below:

Concentration

Step 1.   Focus Your Attention

Step 2.   Use Performance Cues

Step 3.   Search for Ways to Improve Performance

Step 1. Focus Your Attention

Sport psychologists have found that physiological changes take place inside the brain as athletes focus their attention on performance. For example, sport psychologist Dan Landers and his colleagues at Arizona State University have studied the brain-wave activity of athletes during performance. They found that one of the things that happens in the brain is a marked **decrease** in activation of the left hemisphere immediately before successful performance. Conversely, poorer performance is related to increased brain activity in the right hemisphere of athletes. These studies have been conducted with elite marksmen, elite archers, and excellent golfers, so the findings appear to be consistent.

Similar findings emerged in England when the brain waves of high-level karate athletes were examined as they attempted to break a piece of wood. Psychologists found that the number of **relaxed,** slow (alpha) brain waves increased immediately before performance. Indeed, an athlete who failed the task showed no increase in alpha brain waves.

Psychologist Michael Posner of the University of Oregon used a new technology called PET scanning to look at the brain activity of people who were paying attention to a new task. When they tried the task for the first time, their blood flow increased in the brain. But as they had more practice with the task, the blood flow and brain electrical activity **decreased.**

These studies tell me that good performers learn to *quiet their brains* during successful performance. Their attention is focused entirely on what they are doing. They are mentally very relaxed. This is indicated by the increased relaxation of their brain waves. At the same time, however, they are very alert to what is going on. This attitude of quiet alertness is a characteristic of top-level performance.

How does it feel when your mind is relaxed but alert? Another researcher who has studied Concentration intensively is University of Chicago professor Mihaly Csikszentmihalyi. He has developed the theory of *flow* over the last twenty years to explain the psychological state people reach when they are fully focused and performing at a very high level. Dr. Csikszentmihalyi has found that typical experiences of people in the flow include the following:

■ Time seems to slow down. A tennis player in the flow reports that "everything seemed to be happening in slow motion, so that I had lots of time to make good decisions."

- You seem to have more control over what you're doing. A golfer found that "I could shoot right at the pin every time. I wasn't worried about the traps and hazards. I was in control of my game."

- You stop worrying about how you appear to others. While you're in the flow, you forget about the past and future and focus on the present. The actor in the flow doesn't worry about what people think of him. He's not thinking about performing; he's truly "lost in his performance."

- Performance becomes almost automatic. Even when great effort is required to succeed, it seems almost effortless. A skater describing the flow experience said, "It's like you're on automatic pilot, so you don't have any thoughts. You hear the music but you're not aware that you're hearing it, because it's a part of it all."

These characteristics describe what it's like to be fully focused on what you're doing. I have found the same characteristics in athletes who report very high levels of Concentration. I believe that flow is the ultimate in Concentration. If we could measure the brain activity of persons in flow, I believe we would see the very relaxed, alert patterns of activity I described earlier. Flow is a state of intense Concentration, and it is an enjoyable experience. What can you do to become better at focusing your attention and entering the flow?

Learn to Quiet the Mind

The researchers who studied the brain waves of athletes in action found that there is a period of mental relaxation immediately before performance. This mental relaxation occurs even though the athlete is still physically active. For example, it takes a lot of energy to break a piece of wood. Yet the karate athletes were able to quiet their mental activity as they performed. How do they do it?

First, you must gain some control over what you choose to think about. It's impossible to focus your attention if your mind is racing. When I'm with a client, I must *listen* to that person with all my energy. I can't afford to be thinking about the next appointment, about the terrible traffic on the way to work, about the fact that I'm hungry, or about the five phone calls I need to return. If I don't focus my attention on my client, I might miss the critical piece of information I need to help him. It's difficult to learn to focus attention on one thing for an extended period of time, but with practice it becomes easier.

A good way to learn this self-control over what you think about is to practice some simple meditation techniques. Many athletes practice meditation to help them learn how to focus their attention. Greg Norman, for example, one of the world's best golfers for more than ten years, incorporates many aspects of the Zen approach into his game. His fascination with this approach began after he read a book on Zen and the martial arts. A surprising number of successful executives I work with make the time during their day to take a time-out, a short period for meditation or reflection. Here are some suggestions for putting this approach to work for you.

Meditation

Meditation teaches you to relax the mind and to focus your attention. This is a very useful skill for the high achiever. Some people are scared of meditation because of its religious or spiritual connotations. But meditation is simply a way of developing your powers of Concentration. With practice you can become very good at meditating on your own. You don't need to join a group, and there is no need to study it in a religious context.

The following exercise is one of my favorites. Try it to find out how hard it is to relax and clear your mind!

MEDITATION (THE BUBBLES EXERCISE)

Choose a comfortable position. Make sure you won't be distracted while you are doing this exercise.

Take some deep breaths and release the tension in your body.

Let your attitude become one of simple awareness. Let go of any thoughts about what is happening in your day or in your life. Don't *try* to think about anything. Don't even worry about whether you are meditating properly or not. Allow your mind to become calm.

Once you have been quiet and still for a few minutes, you will notice that you are still thinking. Thoughts will drift into your awareness. Some of these thoughts may be about the meditation. Others might be about events in your life. Some thoughts may be simple, others complex. Every time you notice such a thought, imagine placing it in a bubble. Let the bubble float away. See it rising, rising, and disappearing from view.

Return to an attitude of peaceful observation. You're not trying to think. Wait until another thought occurs to you. Put it in a bubble too. Again watch it drift away.

Stay with this attitude of peaceful observation. With practice you will find it possible to relax with a clear mind for longer periods. But don't worry if thoughts come. Just put them in bubbles and let them float away.

Some thoughts may come back more than once. Some may upset you. Some may be confusing. Always put them in a bubble and let them go.

Stay with this exercise as long as you like. It may last ten minutes or half an hour. Simply observe what happens when you try to clear your mind as much as possible.

This exercise is a wonderful way to relax when you feel overloaded. It is also an interesting way to calmly observe what's on your mind. But don't try to solve problems with the Bubbles Exercise. Stay with the attitude of peaceful observation.

A variation on this exercise involves focusing your attention on a single object. For example, sit in front of a vase and simply gaze at it, emptying your mind of all thoughts except observation of the vase. Your mind will keep trying to wander away to thoughts of other things. Gently let go of those thoughts and return to observation of the object you have chosen.

Most of my clients find that daily practice in this method, even if it's as little as fifteen minutes a day, gradually improves their ability to focus their attention. It's important not to get frustrated if you don't seem to be making progress in your ability to meditate or focus. Often the improvement is so gradual that you don't realize how much you've gained until several months have gone by. Remain patient and stick with it.

You must also practice focusing your attention on what you're doing in performance situations. Take a moment or two before beginning a task or project to get into the relaxed, attentive frame of mind. You'll find that the results are worth the effort! This attitude will help you Concentrate on what you are doing.

I believe that many athletes achieve a form of meditation during workouts. They merge action and awareness. Runners, for example, speak of a "runner's high," which appears to be very similar to a sustained meditation. You can try this approach yourself—an excellent way to develop your Concentration is to physically exercise and to really pay attention to your body while doing so. There is a special state of awareness or consciousness that comes through immersion in the physical activity of the body. A popular misconception is that meditation is always a passive, quiet process. In fact, there are many meditations that include very active exercises such as dancing.

Finally, any of the relaxation techniques you learned from the Keeping Cool skill can be used as you prepare for performance. These techniques help calm the mind, which will in turn help you develop that state of relaxed alertness you need to concentrate. Centering is used by many athletes to help them Concentrate.

Remember that the mental relaxation that is so vital for successful performance doesn't require physical relaxation. I work with athletes in sports as different as archery, boxing, and weight lifting, and they all agree that they perform best when their minds are relaxed and focused. Yet a weight lifter preparing to lift a 500-pound weight over his head is usually far from relaxed physically. Indeed, he needs tremendous energy. This physical energy, however, cannot be allowed to interfere with total Concentration on this difficult task.

You can apply the same lesson in your life. Your days may be very hectic and require lots of activity, but you can still learn how to focus your attention and achieve high levels of productivity.

Once you've developed the ability to focus your attention, you must then identify the critical aspects of performance to which you wish to pay attention. The next step in Concentration is to learn how to keep a simple focus on the essential elements of your task or project.

Step 2. Use Performance Cues

When we focus on the right things during a project, we increase our chances of success. But when we get sidetracked into thinking about things that are irrelevant—or worse, counterproductive—we increase our chances of failure. Top athletes learn that during the heat of competition, it helps to focus on one or two simple things that remind them what to do in order to succeed. Sport psychologists call these simple reminders **performance cues.**

In winning the Olympic Trials, Carl Scheuler used performance cues to help him concentrate. One performance cue was the image of reeling in the walker in front, which reminded Carl to focus during the final stages of a four-hour race that saps energy from the body and the soul. Another cue was the phrase *good turnover*, which allowed Carl to survive the pain of his cramp.

Skier Tommy Moe used a performance cue with great effectiveness at the Winter Olympic Games in Lillehammer. Tommy was the surprise winner of the men's downhill alpine ski racing competition. Although he'd never won a World Cup event in his career, Tommy blasted down the Olympic course on Kvitfjell faster than any other competitor, winning the first gold medal of the Games for the United States.

Asked after the race to comment on his strategy, Moe replied,

"I just kept my thoughts real simple. I wanted to focus on making my turns with a strong edge on the outside ski, and keeping my hands forward. I knew if I concentrated on those two things, I would ski fast. That's all I wanted to do."

By winning the Olympic gold medal, Tommy Moe could lay claim to the title of the fastest man on skis in the world. Yet his performance cue on race day was surprisingly simple. Even rank novices are advised to make their turns by edging the outside ski and to keep their hands pointing down the hill. But by keeping his focus simple, Tommy was able to enter the Achievement Zone where the body and mind work together as one. Tommy Moe proved that his Olympic performance was no fluke by winning a World Cup event three weeks later and placing third in the World Cup Downhill Finals at Vail in March of 1994.

In the study I discussed earlier of elite karate athletes, the researchers found that at the same time that brain-wave activity became relaxed, the athletes said they were focusing very intently on the wood-breaking task. The most common strategies used were visualizing the wood breaking, or concentrating on just one part of the technique, such as "dropping the hips." These, too, are effective performance cues.

Selecting a Performance Cue

In all pressure situations, there are thousands of possible thoughts for you to concentrate on, but only a few will help you get the job done successfully. How do you choose your performance cue?

I have three simple rules to help you. They're based on the experiences of thousands of athletes in must-win situations.

Rule 1: Your performance cue should be simple

When you need to perform at your best, your mind/body is looking for direction and guidance. You can confuse yourself with thoughts that are long and complicated. Many clients I work with have experienced the disaster of "paralysis by analysis," the problem of thinking too much during a competition. That is why top athletes often talk about "playing brain dead," or "not thinking about anything at all" when they are trying to perform at their best. Sport psychologists call this "automatic" behavior, and indeed, it sometimes feels as if you are performing on automatic pilot!

So program yourself to think in simple terms. Remember gold-medal winner Tommy Moe. He chose two of the most basic thoughts any skier can have to guide his gold-medal run down the mountain.

Jack Nicklaus gives the following advice on the mental aspect of golf: "Boil down your swing thoughts to the simplest two or three that have worked for you in the past." These "swing thoughts" are Nicklaus's performance cues, and he says he never changes them during an important round. Nicklaus describes using cues such as *Head still* and *Complete the backswing*.

Rule 2: Your performance cue should be positive

It seems such a simple idea to avoid negative thinking when you're trying to concentrate, doesn't it? Yet time and time again I see athletes and other performers in high-pressure situations who fall into the trap of programming themselves for failure. They do this by worrying about, or trying to avoid, mistakes.

Brian Boitano's experience at the Winter Olympic Games in Lillehammer in 1994 showed the danger of negative thinking during a performance. He fell during his technical program, skating himself out of medal contention. Brian is one of the most focused competitors we've ever seen in the sport. This opening gaffe on a triple-double combination was the first time most skating observers had ever seen him fall in a big competition. Interviewed immediately after the program, Brian acknowledged that negative thoughts had prompted his calamitous spill. "Going into that jump, I always concentrate on something technical," said Brian. "Usually I think about things like 'sit on the edge' and 'kick the knee forward.' It's always a technical thought. But today, I don't know why, I was saying to myself, *Just land it, please just land it.* Of course, I didn't."

Most people recognize what happened to Brian Boitano because it has also happened to them. When we think of something bad and it ends up coming true, we call it a self-fulfilling prophecy. Why does this happen?

When we're in a situation where we really want to do well—for example, the Olympics or a big customer presentation—the thought of failure makes us anxious and fearful. When we tell ourselves *not* to do something (*don't fall down on this jump, don't look nervous in front of the boss*), we're actually reminding ourselves of failure. Naturally we don't want to fail, so that makes us anxious. The anxiety causes several mind/body effects, such as the muscles getting tense, the heart racing, and poor Concentration. We lose the control we need to perform at a very high level, and we start making mistakes—the very thing we wanted to avoid!

Successful athletes avoid such Concentration lapses by concentrating on a performance cue to keep their thoughts positive. They never think of failure (unless they are planning strategies for dealing with setbacks). If you're serious about being successful, you should do the same.

Rule 3: Focus on your strengths

Top athletes know that the time to worry about weaknesses is during practice. When they get to competition, athletes build on their strengths. In a study of elite skiers, Bob Rotella and his colleagues found that in the months leading up to the racing season, the best skiers focused on their weaknesses, seeking out ways to improve their skiing. But the night before a race, they focused on their strengths, one of which was all the hard work they had done.

The poorer performers did just the opposite. During the year they thought about their strengths and how good they were, but on the night before a race they started thinking about their weaknesses. Don't fall into the same trap. Work on personal improvement when you have the chance, and when it comes time to lay it on the line, remind yourself of your strengths.

The use of performance cues to maintain excellent Concentration is vividly illustrated in this story about an amazing Olympic feat by kayaker Greg Barton.

NINETY MINUTES TO A SECOND GOLD MEDAL

At the 1988 Summer Games in Seoul, I was privileged to witness a rare event in Olympic competition. U.S. flatwater kayaker Greg Barton won two gold medals in less than two hours! Greg was a favorite in his specialty event, the 1,000-meter singles kayak, but he and partner Norm Bellingham were also very competitive in the 1,000-meter doubles. The problem was, the final of the doubles event took place only ninety minutes after the final of the singles event! For that reason, very few athletes even thought about, much less attempted, the exhausting double.

But Greg and Norm weren't ones to give up on their Olympic dream easily. The previous year, at the 1987 world championships, Greg had won the singles, but together they had faded badly in the doubles final. So they knew exactly what their problem was—they needed an extra surge of energy at the finish of their doubles race.

Now that they had identified their problem, they had to solve it. They decided to work hard on developing a kick late in the race. They would try to surge ahead with just 200 meters to go. Their performance cue was the word Hup. *When they heard that, it was the signal for a final, supreme effort.*

Knowing how tired they would be at the end of a race, they trained until they were exhausted and then *practiced their kick finish. It was up to Greg to give the signal* Hup. *When I interviewed Norm for this book, he confided to me that his greatest fear was that Greg would have nothing left after the grueling singles final. Norm worried that he might never hear that cue,* Hup.

The 1988 Summer Games was the testing ground for their new strategy. In the 1,000-meter men's single final, Greg Barton paddled an incredible race to beat Australian Grant Davies by just five thousandths of a second. The finish was so close that the official scoreboard announced the Australian as the gold-medal winner, and Barton had to wait over fifte minutes to find out that he had won. Bellingham, waiting in the locker room, didn't know who the winner was until the medal ceremony. "I was trying to hear the anthem, but the wind was blowing and I couldn't," recalled Norm. "Then the wind hit the flag, and the stars and stripes unfurled, and tears began rolling down my cheeks."

Norm and Greg could only hope that Greg's body would recover sufficient energy in the brief time between the races. Would their training be enough? As they went to the starting line, Norm thought about the gold medal and said to his partner, "Let's make sure you get two of those darn things."

The eight pairs in the final were all strong, but Bellingham and Barton were still shocked to find themselves in fifth place after 250 meters. "It was a nasty feeling," recalls Norm. "You've trained for four years for this one moment, and you feel it slipping away. I was scared to death on every stroke. I was working incredibly hard, but my right hand was shaking, I was so nervous. It was very hard to concentrate." But their increased efforts paid off, for at the halfway mark they were equal with the Romanians in third.

The pain was etched on Barton's face as they struggled over the last 250 meters. "I was terrified he would be too tired to kick," Norm explained. "But then at 200 meters Greg called Hup *and we just exploded. It was amazing that Greg had something left. I could feel Greg put all his guts into it. He was on fire with such passion that it completely energized me. I was running on adrenaline." In the closing moments they overhauled the race leaders and won the gold by three-tenths of a second.*

"I think it was our ability to analyze our weakness, the finishing kick, and to come up with that simple reminder to give it our supreme effort which helped us win that second gold," said Norm. "At the end I felt like I had been whipped with a cat-o'-nine-tails, but it was worth it." Greg and Norman rode their performance cue, Hup, *all the way to the Olympic gold medal.*

I want you to generate effective performance cues for the important parts of your life. Think about these performance cues ahead of time. It is difficult to think clearly when you're under pressure, tired, or you don't have much time, so you need to have your performance cue ready to go. Rehearse it often before pressure situations so that you can rely on it when you really need it.

When you're being productive at work, what things are you thinking about and focusing upon? Make a list of these things that promote success. Now simplify these into short phrases that will remind you to focus when your Concentration is slipping. Can you come up with a one- or two-word reminder to help you maintain an effective focus? How about a short phrase of no more than five or six words?

Here are some ideas from others who have discovered effective performance cues. Use their ideas to stimulate your thinking about creating your own personal performance cues for success.

▪ World-champion diver Megan Neyer emphasized the link between Concentration and success in her career. "I could never not think during competitions. That was unrealistic for me. My mind was always active. The trick was to acknowledge all these thoughts but leave them behind and focus on the present. So going into every dive, I tried to focus on one or two simple things.

"For example," continued Megan, "before every hurdle dive I said *knee down* to myself, which was a good reminder of the proper technique. If I was doing a dive where I needed good height, I imagined *jumping over a bar* like a high jumper. It really helped my diving to concentrate on these one or two things before the dive."

▪ Master golf instructor Harvey Penick was fond of giving his students something concrete to think about during their performance. For example, to help a player develop the soft touch necessary to excel at putting, Mr. Penick would tell the student to imagine the ball disappearing into the cup *like a mouse slipping into a hole*. This lovely image is a great example of a performance cue, because it focuses attention on something—the speed of the putt—that will help performance.

Notice that a performance cue can be an image as well as a verbal reminder. The essence of an effective cue is that it directs attention to something that enhances the chances of success. It could be a word, a phrase, an image, or even a piece of a song.

▪ Performance cues can remind you of a feeling that helps you compete well. Jason Morris, judo silver medalist at the 1992 Olympics in Barcelona, knows that he competes best when he's loose and relaxed. He reminds himself to *have fun* when he's preparing for a match. "I can be joking around and discussing the weather until two seconds before my match," says Jason. "But *having fun* helps me perform well, and that's the main thing. It keeps my mind uncluttered, so I'm ready to Concentrate when I hit the mat."

It's important to realize that a performance cue which works for someone else may not work for you. Discover your own cues for success. Jason's main rival in judo, Dave Faulkner, had a more serious manner in his preparation for competition. But he was just as careful as Jason Morris to practice his performance cues. "I discovered that I was most successful when I stuck to the same routine before matches. It helped me to feel *aggressive* before matches, so I remembered certain matches when I felt *aggressive and strong.* I didn't concentrate on particular moves or specific strategy. I always tried to recapture that *aggressive feeling* before a match." Dave Faulkner's approach brought him three national championships and three U.S. Open titles.

▪ I was working with Sam, a client who wanted to improve his presentations in front of groups. His problem was that he got nervous in the middle of his speeches and forgot what he wanted to say. The first performance cue he developed was a simple one— *Smile.* Just remembering to smile at his audience helped him relax and stay focused. He used this cue every minute or so.

The second performance cue that helped him was *Take a sip of water and think about it.* This is based on a little trick I shared with him about dealing with those tense moments when the mind goes blank. I suggested that he pause and take a sip of water from a glass placed near his notes, while he used the opportunity to glance at his index cards and read the next point in the speech. As I have found from experience, the audience has no idea you've forgotten where you were in your speech. They're prepared to wait patiently until you resume. Sam used this cue whenever he forgot what was supposed to come next.

Finally, every time he felt anxious he took a deep breath and said to himself, *It's OK, I know more about this than anyone else.* It was a good performance cue because it was true. Sam had terrific knowledge in his area. Once he relaxed and smiled, he was very good at sharing that knowledge with others.

Try various performance cues and see which ones make a difference to the way you perform. If you think a cue might be effective, give it a fair trial. I've seen athletes who give up on a potentially effective cue because it failed them the first and only time they tried it. Just as it takes time and practice to perfect a technical skill, it also takes some time to become comfortable with performance cues, especially new ones. Use the cue several times before you judge its effectiveness.

Don't change your performance cues in a big pressure situation. Many athletes I know have made the mistake of experimenting with their performance cues *during an important competition.* Instead of using the performance cues that earned them a spot on the Olympic Team, for example, they change their cues—because it's the Olympics! Invariably, such experiments end in disaster. That's because changes in Concentration focus produce doubt and uncertainty—which is the opposite of what you need to perform well. So save your new cues for practice or for less important situations.

Step 3. Search for Ways to Improve Performance

The final step in the process is to maintain your Concentration by staying fresh. Top performers never let themselves become stale or burned out. They renew their Concentration by challenging themselves in new ways, by asking more of themselves. High achievers push the envelope of performance.

Mihaly Csikszentmihalyi discovered that the experience of flow is a direct result of this ability to challenge yourself at an optimal level. People experience flow when they feel truly challenged to do their best. If a task is too easy, they become bored and their Concentration wanders. If a task is too hard, they become anxious and their Concentration suffers. Optimal Concentration occurs only when you feel that you have the ability to match the challenge you set yourself.

Csikszentmihalyi tells the story of an assembly-line worker who had what seemed to be a very boring job—putting parts together on a small unit, the exact same task six hundred times a day. But this worker enjoys the job and has been doing it for five years. How can he maintain Concentration on such a boring task? The answer is that this worker looks at his job in the same way that an Olympic athlete approaches her training: *What is my personal best? How can I beat my record?* He continually looks for ways to be more organized and to improve in some fashion, no matter how small. The job usually takes about forty-three seconds to perform per unit, but this worker's personal-best time is twenty-eight seconds and he's still searching for improvement. He's trying to push his envelope further.

Look for ways to improve your performance, however small. This process of searching for improvement will help keep your Concentration sharp. Set new challenges for yourself, especially if you find that a project is becoming boring. If you can't think of ways to improve, or if you're stuck in a rut, there are two ways you can seek out a new angle of attack: experiment with a new approach, and get good coaching.

Experiment

The best way to develop good Concentration at something is the simplest. Keep trying. Every experience, even a failure, is a learning experience. With experience, situations that at first seemed confusing and hopeless become orderly and predictable.

Often even experts don't realize how much the mind/body has

learned from experience. Professor Bruce Abernethy, head of the Department of Movement Studies at Queensland University, illustrated this when he studied the reactions of the world's top squash players. He wanted to know why the best players were able to react so quickly to their opponent's serve. Contrary to what he expected, he found that the best players didn't have amazing reaction times. Testing showed that their reaction times were the same as those of less experienced players. Instead, he discovered that the best players could successfully predict where the squash ball was going to land *before it had even been served!* But they couldn't tell Professor Abernethy how they did this. Abernethy found that the top players had learned to read the upper-body movements of their opponents. By Concentrating on cues provided by their opponents' arms and upper bodies, they gained crucial extra time to prepare for the serve.

Less experienced players concentrated on the cues provided by the wrist and racket movements of their opponents. Because these occur later in the process of serving, they couldn't react as quickly to the serve.

Such research tells me that experience is a wonderful teacher. Often we aren't even aware of all the information we are learning from our experience! So even if your initial experiences with a new project seem disastrous, persist. The more you try it, the more you will learn about what you need to focus on in order to be successful.

Remember that your Concentration will vary depending on the task you're trying to accomplish. Many people think that if you have "good Concentration," you'll be able to Concentrate well in every situation and on every task. Not true! You might have excellent Concentration in one activity, but very poor Concentration in another. For example, I love reading, and I can concentrate for hours while I'm reading the latest scientific journals. Often I don't notice that dinnertime has come and gone while I'm studying. But give me something mechanical to assemble, and my Concentration disappears! I find it difficult to focus for more than a few minutes on screwing those tiny bolts into those teeny holes. Often I get frustrated and have to ask for help to get the job done.

So beware of those who offer you "easy" ways to improve your Concentration. For example, as Head of Sport Psychology for the United States Olympic Committee I've investigated lots of methods that were supposed to "improve concentration and attention" but that turned out to be worthless. Most of them helped you concentrate on a special task, but that was the end of their benefits. One such "aid" was a very large board that contained 300 squares. When the power was turned on, the squares lit up in a random order, and the athletes had to punch the squares in a short time period to score points. As they learned to Concentrate better on this task, they scored more points in the same amount of time.

Another popular Concentration training tool was a piece of paper with the numbers from 1 to 100 written on the page in a scattered fashion. Athletes took a pencil and were asked to cross off the numbers in order, beginning with 1, until time (usually one or two minutes) ran out. As their Concentration on this task improved, they could cross off more and more numbers in a minute. I used these devices and many others with athletes. However, when they went out on the practice field the coaches told me that they didn't see any improvement in Concentration. But the athletes were terrific at punching squares and crossing off numbers!

To learn about the critical aspects of any task, you must spend time on *that task*. You must learn about it and understand it. Practicing the task at hand is the best way to do this. The more you practice, the better you will be able to concentrate. Experiment with different ways of doing something, or try a fresh approach and see what happens. Keep an open mind, and you'll be pleasantly surprised at the benefits to your Concentration level.

Shirley and Juanita were freshman college tennis players who were paired up as practice partners. They quickly found that just hitting the ball back and forth was boring, so they devised a variety of practice routines to challenge themselves. They had to

*hit ten successful cross-court forehands, or ten backhands down
the line. If they made a mistake, they had to start all over again.
As they improved, they devised ever more intricate practice routines. It became a matter of pride not to be the one to make the
first mistake. Their Concentration remained sharp throughout
practice.*

Get Coaching

While you can often come up with new ways to improve your
performance through trial and error, good teachers can make the
learning process much less painful. I remember my own experience
with the game of golf. It seemed like a fairly simple game when I
first saw it. You pick up the club and hit the ball. I was good at similar sports such as tennis and cricket, so I thought golf shouldn't be
too hard to learn.

Was I wrong! I tried to play the game without coaching for five
years without ever improving. I rarely broke 100, and the game always frustrated me. I never developed good Concentration at the
game. Then I finally gave in and got some coaching. It was a reve-
lation. Golf turned out to be nothing like tennis or cricket. I learned
that I should be paying attention to things I had never considered,
such as the angle of my wrists as I swung the club and the weight of
my body over my right leg. As those things became automatic, I
learned what a great drive feels like and how to stroke a good putt.
I began to make lots of pars and experience the joy of an occasional
birdie. Now golf is fun and my Concentration is excellent.

A very successful athlete told me at one of my workshops: "I
regard my ability to get help when I need it as one of my most important skills. Some of my competitors like to go it alone, but I don't
see the sense in that. If help is out there, why not use it? But it's
not enough to just ask for help; you have to listen to what people
tell you. I can take criticism and learn from it. I think that's a real
talent."

The trick in reaching your goals is to discover who the good
coaches are in your life. While a good golf coach is not hard to find,

it's tougher to know where to go for coaching in your relationship, for help with your children, or for assistance in making more contacts and connections at work.

Go to the people you admire, the people whose success you wish to emulate. A terrific way to get started is to find out who are the success stories in your chosen field. Talk to these high achievers, or read about them, or talk to people who know them. Find out what it took for them to achieve their success. If you can find these "coaches" to help you understand what's important in your projects, you will accomplish great things together. It's a great joy when you discover a new approach that takes you beyond what your coach has taught you.

Mentoring is very similar to coaching, but instead of working with someone who observes you and tells you what to Concentrate on, you observe your mentor to discover what is important. If you are serious about success, study the mentoring opportunities available to you. Which projects do you need the most help in? Identify some people whom you might work with on that project. If you do get the opportunity to learn from a mentor, take as much advantage of it as possible. Learn the technical knowledge your mentor shares with you, but also observe what he or she focuses on at work. Pay attention, and learn as much as you can.

Norm Bellingham, Olympic kayaking gold medalist and World Cup winner, decided prior to the 1988 Games in Seoul that he needed a mentor. He wanted to learn from kayaking legend Ian Ferguson of New Zealand, who had won three gold medals in the 1984 Games at Los Angeles. So Norm went to New Zealand and trained with Ferguson. Norm credits his mentoring experience with Ferguson for much of his subsequent success. For example, he learned the skill of Action Focus from the Kiwi legend. Ironically, in that gripping final in Seoul, it was Ian Ferguson and his partner Paul MacDonald whom Norm and Greg Barton narrowly beat for the gold medal.

If you try these two approaches in your work and play, you should be able to keep improving your ability to Concentrate. Successful athletes quickly learn that it's often easier to *get* to the top than to *stay there*. In order to remain on top of the mountain, great athletes maintain Concentration by continually challenging themselves to new heights of performance. Adopt this approach yourself, searching for ways to improve performance, and your own Concentration will stay sharp.

When you learn how to concentrate, you'll discover how rewarding it can be to encounter challenging situations that you previously dreaded. When you push yourself to your limits, you're more likely to experience the total flow of an Achievement Zone experience.

Athletes describe total Concentration as a wonderful experience that allows their best performance to flow freely. Work on your ability to be relaxed and alert, keep your focus simple and positive, and keep searching for ways to improve your work. Then you will have an excellent chance of experiencing the same mind/body harmony described by the following athletes:

> *It's when everything becomes clear and focused. Things are happening around you and you are aware of everything, but at the same time nothing affects you—you know instinctively what to do. It's an incredible feeling—you know that whatever happens your reaction will be the right one. Nothing will rattle you.* [OLYMPIC GYMNAST]

> *In our team sport, rowing, it's people acting exactly together in synchronicity, and I want to say it's thoughtless, automatic. You take a stroke, hear the catches enter together, feel the simultaneous drive, but it feels almost out of conscious control. You are absolutely aware—it's a sensual awareness. Whenever I enter The Zone I surpass my previous last performance.* [OLYMPIC ROWER]

> *It was just one of those programs that clicked. I mean everything went right, everything felt good. . . . It's just such a rush, like you*

feel it could go on and on and on, like you don't want it to stop because it's going so well. [OLYMPIC FIGURE SKATER]

Somehow I am completely inside myself. Almost an alpha state where my body and mind are relaxed but my muscles are able to take over and push me to a higher level of performance. My running is at its maximum. [OLYMPIC RUNNER]

Concentration Tips

▪ Be physically active. In the Energizing skill I will describe the benefits of physical activity, especially increased health, fitness, and energy. Another benefit is increased Concentration. Physical activity wakes us up, makes us more alert, and helps us pay attention to what's happening around us.

▪ Try something new. The experience of trying something new stimulates our minds. It could be learning a new language, reading a new book, learning how to crochet, or bringing home a pet puppy. Whatever the stimulus, it will help you increase your awareness of focusing on the important things. If you're doing something familiar, make it "new" by setting yourself a challenge.

▪ Seek out role models. Others have gone before you in the quest for improved Concentration. How did they do it?

SUMMARY

How to Learn Concentration

Step 1 ■
Focus Your Attention

Step 2 ■
Use Performance Cues
Keep Your Cues
- Simple
- Positive
- On Your Strengths

Step 3 ■
Search for Ways to Improve Performance
- Experiment
- Get coaching

Emotional Power:

Respond Effectively to Strong Feelings

The falling snow was cold and wet, and I huddled into my parka for warmth. I was waiting for the gondola to make the long ride from the Olympic Athletes' Village in Brides-les-Bains up the mountain to the ice hockey arena in Méribel. I was going to watch Mark, a hockey player I had worked with for several years. He was finally fulfilling his dream of playing for his country at the Olympics. As our gondola sliced through the soft flakes I thought back to my first meeting with Mark.

At that time he was a raw sixteen-year-old with lots of talent. Along with other young stars from around the country, he was attending a two-week training camp in Colorado Springs. The country's top youth coaches were there to select a national under-seventeen side to travel to Japan for a series of international games. Mark had the talent to make the team, there was no question about that. But there were questions about his ability to stay focused and calm during an entire game. The rap on Mark was that he was prone to lose control if he took a hard hit.

Mark came to see me after a talk I had given to the teams. He was worried that his tendency to fight and take bad penalties would cause him to miss the trip to Japan. During a recent game, for example, he had earned a five-minute major penalty for retaliating to a high sticking and his team soon gave up a goal that cost them the game. I asked Mark to help me identify the situations that triggered his outbursts. I call these situations "hot buttons." The hot button that gave Mark the most problems was being checked into the boards from behind. Even if it was a clean hit, Mark would immediately feel strong anger and look for a way to "get even" with his opponent. Mark also lost his temper whenever he felt the referee had made a bad decision against him or his shift. He admitted that his anger clouded his judgment and that he often made bad decisions while he was angry.

I could have tried to find out reasons why Mark became so angry in these situations, but that would have been a waste of his time. What he needed was help in refocusing from anger toward constructive action. So I asked Mark to describe how he wanted to act after a check. He told me he wanted to feel strong after a check, to rebound and play harder than ever, but without anger.

To help Mark deal with his anger we watched his old game videos together. When he saw himself get checked he turned off the VCR and imagined how he usually felt. Mark told me he experienced the same angry, vengeful emotions that he did during a game. I then asked Mark to imagine himself responding in the way he wanted. He saw himself get checked, recover, take a deep breath, and then refocus on the puck. He imagined how strong he felt. In his mind he saw himself back in the game, more determined than ever.

Mark carried this image everywhere. Before he practiced he would imagine his strong, determined response to hits. At night he would visualize his new poise and would see himself recovering from hits quickly. Whenever Mark had some spare minutes he would rehearse his new approach.

Mark was practicing the skill of Emotional Power. I call this strategy "rewiring" your hot button. To help him put his skill into practice, I taught Mark a simple four-step approach to calming down and refocusing that he could use whenever he became angry. Soon Mark was able to see the change in game situations. He still felt angry when he took a hit, but now he took a *deep breath and recovered quickly. He took pride in rechanneling the negative emotion of anger into a positive response of playing hard. His coach also noticed the change. Once the coach had benched Mark whenever the game got tight, afraid that he would give away a stupid penalty. Now the same coach put him on the ice in pressure situations so that Mark could lead by example.*

Mark's career flourished after he learned Emotional Power. He became known as the coolest player on his team. Having worked so hard to cope with his anger, he became a leader to other players in stressful situations. Mark's reward came in 1992 with selection to the U.S. Olympic hockey team to play in the Games at Albertville, France. My reward was to walk out of the snow that night into the hockey arena in Méribel and watch Mark play a great game against France. I was surely one of the few in the stands who knew just how long and hard had been Mark's road to his Olympic dream.

What Is Emotional Power?

Emotional Power is the skill of coping with your emotions so that they don't interfere with your performance. Strong emotions are a double-edged sword. Sometimes positive emotions can lift athletes to new heights of performance. The excitement of a big win in the semifinals may give a team the energy it needs to win the finals, despite fatigue.

But negative emotions can cause you to lose control and perform well below your abilities. You may have difficulty controlling your temper and find that you make irrational decisions when angry. Or you might become so depressed by a criticism from your boss that you feel sad and blue and unable to work effectively for days. You might become so upset at failure that you avoid any situation where it could happen, just so you don't have to deal with your emotions. All of these are common symptoms of someone who hasn't learned Emotional Power.

Strong emotions are a natural part of competitive sport. Athletes feel these emotions almost automatically—anger, fear, frustration, despair. The key is not to respond automatically. A blind response based on feelings is almost always a bad one. Instead, top athletes must learn to choose an effective response to their feelings. The best athletes are those who keep their poise in emotionally charged situations. They experience the same feelings that the rest of us do, but they have learned how to handle them effectively.

Golfer Nick Price was asked if there was any secret to his success during his amazing string of victories in 1993 and 1994. He replied, "There's so much emotion that you go through. I would say the best thing is I have a lot of control over both my golf game and my mental well-being in the game right now. I'm not getting too hot and flustered when I make a bogey and I'm not getting too excited when I make a birdie."

That's the essence of Emotional Power. The skill can be applied in many situations outside sports, because strong emotional reactions to setbacks, mistakes, and disappointments are common in competitive situations. I've heard of many bad business decisions made in the "heat of battle." Decisions clouded by negative feelings often turn out to be mistakes. Poise is a valuable trait in both sports and corporate settings.

Emotional Power boils down to a very simple idea. When you feel strong emotions, don't respond to them automatically. Learn how to take a moment to choose an effective response to the emotional situation. Then use the energy of the emotion to make things happen. Don't let your emotions control you.

How to Put Emotional Power into Practice

There are three simple steps to the skill of Emotional Power. They are:

Emotional Power

Step 1. Respond to Emotions, Don't Suppress
- If Something's Wrong, Change It!

Step 2. Rewire Your Hot Buttons

Step 3. Refocus If You Get Upset

Emotional Power is all about choice. Because emotions are so powerful, we often allow *them* to control *us*. "I couldn't help it, I was so angry" is a typical comment in this vein. Or someone might say, "I'm not getting anything accomplished today. I'm just too depressed." But we do have choices, and making the right ones helps us be productive and effective.

In this chapter I'll show you how to handle negative emotions. You can learn to use your emotions as signals—if something keeps upsetting you, it's time to make a change. You can make that change in your environment, or by changing the way you react to certain situations. And for those times when you still get angry or upset while you're performing, I'll show you a surefire way to calm down and make wise decisions.

Let's take a good look at each step in turn.

Step 1. Respond to Emotions, Don't Suppress

It's easy to respond ineffectively to your emotions. You automatically lash out at someone if you get angry. Or you mope around gloomily if someone criticizes you. However, these responses don't lead to success. It takes more effort to make a constructive response to a strong emotion, but it's much more rewarding.

Responding effectively to emotions begins with the understanding that there are no "quick fixes" to make you feel better.

The "magic pill" approach can lead to some big problems. People look for something to instantly make negative emotions "go away." Drugs or alcohol are popular choices. But the emotions don't vanish, and the "cure" is only temporary. Most cases of alcoholism and addiction begin with this approach. While appropriate medication can be very helpful for real mental health problems (such as depression), the magic pill approach doesn't work for most of the problems in life.

It would be nice if we always felt great. But nobody wins all the time. Sometimes you'll be called upon to do your best when you're feeling bad. If you can handle the down times, you'll be a success in whatever you do. It's those negative emotions—fear, anger, sadness—that stop most people from achieving their goals. Athletes have to get used to dealing with negativity. The most successful athletes can give their best effort even when they're disappointed, frustrated, or feeling down. How can you learn this skill?

Most of us hate negative feelings so much, we try to block them out. We try to control them. Often, we try to suppress them completely. But ignoring your emotions is also a recipe for disaster. This attitude may work for a short while, but in the long run there's no avoiding some of the pain in life. Successful athletes know that when they get into competition, they're in for a bumpy ride. They may experience great elation at achieving their goals. Or they may feel the crushing disappointment of defeat.

I once worked with Tom, a tennis player who had problems with strong feelings. When he missed several shots in a row, he would get very angry. He tried hard not to let his frustration show, but by "acting" as if he didn't care, he only made his play worse. The outcome when athletes try to push their emotions inside and control them is what I call "tanking." It's a recipe for performance disaster. You may have noticed this same reaction yourself on occasion. By suppressing your negative emotions, you also suppress the energy you need to perform at a high level, and as a result, your efforts are flat and uninspired.

The only cure for this problem is to recognize your strong emotions and stop trying to suppress them. It's OK to care when you're concerned about the outcome.

Sometimes people talk about "emotional control," as if we could turn our emotions on and shut them off. But emotions aren't controlled like the flow of water through a tap. There's no such thing as emotional "control." If you could turn your emotions on and off at will, you wouldn't be human. To master Emotional Power, you need to recognize and acknowledge your negative emotions, not avoid them. Only then will you be able to deal with them in a constructive manner.

If Something's Wrong, Change It!

If trying to control your emotions is the wrong way to deal with them, what is the right way? How should you handle it when you feel angry, scared, or depressed?

One of the main reasons we experience negative emotions is that they *tell us something is wrong in our lives.* They are a signal that something needs fixing. If we try to press on and ignore the bad feelings, sooner or later the problem will catch up with us.

Instead of trying to avoid the bad feelings, recognize them as the sign of a problem. If you fix the problem, the negative feelings will disappear.

What's causing you to feel bad? That's the first question to ask when you get upset. For example, I worked with a diver who told me she was feeling depressed and irritable. What had once been her greatest source of joy, diving, was now a source of stress. At night she had trouble sleeping, and she was so worried about being overweight that she was developing an eating disorder.

As we discussed the changes in her feelings about diving, it became clear that they had begun soon after her move to a new coach. This coach was extremely critical of her performance. He motivated his divers by pointing out all their faults and then asking them to practice twice as hard. Particularly disturbing were his comments about this diver's weight. He nicknamed her "Thunder

Thighs" and suggested that she could never win until she lost fifteen pounds.

Her negative emotional state was a natural reaction to a bad situation. It was tough for her to stand up to her coach and make a switch, but with help she did. As soon as she found a supportive, encouraging coach her mood improved and her self-confidence came back.

When you run into negative moods, ask yourself what's going on. The anger you feel over a work assignment may be a signal that you need to improve communications with your boss. You may feel you are being asked to shoulder an unfair percentage of the workload. The lethargy and boredom you experience on a project may be telling you that you need a new challenge. You may have become bored at work because you aren't learning any new skills.

Once you've defined a problem, you can work to change it using your mind/body skills. Consider the following options:

- What steps do you need to take to solve your problem? Make action goals out of these steps and get to work on them right away.

- Use your Creative Thinking skill to generate a list of alternative solutions to your problem. Don't throw any of your ideas away. Think about them for a while. After you've had a chance to consider the options, which solution appeals to you? Make that solution your first priority.

- Make use of Productive Analysis. Change the way you talk to yourself when you feel down. Instead of saying, "I feel bad. Things are hopeless. There's nothing I can do about it," tell yourself "I'm in an unusually bad mood. What's going on? There's no sense in moping around. I need to make some changes." Use your negative emotions to *help* you change. Don't let them drag you down.

- If you're stuck for a solution to a problem that's making you feel bad, write down your thoughts about it. Often just the process of putting your thoughts down on paper will help you think of some potential solutions. Take some space in your Achievement Zone diary to write down how you feel and explain why you feel that way. Put your writing away for a few days and then come back and reread it. Often you'll see your problems in a new light.

These steps should help get you back on track. Don't let negative feelings stop you from going after your goals. If you can make some life changes that will improve your situation, now is the time to do it.

What if you can't change your situation? For some people, strong negative feelings are a result of a history of problems they cannot change. For others, their body chemistry may be unbalanced to the point where they need medical help. In both these cases, I strongly recommend that clients get professional assistance. Therapy and counseling can often make a world of difference in these situations.

But if your problems aren't so severe, there may be changes *you* can make in the way you respond emotionally to situations. The second step in learning Emotional Power is finding out how to change the way you respond to pressure situations.

Step 2. Rewire Your Hot Buttons

Sometimes you won't be able to change the situation that is making you feel bad. In this case, you need to learn how to change your response to the situation. You can tell if someone has the skill of Emotional Power. In a situation that would upset most of us, or make us see red, the person reacts calmly and effectively.

One hockey player can get upset about a bad call and come out on his next shift playing brilliantly. Another player on the same team might get upset and retaliate, earning a five-minute major penalty and hurting his team's chances of victory. Both players got upset. One handled it, one didn't. The difference is that one had learned the Emotional Power skills necessary to deal with adversity.

We all have weak spots in our emotional armor. Some situations just make us angry, no matter how often we experience them. I teach athletes to think of these situations as "hot buttons." When the hot button is pressed, it triggers an immediate, strong emotional reaction.

For example, if you had a teacher who always criticized you

for bad spelling, you might overreact to criticisms of your writing. Or some bad experiences with a particular judge might make the sight of that judge a hot button for a figure skater. When she sees him on the panel her heart sinks and her stomach tightens. She finds it difficult to concentrate because she's so worried about how he will judge her.

Think about the hot buttons in your life. What situations provoke a strong negative emotional reaction in you? You might find such hot buttons in a variety of areas. At work, hot buttons can hurt your performance because powerful negative emotions weaken your decision-making ability. It's hard to think clearly when you're very mad or very scared.

For example, I recently visited a company where one of the top executives had become a hot button to many of his staff. The manager was legendary for his angry outbursts when he thought a poor decision had been made. Even staff who had not experienced this man's wrath directly became overly tense and anxious when he appeared. Because of this, many staff had problems making effective presentations to this executive.

Emotional Power means having the skill to choose a new, effective response when confronted with one of your hot buttons. You may not make the hot button go away, but you *can* learn to *cope* with the situation. Instead of allowing the situation to control you, you can control the response you choose. Remember, when we strive to achieve our goals, it's not the setbacks themselves that hurt our performance. It's the emotional way we behave when we experience a setback.

And with practice, you may be amazed at how much you can change your behavior. I have worked with athletes who have transformed their hot buttons from personal weaknesses into strengths. The figure skater who was intimidated by one judge now has an excellent relationship with her former nemesis. Once she learned how to relax and stay calm when she saw him, she found that he could be a useful source of feedback on her technical progress.

The staff who worked with the angry executive were taught

skills in dealing with difficult people and learning to communicate effectively. Once they learned how to stay focused even when he became upset, their effectiveness greatly increased. And the angry boss received some executive coaching to help him become a better role model to his staff, which helped a lot!

Let's identify your hot buttons.

IDENTIFY YOUR PERSONAL HOT BUTTONS

First, I want you to identify just *one* hot button in your life. Once you learn how to deal with this hot button, you will have the skill to tackle others.

Think about *one* of the following three areas in your life:

- Personal relationships
- Work
- Sport and play

Can you think of a situation that always gives you problems in the area you have chosen? It will be a situation you dislike or fear because it makes you feel bad. Even thinking about the situation now might make you upset. It will be a situation you want to change, because you know your automatic negative emotional response is hurting your effectiveness whenever you encounter it.

When you have selected your hot button, take your Achievement Zone diary and write down your answers to the following questions:

1. Describe this situation. What typically happens?

2. Describe your emotional response in as much detail as possible. How do you feel? How strong are your emotions? What

words would you use to describe your feelings? How long do the feelings last?

3. Write down the events that lead up to this situation. Who else is involved? Is there a chain of events that typically unfolds every time you get in this situation?

4. What steps have you taken in the past in order to try to change this hot button situation?

A helpful tip. It is a very good idea to get some help with this exercise. Others often see our hot buttons more clearly than we see them ourselves. If you think you can take it, ask a friend, family member, or colleague for help. Describe your hot button problem and ask them for input. It will be helpful to ask them the same questions you answered.

Warning! If you ask for help, abandon your usual defensive attitude to criticism. Hot buttons are a problem because we hang on to them. We may have once had a set of very good reasons as to why our strong emotions were justified, but not anymore. It's time to change.

Athletes are experts at accepting criticism. They have to be. Without criticism, they can never hope to make the changes to get them to the top. Good athletes not only accept criticism, they love it! They seek out critical feedback in their constant quest to improve.

Adopt the same attitude toward this exercise. If you ask for input from friends, don't argue with them when they tell you what they think. Act like a reporter. You just want to get some more information. Ask your questions and write down the answers. Don't try to justify your actions.

You can use this exercise to identify other hot buttons in your life, but for now, change one hot button at a time.

The trouble with hot buttons is that they take away your control over life. Someone else can come along, push one of your hot buttons, and Bang! Suddenly you're mad, upset, or flustered. It's hard to be effective when you're emotionally upset. You need to regain control over your reactions. You'll be much more effective when you can choose your response in a stressful situation.

Rewiring your hot buttons means replacing your old negative reactions with new effective ones. Let's return to the hot button you identified. The next exercise will show you how to go about choosing a new and more effective response to that situation.

REWIRE YOUR HOT BUTTONS

What was the hot button you selected to change? Let's rewire that automatic response.

First, think about how you want to feel and act in that situation. Remember that Emotional Power means choosing a new set of responses.

In your Achievement Zone diary, take some space to describe the new you in this hot button situation. These two questions might help:

1. What feelings will help you cope with this situation?

2. How could you act more effectively in the event this hot button occurs?

You must be able to clearly and vividly describe the new you in this situation. You can't begin to change into an Emotionally Powerful person until you can see the person you want to be. Until then, you will always be struggling with the old, ineffective you.

Once you've described the feelings and actions you'll choose in this situation, enlist your imagination to help you rewire the hot button. What's the best way to overcome a mistake? Practice the correct answer until it's natural! In your case, the mistake is your old, negative emotional response. The correct answer is the new set of feelings and actions you have chosen. The best place to practice is in your imagination.

Enlist your best Creative Thinking to help you rewire that hot button. In your imagination you can try out your new choices until they become second nature. Practicing in your imagination will make you confident that you can choose effective reactions over hurtful ones.

- Imagine coping effectively as you lie in bed waiting to go to sleep.
- When you have some spare minutes in the day—perhaps waiting in line, for example—rehearse your new coping strategy in your imagination.
- Whenever you think of acting in the old, ineffective way, tell yourself, *That's the old me. Those days are behind me.* Then imagine the way you want to act.

Once you are comfortable with this, you can try out your skills for real. At first you might try a "dress rehearsal." If making a budget presentation to your boss is a hot button, generating feelings of anxiety and unease, rehearse the presentation first with a colleague. Imagine the feelings and actions you want, and then make the desired presentation to your friend. After one or two run-throughs, you'll be ready for the real thing. Go into your boss's office with confidence. Imagine the effective presentation you've been preparing. Then do it. Remember to pat yourself on the back when you're finished with the successful presentation. It will become easier every time you do it.

The way you respond to an emotionally charged situation can mean the difference between success and failure. You can't make negative emotions vanish from your life, but you can learn how to respond effectively to them.

Step 3. Refocus If You Get Upset

The last step in mastering the skill of Emotional Power is knowing what to do if you get upset because of a distraction or mistake. If there is one characteristic that sets the successful athlete apart from his fellow men and women, it is the ability to handle his own negative feelings successfully. Such setbacks *will* occur from time to time. Performances, projects, or tasks rarely go according to plan. Murphy's Law inevitably intervenes. Because of this, you must be ready to deal with the distractions you encounter.

The best way to deal with getting upset is to be prepared for it. Athletes need to refocus quickly after they get distracted. They do this by letting the upsetting moment go and focusing on the next step. You can use the same refocusing skill in performance situations. To refocus effectively after becoming upset, use the following four-point plan.

The Four-Point Plan to *Refocus*

- React
- Relax
- Reflect
- Renew

Let's go over each of the four points.

React

Setbacks cause emotional reactions. It's hard not to get upset when something blocks your quest for success. The first reaction after an athlete makes a mistake or gets a bad call is likely to be "@&*#*!!" There's no sense in trying to block this reaction.

As discussed earlier, emotions cannot be suppressed. Attempting to bottle them up usually results in a lack of energy that creates a flat performance. It's difficult to perform well when you are trying to control your emotions.

But emotions should not be allowed to take over, either. Some athletes become so emotional after a mistake or setback that it affects every aspect of their game. I worked with a figure skater who blew up every time she fell down on a jump in practice. She would scream, kick the ice, and in some cases storm off into the dressing rooms. Naturally her practice sessions were very poor. Her improvement was slow, because she rarely made it through a whole practice session.

The best athletes acknowledge the fact that they are human. They realize they make mistakes and understand that they will get upset. They don't try to shut off their emotions. But if a distraction knocks them off balance, good athletes look for a way to get back on track quickly. Learn from them. Recognize that you will become upset at times during the process of achievement. It's a good sign. It shows you care. But get ready to move on.

Relax

If negative emotions occur, you need to calm down quickly. Most athletes I work with have a quick method they use to calm down if they get upset or angry. Many of them use deep, abdominal breathing. For example, a pitcher who throws a wild pitch might get mad at himself for making a mistake. But he knows from experience that he throws poorly when he's angry. So he takes three deep breaths to refocus.

Other Keeping Cool skills are also useful when you need to relax and refocus quickly. A golfer I worked with discovered that when he made a bad shot, his frustration caused his muscles to tense. His hands and forearms became especially tight. This made it difficult for him to stay loose on his next swing. I showed him how to use the muscle-relaxation method, particularly on his forearms, to get rid of his tension after a bad shot. This allowed him to hit the ball the way he wanted on his next shot.

Decide that you will use a Keeping Cool method to restore calm whenever you get upset. Try out your method to see if it works. If it doesn't, try a different method. Use it consistently whenever you get upset so that it becomes a good habit.

Reflect

By using a Keeping Cool skill to calm down when you get upset, you achieve two things. First, you get rid of negative energy. This helps restore you to the Achievement Zone. And second, you give yourself time to think clearly. When you get upset and distracted you make bad decisions.

In order to make good decisions, we must think clearly. Calming down helps us do this. Now is when you should decide if the distraction taught you something. Mistakes happen for a reason. If your distraction is a mistake, decide why the mistake happened and how you can rectify it the next time. The top shooters I work with take this approach when they miss the bull's-eye. In a match of forty shots, they can afford no more than five or six mistakes if they hope to win. They analyze each mistake they make. Was the last miss caused by the wind, a bad hold, poor stance, rushing the shot, or by waiting too long? They make the correction, then forget about the last shot and focus on the next.

Putting the distraction behind you is essential for Emotional Power. Learn what you can and then forget about it. Mistakes happen, but more mistakes happen when you stay upset because you screwed up. Have you ever seen this happen to a professional athlete? Perhaps the field-goal kicker misses his kick. On the next field-goal attempt he's still bothered by his last miss, and he misses again. When the next kick comes, the pressure is really on. Can he forget about those two misses and focus? Sometimes a serious slump occurs in just this fashion.

Using a cue word or phrase can help you shift your attention *from* the frustration caused by the mistake *to* the next step. Just think to yourself, *Let it go, Let's move on, Put it away,* or *Let's go.*

Renew

You can refocus on the achievement process once your negative feelings are behind you. What do you want to accomplish next? The shooter who decided that the wind caused her to shoot poorly might allow a little more for the wind on her next shot. A speaker who became flustered by an unexpected question might decide that now is a good time to tell that funny story she's been saving. To recover fully from a setback, make a firm commitment to an immediate positive course of action. Renew your commitment to your goal.

An excellent way to help you get back in the flow of your performance is to rehearse your next move in your imagination. A mistake or interruption in the middle of a performance can knock you off balance and out of your Achievement Zone. You lose that feeling of being in the flow and find you are anxious instead. That's where your imagination can be a huge help. Imagine being back in the Achievement Zone. How does it feel? What do you imagine yourself doing next? Then do it.

Top figure skaters use this trick to help them if they lose focus during a competition. A skater may be suddenly distracted by a missed step in the program, or by a slip on the ice. Quickly the skater thinks, *What's next? My triple toe loop. Imagine landing the jump perfectly. I take off with speed and power, spin through the air, and land smoothly. OK, here it comes, let's do it.* The skater uses this approach to land a great jump after an unexpected slip.

You, too, can use your imagination to refocus after any unwanted setback. Your report was going so well, but that urgent telephone call distracted you. Now you're upset over this new problem. How do you get going again? Imagine yourself before the call. You were thinking clearly, writing well. Where were you going? Picture what you want to accomplish in your mind, then open your eyes and make it happen.

Sometimes we want to give up. *That's it, I can't concentrate anymore with all this noise. I'm stopping for today.* But often great achievements are accomplished by going on when everyone else gives up. Help yourself persist by keeping a reminder close by of your final objective. It may be a photo of your dream home, or a brochure on the college your child wants to attend. Remind yourself that you must renew your commitment to being in the Achievement Zone if you wish to reach that objective.

This whole four-point procedure should only take a minute, and can be modified to meet your particular needs. Even if you have only seconds to recover, you can use this strategy to refocus quickly.

I have used the four-point plan for refocusing to help athletes and performers in many different situations. Experiment with it and change it to suit your individual style. But whatever your final approach, please practice it. Setbacks will occur as you pursue your goals. Be ready for them.

To give you an example of putting this refocusing plan into practice, I'll tell you about my experience with a competitive young tennis player who had a tendency to "lose it" during play.

PAM'S DISASTER ON THE COURT

Pam was a young tennis player who came to see me with her father. Her dad, Jack, was a dentist and a hard-driving success story himself. He did most of the talking during their first visit. Jack told me that Pam was an excellent tennis player, perhaps the best in her state, but he said she was wasting her talent. Her problem was her angry outbursts during competition.

According to Jack, once she took the court, it was only a matter of time before she lost focus. Sometimes a bad call upset her, sometimes her own bad shot did the trick, and sometimes she seemed to get distracted for no reason at all. Jack was fed up, and told her that he would no longer pay for her coaching or travel. He hoped I could help Pam. I told Pam that she would have to set up the next appointment with me, because she needed to be the one that wanted to change, not her father. Pam agreed, but I didn't hear from her again for five weeks.

Then one Monday I got a call. Pam was in tears. Over the weekend she had played in a state high-school final and had "lost it" after a close call went against her. Her dad was furious. Jack told her she couldn't travel to a regional tournament the next weekend. Pam wanted to go, so she called me to see if we could work on the problem. I set up a meeting for the next day.

Over the next three months Pam and I worked together once a week. First she helped me understand what tennis meant to her. It turned out that she loved the game, she enjoyed the battle against an opponent, and she loved the attention she got for doing well. But she felt a lot of pressure from her parents to succeed. Her younger brother had taken up the game and was turning into a real star. He was getting lots of attention, which she used to receive, and this made her resentful.

Pam told herself that her occasional lapses didn't matter because she couldn't do anything about them. But deep down, her mistakes really bothered her. She felt like a failure and suffered terrible guilt for days after blowing a "sure win." She wanted to apologize to everyone, but her dad got so angry that she was afraid to bring the issue up. Now she was afraid she wouldn't be able to play anymore.

I explained to Pam that dealing with the emotions of competition is a skill and must be learned, just as one needs to learn and practice a topspin backhand. Obviously Pam's ability to handle negative feelings was poor, but that just meant she needed to improve. I also explained that it's natural to get upset during competitions. Pam simply needed a way to refocus when she became upset.

Together we put a four-point refocusing strategy into practice. First, Pam allowed herself a moment to express her disgust at a bad shot. Next, Pam told herself to take a "ten second time-out" every time she felt frustrated. Instead of hurrying into the next point, still mad, Pam took two deep breaths and "let go" her frustration at her miss or the bad call. She decided quickly whether she needed to change strategy. Finally, to refocus, she thought about what she wanted to accomplish on the next point. Only then did she prepare to serve or receive.

The changeover was a crucial time for Pam. Every two games she changed ends, and she usually sat stewing over missed opportunities. When she went out to play again she was often lost in thoughts about past mistakes. I asked her what she looked at during the change of ends. The eyes are very important in determining where we focus our attention. Pam's answer was telling. She looked into the stands, searching for her parents to see how they looked.

I asked Pam what she wanted to achieve during changeovers. She wanted to relax and refocus. I suggested that she pick out just one place to look during changeovers. Pam had told me that the color blue made her feel peaceful and relaxed, so we decided she would buy a blue bracelet and wear it every time she played. During the changeovers Pam would sit and stare at the deep blue of the bracelet. This helped her to release her frustration and regain a sense of calm. Before she went back on the court she would decide on her strategy for the next game.

We also had a couple of meetings with her parents. At these meetings Pam finally told her parents how much she appreciated their support. But she also asked them to ease off in their constant pushing for her to succeed. Pam also asked if they could sometimes allow her to go to a tournament alone. They readily agreed, somewhat surprised that she had shared her feelings with them.

The change in Pam was remarkable. Within weeks of learning these skills, her angry outbursts ceased. The new Pam was a cool and calm customer who seemed to relish fighting back in difficult situations. Jack told me that I was a miracle worker, but I pointed out that it was his daughter's own hard work that had led to these improvements. Pam no longer needed to work with me, but Jack sent me occasional updates on her progress. She won the state singles championship as a senior, earned a tennis scholarship to an excellent college, and was an All-American at university.

You recognize Emotional Power when you see it. It's the ability to stay confident and calm when everyone else is stressing out. Such poise is invaluable when handling the ups and downs of competition. Negative emotions are inescapable in the heat of battle, but with Emotional Power you can make the right decisions despite emotional turmoil.

By learning to handle the negative emotions you experience, you'll be able to spend more time in the Achievement Zone. And by spending more time in the Achievement Zone, you'll create more positive and empowering feelings in your life. That's Emotional Power.

Emotional Power Tips

During most of this chapter I have focused on dealing with negative emotions, because these are usually the ones that hurt your performance. However, there are occasions when powerful feelings of joy or elation can interfere with performance. It's possible to get too excited during competition. When this happens, you will see an athlete making mistakes and losing control.

For example, one of the greatest challenges for the U.S.A. hockey team in 1980 at Lake Placid was the gold-medal game. It's often forgotten that after their dramatic semifinal victory against the U.S.S.R., the Americans still had to play Finland in the Final. After the euphoria of the improbable win against the almost invincible Soviets, it was tough to refocus for the Finnish team, and the U.S. team trailed during the first two periods of the game. It wasn't until they got the wake-up call they needed and refocused that they were able to pull ahead and win.

The best response to overly strong positive emotions is to calm down and relax. Although Keeping Cool is usually used to deal with the problems caused by anxiety and nerves, the same methods can be employed to regain composure after great joy or happiness.

SUMMARY

How to Learn Emotional Power

Step 1 ▪
Respond to Emotions, Don't Suppress
   ▪ If Something's Wrong, Change It!

Step 2 ▪
Rewire Your Hot Buttons

Step 3 ▪
Refocus If You Get Upset
   ▪ React
   ▪ Relax
   ▪ Reflect
   ▪ Renew

Energizing:

Turn It On When You Really Need It

One of the most stunning upsets in Olympic history, and also one of the great track races of all time, took place at the 1964 Olympic Games in Tokyo. Everyone believed that the 10,000-meter event would be a showdown between world record holder Ron Clarke of Australia, defending champion Pyotr Bolotnikov of the Soviet Union, and the defending champion in the 5,000 meters, Murray Halberg of New Zealand. The American runner, Billy Mills, was a complete unknown whose best time in the event was nearly a minute slower than Clarke's world record. But Mills astonished the world when he defeated these heavyweights and won the gold.

Halfway through the race, Mills thought he would have to quit. Clarke had a pattern of surging on every other lap that made it extremely difficult to keep up with him. "At one point I was going to go one more lap, take the lead, and go one more. That way, if I did have to quit, it would be while I was winning," said Mills. But at just that moment, Mills noticed Clarke looking back over his shoulder. My God! He's worried, *thought Mills.* "From that point on, it was I'm here to stay."

With less than three laps to go in the race, the clear leaders were Clarke, Mills, and another runner, Mohammed Gammoudi of Tunisia. In the backstretch of the final lap came the moment that electrified the crowd.

As they lapped some of the other runners, Mills was on the outside of Clarke, a perfect tactical position. Desperate to get space, Clarke gave Mills two nudges before shoving him out of the way, sending him sprawling to the outside. At that moment Gammoudi shouldered between both of them and sprinted into a ten-yard lead. Mills describes the closing moments.

"*There were probably seventy-five thousand people screaming in the stadium, but all I could hear was the throbbing of my heart. In my mind, in a kind of self-hypnosis, I was reliving my training sessions at Camp Pendleton. . . . Every day of my training, in my mind, I went by Clarke just a second before the finish, and I'd win. But this was real. . . . I kept thinking,* One more try. One more try. *. . . With about eighty yards to go they were five or six yards ahead of me, and I thought,* I may never be this close again. Drive! Drive! *. . . I knew I had won. I knew I might not get to the tape first, but I knew that at that stage I was the fastest man on the track, and if I had enough time I would go past them. . . . Then I felt the tape break across my chest. I came to a stop, and a Japanese official came running up to me and said, 'Who are you? Who are you?'*"

With his dramatic gold medal, Billy Mills, a twenty-four-year-old man of Sioux heritage, became an American legend. He proved his win was no accident by breaking the world record the next year.

What Is Energizing?

Energy is a critical component of the Achievement Zone. When your energy is too low, you perform poorly. If this situation is prolonged, you risk becoming ill or burned out. Low energy can result from having worked too hard, or from having used up too much energy in a previous project. It's also common for people to feel underenergized when they believe they won't be challenged. Athletes who play with low intensity because they thought the game would be easy call this "coming out flat."

How do you make certain that you will have lots of energy when you need it? First, you need to learn how to give yourself energy, to "psych yourself up" at critical moments. Your thoughts and feelings, the attitude you bring to a performance and what you tell yourself, all affect your energy level. Second, you must ensure that your body has energy reserves stored up. In this chapter I'll show you how to Energize whenever you need to. And I'll also show you how to take care of your body so that your available energy charge is always high.

Learn Energizing

Maintaining a high degree of productivity and knowing how to call upon extra energy reserves when you need them is the mind/body skill of Energizing. In Billy Mills's case, the physical training he did at Camp Pendleton was critical for his development as a runner. But his mental preparation helped him develop Energizing thoughts that gave him the extra boost when he really needed it. He used these thoughts in the Olympics when he told himself *One more try, one more try*, and when he yelled to himself, *Drive! Drive!* You can easily learn to Energize yourself, too. The steps are shown below:

Energizing

Step 1. Energize Your Thinking!

Step 2. Keep Your Energy Battery Charged

- Fitness

- Sleep

- Nutrition

Let's look at how Energizing can help you perform in your Achievement Zone.

Step 1. Energize Your Thinking!

No matter how much you enjoy what you do, there will be times when you'll need to psych yourself up for an extra effort, or dig within to keep going when you feel like quitting. If it's the end of a long day at work or the last few minutes of a tough race, you're going to be tired. At these times, your mental state is critical in determining your energy level. Your thoughts can either drain energy away, leaving you listless and unable to perform, or they can give you new energy and excitement.

Energizing Thoughts

The following story demonstrates the effect that your attitude can have on your energy level. A colleague of mine was once traveling back to Colorado Springs in the evening. Snow had shut down the eastern seaboard and flights everywhere were late. Finally he arrived in Denver at 11 P.M. and waited until midnight for the connecting flight to Colorado Springs.

Understandably, the waiting passengers were tired, grumpy, and frustrated. Everyone was late, luggage was lost, and personal plans were in a shambles. That's when a gentleman of about fifty began approaching passengers and asking them for a favor.

"Good evening, I'm Carl and I'm flying to the Springs to meet my fiancée, Marlene. I wonder if you could help me wish her a happy birthday? She turns fifty today and I have fifty red roses here. Could you please give her this rose and say 'Happy Birthday' as you leave the plane? It will be a big surprise for her."

Who could refuse such a request? People smiled and took the roses. They watched as Carl repeated his request fifty times. Soon the plane arrived and everyone trooped on board. But the atmosphere of fatigue and irritation had disappeared. People were awake and interested. Whereas before they had avoided eye contact, now they spoke to each other and laughed about Carl's surprise. Everyone looked forward to meeting Marlene.

The plane touched down. The passengers let Carl get off first, and as they came out they each gave Marlene a rose, offered heartfelt birthday greetings, shook hands with Carl—and usually gave Marlene a hug. Through it all she stood in amazement, laughing and repeating, "I don't believe this, this can't be happening!" My friend says he, like the other passengers, left the airport with a warm glow. Carl's gesture had touched everyone.

Yet what did Carl do to restore everyone's energy and good cheer? Did he hand people an energy pill? Did he deliver a rousing pep talk to the passengers? No, by his own actions he quietly changed the way they were looking at things. He gave them something wonderful and happy to think about. And it wasn't even a thought about themselves! That's why I say that your energy level depends on your thoughts.

Use this basic principle to help you stay Energized during the workday, at home, on a project, or during a workout. There are lots of ways to increase your energy level using your mental powers. Here are some of the methods that the athletes I have worked with find most effective.

Focus on energizing images. Experiment with your Creative Thinking skills. Visualize yourself as a machine with incredible power, a train that is unstoppable, a fish that glides effortlessly through the water, or a greyhound moving quickly. Imagine that you are carrying a spare fuel reserve with you, and think about pouring the extra fuel into your tank. Feel the renewed power flowing into your body. Try different images to find ones that create just the right feeling of energy for the task facing you. Use all your Creative Thinking skills to capture the *feel* of the energy you need.

When you have high energy, try to think of an image that captures the way you feel. Think of that image whenever you feel especially Energized. Your image will become automatically associated with the energized feeling. From then on, focusing on the Energizing image will help trigger the feeling that is needed when you're tired.

Imagine excellence. I worked for some time with Maria, a world-class figure skater preparing for the Olympics. Maria's main problem was a lack of energy in the last minute of her four-minute-long program. Her skating routine included a couple of tough jumps at this stage, but she felt so fatigued after three tiring minutes that she often fell. When we took a look at what she was thinking at the end of the program, it was *Don't screw up now. You're very tired so just don't make a mistake.* I explained that these thoughts were just reinforcing her fatigue. Instead she needed to think of a new source of energy.

She did it by imagining a couple of brilliant jumps at the end of her program. As she skated into her jump, she imagined landing it perfectly and the crowd roaring with delight. This thought sent a shot of adrenaline surging through her body and gave her the emotional lift she needed to combat her fatigue. She used this image only when she needed it—at the end of her long program.

At the Olympics, Maria's strategy worked perfectly. Just as she began to tire, she imagined landing those great jumps. Re-Energized, she skated wonderfully. She was delighted when she really did receive that roar from the crowd.

When you need more energy, imagine doing things exactly the way you want to. See yourself in top form, doing things well and getting lots of positive feedback for your efforts. Make this picture as real in your mind as you can. This will give you the extra energy you need to succeed.

Park the fatigue. Athletes use the term "parking" the fatigue to describe the sensation of putting their tired feelings outside them. They effectively get rid of their fatigue for a short time.

For example, you can imagine your feelings of fatigue flowing out of your body and into the ground. Or you could say to yourself, *I have plenty of time to be tired later. Let's park my tiredness here (and touch an object, perhaps a table, a wall, or a suitcase) and I'll pick it up again later when I'm finished.* Keep going with renewed energy, and when you're finished, touch the object again to pick up your exhaustion. Get rid of it through rest or by a technique I'll explain later—recharging your energy battery.

Use Energizing cue words. Performance cues, introduced in the Concentration skill chapter, can effectively remind you of the feelings you need to keep going. Athletes use cue words such as:

- Go, go!
- Explode!
- Blast off!
- Nothing can stop me!
- Here is where I take off!
- Watch me now!

Don't use the cue until you really need it. Time your energy burst so that it will be most effective (remember Billy Mills surging with 150 yards to go in the Olympic 1,500 meters).

When swimmer Roque Santos pulled off a huge surprise and won the 200-meters breaststroke at the 1992 U.S. Olympic Trials, he used this cue-word method. "During certain times of the race I say, *Now! Now! Now!*" said Santos. "And I mean, *now* is the time to pick it up, *now* go. It's just a positive reinforcement I say to myself. It sounds kind of corny, but try it in a race and it works."

Focus on your desired result. Nothing has more power to Energize you than a vivid thought or picture of the result you desire. When the going is really tough, remind yourself why you are doing this.

Perhaps you're working overtime to help your children through college. Create a vivid mental picture of your child's graduation and think about how excited and proud you will feel. Use that positive energy to help you keep going. When they're tired during a workout, athletes often imagine entering the Olympic stadium and hearing cheers for the red, white, and blue. That picture of their dream pumps them up and gets them going!

Focus on things within your control. Low energy is often the result when you feel out of control. To turn things around, focus on the things you know you can change.

If athletes tell themselves *I must win this race*, they can lose energy if things start going badly. Instead, they concentrate on good execution, sound technique, and giving maximum effort. Look for the things that you have direct control over and think about them. For example, how much time you spend on a project, the quality of your work and your attention to detail are factors you directly control. Next time you feel out of control, stop and focus on these elements of your project.

Challenge yourself! It's common to feel flat if you think you have no chance of reaching your goal. Mark, an Olympic swim coach, told me about a team that was preparing to face the perennial state champions in a meet. The swimmers felt they had no chance of winning, so their workouts were flat and lethargic. The coach tried yelling, tried promising rewards—all to no avail.

So one day, when his first group of swimmers came in, the coach wrote on the blackboard the best training times of all the swimmers in the other group. Naturally, the swimmers thought they could do better than their teammates, and they went out and beat those times. The coach wrote the new records on the blackboard. When the second group came in and saw their times erased, they worked twice as hard to get their names back on the board. In one day, training had been transformed into a dynamic challenge, and everyone was reenergized. The intensity level remained high through a week of training. The swimmers pulled off the shock of the year when they beat the state champions that weekend.

What challenges can you set yourself to sweep away lethargy and bring back that feeling of high energy? A new goal or a new challenge can help you see things in a different way, resulting in revitalization of spirit and mood.

Listen to upbeat music. Megan Neyer, one of the U.S.A.'s greatest divers, won eight NCAA national titles, fifteen U.S. national championships, and the 1982 world championship. I asked Megan how she Energized herself before her dives. "I had to figure out what worked for me," she replied. "No one ever told me about Energizing. I learned a lot from watching the other divers, especially Greg Louganis. For example, music really helped me. Before going into diving I was a gymnast, so entertaining others and expressing myself were natural for me. I loved to dance. Before a competition I listened to dance music, something with a good beat or the right tempo. I would even start dancing, getting my body flowing. I remember at the Olympic Trials in 1980 I listened to the theme from *Rocky,* and at the 1982 World Trials I listened to *Chariots of Fire.*"

Athletes find that listening to the *right type* of music is important. Some types of music can pump you up when you need to Energize, and other pieces can slow you down when you need to stay calm. In fact, researchers are now discovering what athletes already know. A study by the American Medical Association found that surgeons report performing better when they listen to their favorite music in the operating theater. But their choice of good operating music varied all the way from classical music to Pearl Jam. So find out which types of music have the desired effect on your energy level.

Physical activity and stretching. Light exercise and stretching are invigorating and Energizing. Both get the blood circulating and oxygen flowing through the body. This increases the energy available to the brain and to the muscles, where it's needed. Make sure the activity is not so demanding that it depletes your energy reserves before a tough challenge.

Athletes who think they might be facing an easy opponent often find that a really hard workout immediately before competition stimulates game readiness. It gets them in the fighting mood and prevents any possible letdown that might come from taking an opponent too lightly. On the other hand, teams playing a skilled or higher-ranked opponent often benefit from a light workout focusing on technical skills and precision and emphasizing calm and concentration.

When consulting with companies concerning increased productivity, I frequently recommend the addition of physical activity to the office workplace. Managers often seem to expect that staff can plow through a succession of three-hour meetings and remain alert and creative, whereas such work schedules actually reduce productivity drastically. A half-hour break that includes time for a brisk walk or some other activity will do more for increased work effectiveness than any additional reports, lectures, or brainstorming sessions.

Where did we get the idea that a productive staffer has to be sitting behind a desk all day to get lots of work done? Clients tell me that most of their best work ideas occur **away** from the office, and especially when they're out running or exercising. I discovered the truth of this when I was working with athletes at the Olympic Training Center. I began to find that my early-afternoon clients seldom saw me at my best—after lunch I was usually dull and lethargic. So I began the habit of walking around the Olympic Complex with the athletes as we discussed the important issues in their lives. These walks reenergized me, and my athletes enjoyed working with me on the move.

So for increased creativity and productivity, get out from behind that desk and start moving! If your boss wants to know why you're not at your desk, tell her to speak to me.

Breathing. Breathing can be used not only to relax, but also as an effective Energizing technique. Focus on a regular, relaxed breathing rhythm. When you are ready to increase energy, increase your breathing rate. With each inhalation imagine that you are taking in Energizing oxygen. With each exhalation imagine fatigue flowing out. Imagine your mind/body becoming more and more Energized with each breath. You may find it effective to say, *Energize*, with each breath in. When you feel pumped up, return to your normal breathing pattern.

Look Energized! Remember the old adage "You look good, you feel good." Well, the same is true for Energizing. You can make yourself *feel* more Energized by *looking* Energized. Walk, talk, and act as if you have lots of energy. Increase the pace of your activity. Researchers have discovered that acting out a strong emotion can actually cause an emotional physiological response, so act Energized.

Remember a time when you had the right energy. Judo athlete Dave Faulkner told me about a method he used to Energize before matches: "I learned from experience that if I was feeling bad before a match, it helped to remember a time when I felt good. I would concentrate on the memory of that time and try to recapture the feeling I had then. Gradually I would remember how I wanted to feel." Use your Creative Thinking skills to remember the previous event as clearly as possible, and focus on recapturing the feeling you had that helped you achieve success.

Think productively. Use the skills you learned in Productive Analysis to combat feelings of fatigue and lethargy. Talk to yourself in a productive, helpful way. Focus on previous good performances and experiences to stay Energized. For example: *I performed well last time and was able to deal with the fatigue. I will cope with the fatigue again today.* Or: *I've worked hard for this. I'm mentally and physically strong. I'm prepared. Now all I have to do is let it happen.*

Showers and massage. Athletes often use both showering and massage to make them feel more Energized, alert, and invigorated. The temperature change of a hot or cold shower stimulates circulation and wakes the body up, serving as a powerful and quick Energizer. Likewise, a massage by a knowledgeable practitioner stimulates blood flow and aids the body in ridding itself of the waste products of effort or anxiety. A massage can be a very good way to help the body recharge after a long and tiring effort or after a stressful period. The increased energy will usually be available into the next day.

Have fun. Laughing at a joke or a funny memory can be a great Energizer. Dr. Jerry May of the University of Nevada, sport psychology consultant for the U.S. sailing team, has studied hundreds of elite performers in sport and business. He finds that a characteristic shared by highly successful people is a sense of humor.

If having fun and joking around help you reach your Achievement Zone, don't wait for the fun to start—make it happen. You might learn a variety of jokes to tell teammates or colleagues—by getting others laughing you will stimulate an Energized environment. Or if you are getting too serious about an event, rehearse some sayings you can use to stay loose. For example: *Lighten up, this is just an exam, not the End of the World As We Know It.* Or: *Smile. I've been in big competitions before. I always do better if I enjoy myself.*

Learn something new. A characteristic of high achievers is that they love doing new things, learning new skills, starting new projects. They are always searching for new techniques and methods to try. Bob Foth, Olympic silver medalist shooter, told me, "I always ask questions. I really believe there's no such thing as a dumb question. I'm always learning. I talk to the great shooters, I ask questions of the young shooters I'm teaching—I never know when it will make me think of something new."

Use this approach to Energizing by building new experiences and new learning into your life on a regular basis. Try not to let a month go by without enrolling in a course, working on a hobby, going to a play or concert, or meeting new people. Our mind/bodies must be continually stimulated in order to stay alert, effective, and invigorated.

Create stimulating surroundings. Dr. Martin Moore-Ede of Harvard has spent years studying how people in energy-draining jobs—for example, doing shift work—can best stay alert. His major finding is that the work surroundings must stimulate the worker in order to avoid lethargy and fatigue. This principle can also be applied to helping you reach your Achievement Zone. If your work environment is stimulating, you'll find it much easier to stay alert and focused on the job. Here are some of the things Dr. Moore-Ede suggests you can do to "wake up" your workplace:

■ *Use bright lighting.* Workers on the night shift can combat sleepiness by using bright lights. Researchers have found that very powerful lighting (1,000 lux or more) increases alertness and greatly reduces errors. Similarly, a work setting that allows a lot of sunlight in will be more Energizing than an enclosed room.

■ *Change the background.* One of the things that contribute heavily to a lack of energy is boredom. When the background surroundings are always the same, the brain receives little stimulation. In order to stay alert, try adding some spice to your workplace. Music that changes beat, sounds that are unpredictable, a cooling in room temperature, being touched, arresting aromas—all these changes increase your alertness and effectiveness.

The offices I visit in my consulting work are often so dull that it's a wonder that any productive work ever gets done in these drab cubicles. I often suggest a change in physical work conditions as a priority in establishing an Energizing work environment. In one company I worked with that had a high absenteeism rate among secretarial staff, redesigning the office space to make it more attractive, airy, and stimulating reduced absenteeism by 70 percent.

Take advantage of your times of peak energy. All the biological systems of our body regularly cycle on a twenty-four-hour schedule. This rhythmic cycle is called the circadian rhythm. Studies have shown that when our body temperature rises and our hormones surge, we not only feel more alert, we also perform better. But there are times during the twenty-four hours, most noticeably at night and during the midafternoon, when our systems are down and we perform poorly. We make mistakes in our reasoning and we become clumsy.

Keep track of your own periods of high energy. As much as possible, schedule your most challenging work for the periods when you feel most Energized. An executive I work with, Graham, works on his company's most important projects from 7 A.M. to 11 A.M., when he's feeling most alert. After lunch he schedules less challenging activities, such as returning phone calls and dictating letters. In the early evening, when he has another burst of energy, Graham does the long-term planning for his most important projects.

I hope I've given you plenty of ideas about how to stay Energized. Following these suggestions will help you be alert so that you can achieve the results you desire. Now let's take a look at how you can take care of your mind/body so that it has the energy you need, when you need it.

Step 2. Keep Your Energy Battery Charged

If you want to be able to Energize when you need it, your mind/body must have an available store of energy that it can utilize. Think of your body as an energy battery for your mind. Keep that battery charged, and you'll always have high energy. Let it run down, and your effectiveness will suffer. Three essential factors contribute to high energy: fitness, proper sleep, and good nutrition. World-class athletes seek the very latest information on each of these areas. You must also take care of these basics if you wish to use the mind/body skill of Energizing.

Nowhere is the connection between mind and body more clear than in the skill of Energizing. Your mind is not something that floats around in the air above you. It's inextricably linked to your body. If you keep your body fit, well rested, and well fueled, your "mental energy" will be high. But allow your body to become unfit, tired, or badly fueled, and the energy available for your mind will be much less.

It is often said that athletes depend on their bodies for their living. But this is just as true for the rest of us. If you are tired or feeling unwell, you're more likely to make mistakes and miss opportunities to shine. Your performance in all situations depends just as much on the readiness of your body as does the performance of an athlete in competition. If athletes take such good care of their bodies, shouldn't you consider doing the same?

Let's go over the fundamentals in these three important areas.

Fitness

Athletes are among the most dynamic, energetic people I know. This is not an accident. It isn't that people with high-energy personalities are attracted to sport; it is the sporting lifestyle itself that gives athletes lots of energy.

The high-activity lifestyle of athletes provides two benefits, which I believe are interrelated. The first is that being fit gives athletes a large amount of energy to use. The second is that physical fitness promotes good emotional adjustment and an ability to cope with the ups and downs of life.

How important is the effect of activity on your energy level? Some smart scientists decided to compare the energy boost you get from a candy bar with the energy you get from a brisk ten-minute walk. They asked people to either eat a candy bar or take a walk in the early afternoon. They found that the people who ate the candy bar experienced a surge of energy in the next half hour. Isn't that great? Just what the candy makers have been telling us. Except that after half an hour, guess what? The candy eaters CRASHED! Not only did they lose that energy boost, their energy went down to a level lower than it was before they ate that candy bar. And they didn't recover their energy for the rest of the afternoon. It's funny that the candy makers don't put that research in their ads, isn't it?

What about the walkers? Well, after finishing their ten minutes of vigorous walking around the block, their energy also surged. In fact, their energy level was *dramatically higher* than that of the candy eaters. What's more, it stayed high *all afternoon*. Instead of feeling drowsy and tired, they were alert and wide awake for the rest of the day. Just from one ten-minute walk! *That's* how important being active is if you want high energy in life.

Exercise and fitness have also been shown in many studies to have a positive effect on mood. In fact, psychologists now regularly use exercise as an additional treatment method for people who are depressed. In addition to receiving therapy and counseling, depressed clients are encouraged to join exercise classes. Researchers have found that many forms of exercise can promote a positive mood, including walking, running, weight lifting, swimming, biking, and circuit training.

It is not only depressed people who have benefited from adding exercise to their lives. Researchers found that people over age seventy could greatly increase their alertness and vigor by adding daily weight-training exercises to their schedule. Not only did they feel better, but they also increased their muscle mass, proving that physical fitness does not have to deteriorate with advancing years. Indeed, it is never too late to get fit.

Researchers have also found that regular exercisers live longer and suffer from fewer illnesses than people who don't exercise. In people with cardiovascular disease, for example, the death rate among exercisers is only half that among nonexercisers.

So it's clear that staying fit can be a very effective way of maintaining a high energy level. Having said all these wonderful things about fitness, my next piece of advice may surprise you.

Don't exercise. Athletes enjoy exercise, but I've noticed that many people don't. It took me a while to get this message. When I first began work as a psychologist I often advised unfit clients to begin an exercise program. I usually referred them to a local gym or YMCA. But when I followed up with them some months later, they had rarely attended more than once or twice. Gradually I began to realize that many people would rather exist on a broccoli-and-spinach diet than exercise regularly.

Less than a third of Americans exercise regularly. The rest of us are, by and large, sedentary. Those of us who *do* exercise try to make up for everyone else! You exercisers know who you are. You're out there in the fitness clubs and pools, and running or cycling on the roads every day. To all you exercisers, I need only say, Good work. Keep it up. You have a passion for being fit, and that's great.

What's holding the rest of us back? I'm sure studies are being done as I write to try to figure out how to get more of us to exercise regularly. But just from talking to people, asking those clients I told to go to the gym why they never did, I think I know the answer. For them, *exercise is no fun.*

For many people, there is nothing interesting, rewarding, or exciting about a trip to the local gym, pool, or racket club. And if it's no fun, if it seems like hard work (and no one is paying you), people won't do it.

There are many reasons why people don't find exercise fun. Some people have had a bad experience in school with gym class and got turned off to exercise in general. Others have had a coach who was abusive or too competitive, and have steered away from sport ever since. Others feel they don't fit in with the exercisers. Let's face it, most of those folks in the gym are pretty fit already. If you walk into their aerobics class weighing twenty-five pounds more than you want and with little endurance for sustained exercise, you're likely to feel very out of place.

Unfortunately, I find these negative feelings toward sport and exercise to be common. All those of you who are exercising already are having fun. But if you're one of the many who don't like exercise, my advice to you is simple: Don't. Don't exercise. Don't sign up for that expensive fitness club and then never go. There are other ways to get fit.

Be more active. The simplest way to get into shape is to be more active. Since there are so *many* things you can do actively (besides exercise), you are sure to find something that you enjoy. And that's the key to getting and staying fit. Do something *active* and *fun* every day.

With just a few minutes' thought, I came up with the following list of activities (things that require you to be active) you could try.

- Walking your dog
- Hiking
- Jumping rope
- Ballroom dancing
- Rock climbing
- Square dancing
- Tennis
- Racquetball
- Swimming
- Horseback riding
- Biking
- Tae kwon do
- Karate
- T'ai chi
- Yoga
- Canoeing
- Ice-skating
- In-line skating
- Skiing
- Waterskiing
- Kickball
- Basketball
- Softball
- Playing Frisbee
- Orienteering
- Gardening

There are bound to be some things on this list that you would enjoy doing. And if I can come up with that list in five minutes, I'm sure you could come up with more ideas if you put your mind to it. Try one of these activities, or one of your own, today. If some of them interest you but you're not sure how to begin, sign up for lessons or join a local league or intramural team.

If you're having trouble adding physical activity to your daily routine, decide what's holding you back. Not enough time? Then make your activity an action goal and get started on it immediately. Not enough support? Ask your family for suggestions. Get some friends to join in the activity with you. Without increasing your activity level, you have no chance of increasing your energy and getting to work on making your dreams happen.

Stretch! A couple of years ago, the United States Olympic Committee invited noted stretching expert Bob Anderson to Colorado Springs. He did a stretching workshop for our Olympic development coaches. I had the pleasure of sitting (or should I say stretching) through his workshop and was delighted by the philosophy Bob shared with us. Simple stretching is an often neglected energy booster that can be used anywhere, anytime. Stretching increases your flexibility and makes moving around easier; it helps prevent injuries; it increases your coordination; and it's a wonderful Energizer.

Stretching properly is not hard. Stretch slowly with gentle movements and don't bounce. If it hurts, back off. Stretching shouldn't involve pain. Pay attention to your body as you stretch and stay within your limits. Try breathing out slowly as you stretch. For lots of good stretching ideas, read Bob Anderson's book *Stretching*, which is still widely available.

Stretching is a particularly good Energizer if you work in an office. The fact that you can stretch while sitting at your desk, or by just standing up, makes it wonderfully convenient. Stretching is also very important for avoiding problems associated with repetitive movements (like typing) or with long periods of inactivity, problems common in office environments.

For office workers, I recommend five minutes of stretching

every half hour. If you keep forgetting to stretch, think of a way to remind yourself. For example, you could have someone from your computer department program your computer to beep every half hour—the signal for you take a stretching time-out. Stretching can be very rewarding, because it feels so good to loosen up and stretch out those muscles after they've been cramped and inactive.

Before I finish talking about fitness and move on, let me answer some questions that often come up when fitness is discussed.

How often should I be active? Actually, the typical question I hear is "How often should I exercise?" That question comes from looking at exercise as a form of punishment. "OK, I'll exercise if I *have* to. I know it's good for me. But how little can I get away with?"

See how different the question becomes if you ask, *How often should I do something fun and active?* My answer is, as much as you can! Taking care of yourself should be one of your main priorities in life. If you can combine activity with spending time with family or friends, it should become a top priority every day.

So my answer is, try to do something every day. A lot of people try to figure out how much exercise they should get on how many days (for example, thirty minutes a day four times a week). But I believe that not a day should go by when you aren't active—if you want to keep your energy battery charged at all times.

How hard should my activity be? That's the other favorite question of people who think they *have* to exercise and who want to know how little they can get away with.

Well, there are lots of fitness formulas out there you can try. But to be honest, even after working at the Olympic Training Center for more than seven years and working with exercise physiologists every day, I never did figure out the exact equation.

I'll let you in on a little secret. When we test elite athletes at the Olympic Training Center in Colorado Springs, one of the high-tech, sophisticated pieces of equipment we use is a piece of cardboard with some numbers on it. We hold it up in front of athletes and ask them to tell us how hard they're working. The numbers look like this:

20
19 Very, very hard
18
17 Very hard
16
15 Hard
14
13 Somewhat hard
12
11 Fairly light
10
9 Very light
8
7 Very, very light
6

As athletes are running on a treadmill or pedaling on a bike, we ask them to call out a number corresponding to how hard they're working. So a 20 is the most strenuous exercise possible, and under 12 means a light workout.

If you want to get your body moving in a way that will do it good and increase your fitness, stay active until you feel you're at the "somewhat hard" level, and stay there for a half hour.

The beauty of this system is that it's totally individualized. What might be easy for an elite athlete might be very hard for you. This is why reading a typical exercise book may not be helpful if you're out of shape or have been inactive for a while. All those exercises will be too hard. But you can make any activity easy enough or hard enough if *you're* calling the shots.

What you need to strive for is balance. The activity should be hard enough to get you puffing and blowing, hard enough for you to feel your heart rate increasing, but easy enough that you can keep it up for a half hour. If you need little rests periodically in order to keep going, fine. As your fitness increases, you'll find you can stay active at the "somewhat hard" level for longer periods without a break.

As you become more fit, activities that were once demanding will become easier. So keep challenging yourself. If you now rate your activity as "easy," not "somewhat hard," add to it. Increase the length of your walk. Or try to go faster. Swing your arms vigorously, or take longer steps in your stride. (That's a good one. Try it the next time you're out walking and see how it adds to the intensity of your walk.) Just don't overexert yourself. There's no extra fitness benefit to be gained from being at the "very hard" or "very, very hard" levels. You're not training for the Olympics. A daily activity in the "somewhat hard" range will give you lots of increased energy that you can use to stay in your Achievement Zone.

I challenge you—try doing something fun and active every day for a month, and I bet you'll have greatly improved energy by the end of it. If you don't, write and tell me, and I'll put you in my next book.

Sleep

I met Bill when he attended a national training camp for top young soccer prospects. He came to see me because he wasn't getting enough sleep. The problem was nerves. In the last few days before a game, Bill started thinking about the match constantly. His endless thoughts about the game made it tough to fall asleep. Even when he did doze off, he woke up often and had trouble falling asleep again. Bill felt tired and cranky all day after tossing and turning all night. The outcome was that by match day he usually had low energy and low spirits. Bill knew that he wasn't performing up to expectations, and he worried that he wouldn't be selected for the international team.

Our medical personnel thoroughly examined Bill, but they couldn't find a physical reason for his sleeplessness. So I asked Bill to keep a sleep diary. He kept track of the time he went to bed, the time he thought he fell asleep, the amount of sleep he estimated he had gotten, and a rating of the quality of his sleep. After a week we sat down to look at the diary together. Bill was surprised that he was getting more sleep than he'd originally thought. I taught Bill a number of simple strategies to help him fall asleep effectively, encouraging him to lie down only when he was tired and not to watch TV in bed as he usually did. After three weeks Bill rated his sleep as much improved. We stayed in touch, and Bill continued to improve his sleeping habits. A year later he was chosen for a U.S.A. junior soccer team.

It is important to recognize that sleep is an active, not a passive, process. Some parts of our bodies are most active when we're asleep. For example, protein in our brains is made during REM (or dream) sleep. Certain hormones, such as growth hormone, reach their peak of secretion during the deep sleep stage. The division of cells is also at its peak during deep sleep. Sleep experts believe that most of the repair of the body goes on during sleep, and some have guessed that the brain stores new information in memory during dreaming. For these reasons, sleep is much more than just *rest*. Sleep is really a period of *active recovery* and growth.

We've known about the physical changes that occur during sleep for some time. But only recently has the importance of sleep for a healthy mind emerged. Nobel Prize winner Francis Crick has developed a theory of sleep that says it is vital for the brain to have time each night to "flush out" the accumulated debris of the past day's experiences (our dreams). Then the brain can go about the vital work of putting into long-term memory our significant experiences. Studies of sleep-deprived individuals have found that even before the body begins to tire from lack of sleep, the mind begins to suffer from disturbances such as hallucinations.

How much should I sleep? It is important to find out how much sleep *your* mind/body requires for optimal functioning. Surveys suggest that many Americans suffer from a chronic lack of sleep. Quite simply, many people never get the amount of sleep at night that their mind/body really needs. Try going to sleep one hour earlier to see if more sleep is beneficial to your functioning. Give yourself a daily rating of how alert, energized, and effective you are. Compare your ratings before and after the hour's extra sleep. Ask one or two people who see a lot of you during the day to give you some feedback as well, and don't tell them when you're switching to the extra hour of sleep. If you're doing better with more sleep, I strongly suggest that you make the early bedtime a regular part of your lifestyle.

Sleep and performance. The best advice I can give you regarding your daily sleep is to take it seriously. We spend about a third of our lives sleeping, so it clearly serves important functions. A useful way to pay attention to your sleep patterns is to keep track of them in your Achievement Zone diary. Make a simple note every day of the length of time you spent asleep and a rating of the quality of your sleep (3 could be sound, 2 might be OK, and 1 could be poor). As you discover any relationships between your lifestyle and your sleep, make a note of them in your diary.

For example, you might find that you went to bed tired after a busy day that included a good workout after lunch, and the next day you awoke early and had lots of energy until midafternoon. It's important to make such a discovery. It tells you that an afternoon workout helps increase your energy the next day. If you continue to observe your habits, you'll gradually understand the role sleep plays in your life and its importance in keeping you Energized.

Many athletes find that a regular routine helps them stay Energized during tough periods of training. They try to go to bed and to wake up at the same time every day. This approach works because the mind/body adapts to such a routine. The body actually starts waking up an hour or so before you wake up—your temperature rises and your blood pressure comes back to normal. So when you get out of bed, you feel more Energized. It's a great way to start the day! The body cannot establish such a pattern if you have no routine.

Nutrition

Without the proper fuel to keep the body's engine running smoothly, it is difficult to achieve top-level performance. Good nutrition and healthy eating habits can make all the difference between finishing a day with energy to spare and running out of gas in the middle of the afternoon. If you're unsure about how healthy your eating habits are, consult with a qualified nutritionist regarding your daily diet.

Make sure that you understand any nutrition advice you're given. Healthy and effective eating doesn't have to be complicated. Don't let "experts" use big words to confuse you. Just keep asking questions till you know what you're doing.

The following story shows how important proper nutrition can be in performance situations. For this athlete, it meant the difference between a disappointing season and an outstanding one.

"I NEED MORE ENERGY TO REACH THE TOP"

Tanya was one of America's top road cyclists when she came to the USOC's sport science team and requested help. She was concerned because she was losing energy at the end of long road races. The sport science team analyzed her training and competition methods and discovered that she could benefit by changing her habits in three areas. First, her diet; second, her fluid intake on race days; and third, her thoughts during a race.

Our analysis of Tanya's diet indicated that she needed more carbohydrates; she was eating under 400 grams of carbohydrates every day. Based on her weight and training intensity, however, our nutritionist recommended a daily diet of about 600 grams of carbohydrates. This change may seem small, but it can make a big difference to an athlete in a demanding sport such as cycling. Carbohydrates (fruits, vegetables, breads, rice, pasta, potatoes, and cereals) are a critical source of energy, because they provide the body with glycogen, the energy source within the body. Exercise uses up glycogen, and it must be restored by eating foods high in carbohydrates.

Because she was usually nervous on race day, Tanya tended to eat and drink very little before a race. Our assessment indicated that she was not drinking enough fluids to maintain her energy during a grueling road race. When an athlete doesn't drink enough water, the amount in the blood decreases due to sweating. This causes blood volume to decrease. As a result, body temperature and heart rate both increase. These changes hurt athletic performance. Our exercise physiologists helped Tanya learn how to monitor the amount of fluid she was drinking. She learned how to drink enough before and during a race to avoid dehydration. Restoring her fluids had a very positive impact on her energy level.

Finally, I worked with Tanya to find out what her thoughts were during races. She typically began a race with a good plan and a lot of confidence, but as she tired she often lost Concentration. At the end of the race she would forget her plan and think about how much her body was hurting. These thoughts damaged her confidence.

We worked together to develop a race plan for all parts of the race, including the end. She practiced focusing on simple tactical thoughts, her performance cues, at key points. Performance cues must be very simple for the end of endurance events, or else they are forgotten. Hers were Pace and Kick It! The changes she'd made to her diet and her drinking of water on race day gave her increased energy at the end of a race, and her improved mind/body skills helped her concentrate all the way to the finish. Tanya had a much-improved road race season after working with us, and she won the Nationals.

If you're concerned about healthy eating for high-level performance at work, may I suggest you read *Eating for Peak Performance* by Rosemary Stanton. There are several good books out on this topic, but this one is easy to read and follow. Also, consider the following suggestions for healthy eating and high energy. They're the same suggestions we offer athletes at the Olympic Training Center in Colorado Springs. If you're serious about success, you should think about them carefully.

Nutrition Tips for High Energy

1. Eat more:

   - fruit
   - vegetables
   - bread
   - cereals

   These are high-energy foods.
2. Eat fewer sweets, desserts, snack foods, and fast foods. These trigger the insulin response, which rapidly reduces energy.
3. Avoid fatty foods. Cut down on your intake of oils, butter, margarine, fried foods, fatty meat, and creams. Fat is a very low energy food. Once in the body, fat makes you sleepy. At most, only a quarter of your daily calories should come from fat.
4. Drink plenty of water. About a cup an hour should be sufficient. We advise athletes to drink about three cups of water every half hour before competition to make sure that the blood gets enough fluid when competition starts. (Drinks with caffeine, which include most sodas and coffee, don't count because they trigger fluid *removal* from the body.)
5. For women, especially, get plenty of calcium in your daily meals. The best sources of calcium are low-fat milk, fruits, nuts, dairy foods, soya beans, and seeds.
6. Avoid excessive salt, caffeine, alcohol, and sugar. These all waste energy.
7. Eat smaller, well-chosen meals. Eat more frequently. This helps keep your energy level stable throughout the day.
8. Eat small portions of low-fat proteins (lean meat, fish, skinless poultry, legumes, and dairy products). About three to five ounces at one meal a day should be plenty. (Weigh four

ounces of meat, cut it, and take a good look at it to understand the size of the portions you should be eating.) Try having fish (not fried!) once or twice a week instead of red meat. Protein is essential for high energy, but it shouldn't be overdone.

9. Consider your activity level before you determine your daily eating plan. The more active you are (for example, if you get lots of exercise), the more food you'll need.

10. Don't diet. This is such an important piece of advice, I'm going to repeat it.

   Don't diet!

   By dieting, I mean the process of starving yourself periodically, or restricting calorie intake, in order to lose weight. People who starve themselves to lose weight end up gaining more weight over the long term. This sort of dieting can also cause all sorts of nasty health problems. The worst, and I've seen a lot of them among female athletes, are eating disorders. Dieting always causes a reduction in energy.

   If you're overweight, the keys to weight loss are healthy eating and staying active. If you have weight concerns, I recommend the book *Weight Loss Through Persistence* by Dr. Dan Kirschenbaum.

   All of these suggestions depend on your body type, body weight, and present level of fitness. That's why it's so helpful to work with a nutritionist or health expert to get your own individualized nutritional energy program up and running.

These simple steps from a nutrition and health expert will help you begin a lifelong habit of healthy eating for high energy. If you need to make changes in your eating habits, make that an action goal today.

Vitality and good health are the reward for taking care of the three basics of fitness, sleep, and nutrition. If you want extra energy in your day, pay attention to these three elements of your life. Once you've experienced increased pep and vigor, you will never want to go back to a life of lethargy.

Achieving your dreams takes hard work. Roger Bannister, the first human to break the four-minute mile, once said, "The person who can go further once the effort gets painful is the person who will win." You will need lots of energy to overcome the inevitable obstacles that will appear along the way. But applying the skill of Energizing will give you the strength to achieve your goals.

Energizing Tips

If you find yourself in a high-stress situation, make sure that you allow time to recover from the experience. Schedule appropriate sleep times in your day, take care of what you eat, and stay active. Also build a daily energy-recharging time into your schedule. You can recharge your energy battery by using a Keeping Cool exercise to help your mind/body recover. Elite athletes I've worked with typically set aside between twenty and forty-five minutes a day to recharge their batteries. Some athletes use even shorter recovery periods, but use several of them each day.

These recharging sessions will help you deal with stress. Stress has received a bad rap in society, but it's actually beneficial. The only way athletes can get stronger and faster is to *stress* their bodies by working out. The body adapts to that stress, and the end result is a stronger, faster body. You can also learn how to handle increasingly challenging situations, as long as you allow yourself time to recover from stress. To recover optimally from stressful periods, learn one of the mind/body relaxation skills I describe in the Keeping Cool chapter and use it every day. If you can spare just ten minutes, that is much better than nothing, but thirty minutes will give you even greater restoration of spirit. You might be able to close the door to your office and forward your phone for fifteen minutes. Or you might ask your spouse to watch the children while you lie down for a half hour. Try it for a month, and I'm sure you'll notice a difference in your energy level.

SUMMARY

How to Learn Energizing

Step 1 ■
Energize Your Thinking!

Step 2 ■
Keep Your Energy Battery Charged
- Fitness
- Sleep
- Nutrition

Consistency:

Prepare
for Success

The Olympic sport of shooting is a solitary pursuit. There are no opponents to blame for forcing you into errors, no umpires to yell at for making a bad call. And in the modern form of the sport, with television cameras showing spectators the result of every shot, your successes and failures are up there for everyone to see.

In this demanding sport, Bob Foth has emerged as one of the U.S.A.'s best ever. At the 1992 Olympics, he won the silver medal in the men's three-position small-bore rifle event, missing the gold by just one point. Bob is now in training for the 1996 Olympics, which will be held in Atlanta. He has had continued success in recent years, winning many medals in the prestigious World Cup events and earning his way into the World Cup Finals every year from 1988 to 1992.

When I interviewed Bob, he explained that his success comes from a very consistent approach to each shot. He can't afford to be careless, so he prepares thoroughly every time he picks up the rifle.

Bob explains that "for each shot, I go through a sequence that involves breathing six times. During each one of those breaths, I know what I should be thinking; I know what I should be looking at; I know what I want to be visualizing; and I know what parts of my body I should be focusing on."

The attention to detail in Bob's preparation is remarkable. Yet it has obviously been a big factor in his success. He goes through each breath with me and tells me what he is thinking at every stage of the shot. "On the first breath the rifle is still on the stand and my eyes are closed. I'm working on breathing deeply and trying to feel generally relaxed. I want to make sure everything is comfortable and in position. On the second breath I work on relaxing any trouble spots that are still tense. Then I visualize what the perfect sight picture looks like [what Bob sees when he looks through the rifle sight at the target]."

He continues, "On the third breath I open my eyes and pick up the rifle. It's pointed roughly at the target and I let it settle as I exhale. Then on the fourth breath I fit the rifle into my shoulder more tightly." Only now does Bob finally look through the sight at the target. "At the beginning of the fifth breath I look through the sight. My attention is starting to go toward the target. But I'm still very aware of feeling relaxed through my whole body. I make sure that the grip of my right hand on the rifle is correct." Now he focuses intently. "The sixth breath is shallower, it doesn't disrupt me. My focus is becoming very, very sharp on the target. I reach a level of concentration that I can't maintain for long. Then I'm ready to break [fire] the shot."

Bob uses this routine every time he fires a shot, in practice or in competition. "If I didn't practice that way every time, I might get lazy and forget to do it in competition, too. I think it helps me bounce back quickly when things don't go well. Most top shooters can do well when everything's clicking, but it's harder to keep going when you're down," explains Bob.

"For example, at one of the World Cups, in Zagreb, I was in third place and catching up on the two leading Yugoslavians when I took one of my shots on someone else's target! It's an unusual mistake, to say the least. I got no points for that shot because I didn't hit my own target. Suddenly I was back in the pack. I experienced a horrible sinking feeling. I said to myself, I can't believe you just did that! But I had.

"I sat down to get my thoughts back together. I realized that I couldn't give up. Experience has taught me to always keep trying. So I used some of the deep breathing I practice to get rid of that sinking feeling. I fought those negative thoughts and told myself to keep going and just stick to the basics. I knew I needed to have relaxed muscles to shoot well, so I did some muscle-relaxation exercises to get rid of my tension. I imagined shooting well again, hitting tens, and I got up and continued. Somehow I clawed my way back into the match, and I ended up being rewarded with the bronze medal. An experience like that teaches me a lot." I nodded, and wondered how many of us could stay as calm as Bob in our approach if we had just screwed up. But how many of us prepare our minds for success the way Bob does?

What Is Consistency?

Being in the Achievement Zone is widely regarded as an elusive phenomenon. Athletes and researchers describe being in the Zone as temporary, transient, fleeting, short-lived. People are surprised when they reach the Achievement Zone and are not surprised when they leave it.

In a study of elite golfers, researcher Patrick Cohn from the University of Virginia found that all players say their experience of peak performance is "temporary." Why is it that being able to get the very best out of ourselves, performing at the top of our game, seems such a hit-or-miss proposition?

I've found that two things prevent people from being in the Achievement Zone as much as they wish. First, they lack a consistent approach to the Achievement Zone. Second, when the pressure's on, many people panic and change their approach. The skill of Consistency is developing a method that works for you and then sticking to it, no matter what. Once you have mastered this approach, you will find that you can enter the Achievement Zone at will.

Learn Consistency

Who are the athletes you most admire? If you're like me, your greatest admiration is probably reserved for those who have stayed at the top of their game for many years. But even the most consistent athletes don't win all the time. Do you know who has the most second-place finishes in the history of the PGA Tour? The answer is Jack Nicklaus, generally considered one of the greatest golfers of all time. Do we regard him as a failure because he finished second so often? No, because even finishing second is an indication of his ability to put himself in a position to win.

There's a reason why the champions I've worked with are consistently successful. They don't leave the outcome of their efforts to chance. Instead, they do everything in their power to put themselves in a position to succeed. From my work with these consistent winners I have discovered three steps that characterize their approach. These steps make up the mind/body skill of Consistency. Here they are:

Consistency

Step 1. Develop Your Own Plan for Success

Step 2. Stick to Your Plan Under Pressure

Step 3. Expect the Unexpected

Let's take a look at these three steps.

Step 1. Develop Your Own Plan for Success

In a 1994 study I conducted of one hundred athletes at the Olympic Training Center, I asked participants if they could enter the Achievement Zone at will. Eighty athletes said they could. When I asked them how, nearly all of them described some form of careful preparation for their event. For example, one athlete told me, "Yes, I can reach the Zone, but it takes the right preparation. Physically I have to be confident in my training program. Mentally I must trust my teammates and focus on the race."

Another Olympian said, "I think that the way you enter the Zone is by being prepared. You must train every day for the Zone." Although twenty athletes felt they could not reach the Zone deliberately, the majority of these said they were learning how to get there. One athlete summed up this attitude when she said, "I think that as I mature as an athlete it becomes easier to willfully enter the Zone. I'm learning a lot about my abilities and the kind of sharp focus I need to do my best."

Successful athletes find that they can't control the external world in which they compete, but they *can control their own internal environment*. Consistent excellence is a matter of careful preparation— not just physical preparation, though that is extremely important, but also mental preparation, the kind that Bob Foth talked about.

The Achievement Zone is attained via the personal mix of thoughts, images, and emotions that allows you to do your best work. This mix is unique to each individual. Psychologists used to think that being in the right frame of mind was a matter of chance. Some days we're "on," some days we're not. Now we know that belief to be wrong. Once we know what thoughts, images, and emotions help us do our best, we can choose to think and feel in that way. Successful people don't enter the Achievement Zone by chance. They find out what they need to do to get there, and they use that approach in all important situations.

The Importance of Consistent Preparation for Performance

Sport psychologists Steve Boutcher and Debra Crews looked at how long golfers of varying ability take to hit the ball after they select their club. Observers followed golfers around the course with a stopwatch and timed how long the golfers took in preparation for hitting the ball. They found that golfers of all levels usually did the same things before they hit a shot: they stood behind the ball, lined up the club, glanced at the target, and waggled the clubhead around. However, professional golfers were much more consistent in their preshot actions than college or beginning golfers. The successful golfers always took about the same amount of time to hit the ball. The less successful golfers, on the other hand, fluctuated widely in their preshot timing. Sometimes they took ten seconds to hit the ball; at other times they took sixty seconds. They weren't consistent.

Developing a consistent plan for competition provides the following benefits:

■ When you learn which thoughts and feelings help you do your best, you can focus on these in every important situation.

■ Your consistent approach is like a traveler's checklist. It makes sure you won't forget something that is crucial for success.

■ Your approach gives you confidence in high-pressure situations. You know you're using the same reliable approach that has brought you success in the past.

■ In high-pressure situations, many people fail because they panic. Your approach helps you stay in your Achievement Zone, preventing any chance of panic.

Some athletes are very meticulous in planning their approach. Cathy, a runner I worked with, would plan the things she focused on for the week before the race, the night before, and the hour before. Other athletes are much more casual in their approach. For example Ben, a wrestler, knew that he needed to laugh and joke around with his teammates before a competition. This helped him stay loose and wrestle well. His approach was no more complicated than that.

Just as athletes develop a consistent approach to competition, you can develop a winning formula for your work. For example, a salesperson might develop a successful style for handling cold calls. An executive can create an effective way of delivering attention-getting presentations. An actor can craft his own style of preparation for dramatic performances. Use the following exercise to begin putting your approach together.

PUT TOGETHER AN EFFECTIVE PLAN FOR SUCCESS

What makes up a successful performance plan? In creating your own method of preparation it's very helpful to think about each of the seven mind/body skills discussed in the previous chapters.

Think about an important task you're facing. It might be a speech at the local club next month; the final of your tennis competition next week; the delivery of the team report on your project at work. Now ask yourself the following questions:

- What are my goals in this situation? (Action Focus)
- What images help me do my best? (Creative Thinking)
- What thoughts will enable me to achieve success? (Productive Analysis)
- How will I stay calm when the pressure is on? (Keeping Cool)
- What do I need to pay attention to in order to succeed? (Concentration)
- How will I respond to the feelings I have as I perform this task? (Emotional Power)
- How will I maintain sufficient energy to perform optimally? (Energizing)

If you are able to answer these seven questions you are in a position to achieve optimal preparation for performance. Like a champion, you will be leaving nothing to chance. The way you approach work, or any other performance situation, *is under your control.*

Let's take a look at how someone actually went about developing a Consistent preparation strategy for performances. The story of Grant shows how anyone who lacks Consistency can put together a performance plan that is reliable, even under pressure.

GRANT'S SIZZLING STARTS, FIZZLING FINISHES

Grant, a professional golfer, first came to me at the recommendation of his coach. A beautiful striker of the ball, Grant was struggling with his game. He would often sizzle at the start of a round. But he rarely kept it together for eighteen holes. This puzzled Grant greatly. "Why can't I go on with it when I get to three or four under after nine holes?" Grant complained. "I begin to feel really nervous and I just want to get back in the clubhouse with that score under my belt. I want to see my name up on the leaderboard at the end of the day. Instead, I start to make mistakes. I drop shots, and I want to get them back so desperately that I press harder and start making more mistakes. Suddenly I'm rushing and the whole round falls apart. I just need to get a few good tournaments under my belt where I don't collapse. Then I might start believing in myself."

Because he had no history of success, Grant rarely gained automatic entry into tournaments. Usually he relied on his sponsors to get him into the draw. If that didn't work he could also try to qualify, which meant more traveling and more competition. As a result, Grant felt immense pressure to succeed in every tournament he entered. He worked hard on his game, but there were many other talented players competing against him. With every disappointing performance his confidence decreased.

During one tournament I walked around the course with Grant, observing his mind/body approach to the game. As I watched him play I noticed a lot of variability in his approach to shots. Sometimes he laughed and moved quickly, his swing looked relaxed, and the results were good. At other times he lingered over his club selection, looked worried during his setup, and hit a jerky-looking shot. After an up-and-down round he had a chance to make the next day's play with a birdie on the eighteenth. But his eyes looked glazed as he stepped onto the green and he appeared to rush his ten-foot putt. He missed the cut.

When I asked him later what he was thinking on the last green, Grant replied, "I was still shook up after that ball out of bounds and the double bogey on the sixteenth. Until then I knew I was going to make it, but then I said, Uh-oh, same old thing. I just wanted to hurry up and hit the putt before I thought about it too much and messed up. But I missed it anyway."

Grant and I discussed the idea of mind and body working in harmony. I suggested that in his eagerness to do well, Grant was thinking too far ahead. He was worrying about being on the leaderboard before he had even enjoyed his entire eighteen holes. To help Grant focus on the important things (his preparation for the swing), I asked him to pay attention to how confident he felt before each shot.

At first it was difficult for Grant to focus his attention on his own game. When I asked him how confident he had felt before each shot, he would say "I forget." Gradually, he became aware that when he was focused on his shots he was confident, but that when he was paying attention to the leaderboard or his playing partner, he played scared.

Grant and I used this information to come up with a plan that would increase his Consistency. Grant's plan was to "see it, paint it, feel it, and do it" on every shot. These four steps reminded Grant to concentrate on what he needed to do to hit the ball well:

- **See it** reminded Grant to take in all the information he needed to make a good shot selection. When putting, for example, he needed to observe the possible break, the grain of the grass, the speed of the putt, the angle of the hole, and so on. Taking the time to really see all these details forced Grant to slow down and prevented rushing.
- **Paint it** moved Grant on to the point of decision. He would not hit the ball until he could successfully visualize the shot he wanted to make. On every shot, he imagined exactly how he wanted the ball to travel, how it would look in the air, and where it would land.
- **Feel it** helped Grant move from a very analytical way of thinking into a "feel" mode. Grant took the time to imagine his body moving and striking the ball exactly the way he wanted. This put him in the right frame of mind to be successful.
- **Do it** was the final message Grant gave himself as he addressed the

ball. To him, this meant total commitment. He put all his energy into striking the ball just as he had imagined and felt it.

After each shot, Grant took a few moments to evaluate the outcome. If he hit a poor shot, he decided if his mental approach was wrong, if his strategy was poor, or if his technique was incorrect. Each shot taught him a lesson. If the shot was good, he rehearsed it again mentally. He wanted the good shots stored in memory.

Originally there were six steps in his preparation, but he found that this slowed him down too much. For several months he fine-tuned his approach until he felt ready to use it in a tournament. He was immediately rewarded when he made the cut and earned his largest check of the year. After missing the cut in eight of his previous nine tournaments, Grant made the cut in three of the next five. A year later he had climbed from below 150th on the Tour to the top 50, and his best finish was a tie for third.

Grant told me that in addition to playing better, he was having more fun than he had had in five years. Grant enjoyed using all the mind/body skills of success, but he believed that the skill of Consistency was the one that enabled him to put it all together.

Develop your own approach

Jack Nicklaus approaches every golf shot in a similar fashion. You don't see him vary his approach. This helps him remember the critical components of a successful swing. Many baseball players also have a familiar set of actions they go through every time they step into the batter's box. It helps them focus.

As you put together your own approach to success for different tasks, don't be afraid to experiment. Some athletes like the sort of preparation strategy used by Grant. Simple and short. Others have a very detailed checklist, like Bob Foth. Each of us must discover for ourselves what is important and what we should ignore. That's one reason why the Achievement Zone is such an intensely personal experience. What works for you probably won't work for me.

For example, a few years ago I worked with two excellent actors. Both were critically acclaimed and popular. Yet their approaches to acting were entirely different. One of them, George, concentrated on developing his roles by living them out. While rehearsing a play, he would almost become the character he was portraying. There were few moments of the day when he wasn't thinking, *How would my character react in this situation? What would I feel right now?*

The other, Lisa, focused on detailed observation of human behavior in order to bring her roles to life. She prided herself on her ability to mimic people, and she used people she met to give her ideas for the characters she played on stage. Away from the stage, Lisa left her character behind.

Both these actors were very successful. Yet their approaches were very different. They had each learned to prepare for success in a manner that worked for them. As you begin to understand how *you* achieve success, you can stop worrying about the things that are unimportant. Then you can pay more attention to the things that are critical in your preparation. In this way you will develop your own way of reaching your personal Achievement Zone. Whatever approach you use, practice it until it becomes second nature.

In the next exercise I've provided a set of questions that will help you put together a winning formula for consistent success. Use it to help develop your own approach to important projects.

Consistency Checklist

The following questions will help you develop a consistent approach to projects. For the sake of clarity, I have focused my questions on the work environment. However, you can adapt these questions to other settings.

Do you leave things to chance? Or do you have a way of consistently preparing mind and body for success?

- What surroundings do you like to work in? What environment promotes your best work?
- Are there things you can change in your work setting that will help you stay in the Achievement Zone? Get a better desk, a more efficiently organized office? Eliminate poor lighting or an uncomfortable chair?
- When you're involved in a project that lasts many days or weeks, what mind/body factors help you stay in the Achievement Zone?
  - What things can you say to yourself to stay motivated?
  - What images and mental pictures help you do your best?
  - What energizers can you build into your day to help you keep going?
  - In a long project, what distractions typically waste your time? What can you do to prevent or overcome them?
- When you're working on a deadline, under time pressure, what mind/body factors help you stay in the Achievement Zone?
  - What things can you say to yourself to stay calm and focused?
  - What images and mental pictures help you work well under pressure?
  - Do you need to build some Keeping Cool exercises into your schedule to stay focused?
  - When you're working on a tight deadline, what distractions typically waste your time? What can you do to prevent or overcome them?
- Do you have a consistent approach to situations, even when tackling low-priority projects? If you approach low-priority projects carefully, you will be comfortable with your approach when high-priority projects come along.
- How do you prepare for success the night before an important project? What thoughts and images have helped you deliver your best work in the past?
- How do you successfully prepare for excellence in the last hour before an important project? What should you be thinking

about in order to be in your Achievement Zone? What has worked for you before?

- Just before you begin, what is your cue to remind yourself to go for it with everything you've got? What puts you in the right frame of mind to deliver a winning performance? Have you discovered things that help from experience?

If you think about these questions carefully, you will be able to come up with a successful approach to reaching the Achievement Zone. Put all your mind/body skills to work for you, and success will be yours for the asking.

Step 2. Stick to Your Plan Under Pressure

If things start going wrong, having a consistent approach prevents panic. There is nothing worse than entering an important situation and changing the way you do things because of the pressure. Usually, you throw away the very things that made you successful.

Unfortunately, I've seen this happen many times. I remember talking with Jim, a pole vaulter, after his competition in the Olympic Trials in 1988. This was the most important event in his athletic career. So he decided that he'd double-check every aspect of his preparation that day. He got on a bus and went out to the venue several hours early. There he checked and rechecked his equipment. At the pole vault site he stood and imagined his upcoming competition. He dressed early and killed the last hour or two by reading a novel he'd brought along.

The Trials were a disaster. Although Jim was definitely one of the top three contenders coming into the competition, he put in his worst performance in two years. He finished fifth and missed out on his dream of representing the U.S.A. in the Olympics.

As we sat and talked, the painful realization dawned on him that his extra preparation had backfired. Typically, he arrived at the competition venue an hour before competition and had plenty of time to go through all his equipment checks and warm-ups. Today he'd added several hours of preparation, but the result was increased stress, not increased success. As he waited and waited his tension had steadily mounted. Jim was way out of his Achievement Zone by the time the competition began. By the time he'd recovered, the damage was done. It was a terrible lesson to learn so late in a career.

His story is a typical one. Many athletes learn too late that the Olympic Games are really just another athletic event, requiring exactly the same skills they have used in the past. Instead, many athletes let all the hype and media attention get to them. They change their plan, put more pressure on themselves, and court disaster in the process.

The same thing happens in other fields. Students worry themselves sick about passing exams and unexpectedly fail. Employees get tied up in knots about an upcoming promotion evaluation and begin producing inferior work. Even in everyday situations, people get flustered when they run into problems; instead of sticking to a successful plan, they try to change, which only makes things worse.

In a groundbreaking study on achieving athletic excellence, Canadian sport psychologists Terry Orlick and John Partington found that a major cause of failure at the Olympics was altering routines. They interviewed 235 members of the two 1984 Canadian Olympic teams (Winter and Summer) and found that many athletes who had failed to perform up to their potential believed that they had changed too many things before the Olympics. One of the athletes said:

> Even though I had just come off my best year ever, I completely revolutionized the training program I used to prepare for the Olympics. My training changed so much, and I did so much work that I still have physical problems from overworking myself. It was a complete waste of time. When I look back, it makes sense that if you find a training program that works for you, you mustn't go away from it.

When athletes have achieved success, they should stick to their approach under pressure. Last-minute changes inevitably cause problems. The most dramatic example of this that I've encountered is told by the marvelous sailor John Bertrand in his compelling book *Born to Win*. His story illustrates perfectly how failure can be a learning experience. In the Olympics, Bertrand's failure to stick with his approach cost him a gold medal. But the lesson he learned helped him become a national hero seven years later.

A Dream 132 Years in the Making

Bertrand was an experienced young Australian sailor when he won the right to represent his country at the 1976 Olympic Games in Canada. In his book about the 1983 America's Cup challenge, he describes an incident during those Games that had a profound effect on his approach to competition.

"[I] headed for the Olympic regatta site at Kingston, where I carried the flag in the opening parade. I sailed better than I had ever sailed before, of that I am certain. There are seven races in the Olympic classes, and you eliminate your worst result. . . . I was having a terrific time—until the eleventh hour, when something happened that I will never forget and that was to have a profound and lasting effect.

"Five races had been sailed. It came down to a straight fight among Australia, East Germany, Russia, and Brazil. Conditions were perfect [for the sixth race]. I was second, tracked hard by the East German. . . . Approaching the bottom mark I was planing at between ten and twelve knots, and I kept glancing back at this impassive blond German about three feet behind, nearly touching my boat. Until the day I die, I will remember the feeling that rushed over me. Suddenly, from out of the blue, I thought, Am I good enough? *It was my first moment of self-doubt in the entire competition. Defeatism is like a forest fire in a big international event. Quickly I thought,* Can I hold him off? Am I being pushed beyond my normal limitations? *These were my first negative thoughts in the Olympics. . . .*

"Seized by a need to make a positive move, I decided to take a chance that I would never have dreamed of taking in a normal race. I would not

even have done this in practice. But I took the opportunity of transferring the mainsheet from the boom through the ratchet block in the floor of the boat. I was under total stress at the time, and I knew this particular maneuver would save me one step, would save me precious time and inches, would stop the East German from gaining an inside overlap at that mark and from giving him the opportunity to pass me. I could not even bear to think about that possibility.

"Then I lost control of the mainsheet, and the main boom shot out to leeward, beyond the position for stability control of the sail. The boat immediately flipped out of control and capsized to weather. The boat was upside down and I was underneath. Holy God! What have I done? *was my last thought as I hurtled into the water. I had gone from very nearly being in a control position to being totally out of control.* If only I had had the presence of mind to do what I had been trained to do *[emphasis mine]. If only I had made the methodical moves I knew were right under that intense pressure, I would still be sailing along, still in front with miles to go in which to get him, even if he did get an overlap. Instead of that, I tried to drown myself. I had fallen into the trap that nearly every Olympic competitor falls into. I had taken a stupid risk, losing the significance of the race and my position in it. I had done the opposite of everything I had been trained for. And now I was upside down."*

Bertrand sailed conservatively in the seventh and final race and made sure of the Olympic bronze medal. But he felt sure he had learned a very important lesson for the future:

"I took that one negative moment deadly seriously. I reflected on it many times after the regatta because it had happened at a critical time, and it spurred me on to become a keen student of sport psychology, of the psychology of winning. . . . It amazed me how cool, or at least apparently cool, that East German had been, even though he had never before won a European championship or any major regatta. He just kept on doing what he had been trained to do, reproducing his training under extreme pressure. That East German just seemed to be enjoying the atmosphere and the competition, and that was what I should have been doing, achieving that same degree of self-control."

In 1983, John Bertrand was able to use that lesson during the dra-

matic clash for the yachting trophy known simply as the America's Cup. Since 1851 this prize had been held continuously by the United States. Bertrand was captain of the twelve-meter yacht Australia II, *which, with its revolutionary winged keel, was supposed to break the string of successful defenses. But after four races Dennis Connor and his crew had comprehensively outsailed the Aussies and led three races to one.*

It would have been easy to panic and make desperate changes, as every previous challenger had done. But Bertrand had learned his lesson from the steely East German and he stuck with his game plan. He successfully led his crew to a remarkable comeback, winning the last three races. After 132 years a challenger finally took "The Auld Mug" from the hallowed grounds of the New York Yacht Club.

Let It Happen

If you thoroughly prepare yourself for success, you'll be more likely to trust yourself to do well in difficult situations. In any activity, there comes the critical moment when you commit yourself to a course of action. Many people fail because they hesitate at this step. For example, a salesperson may feel ready to begin a sales pitch yet hold back from beginning the call. A writer can be prepared to write but delay sitting down at the keyboard. Trust your own plan for reaching the Achievement Zone. If your preparation is good, your chances of success are high. Trust yourself to succeed. Let success happen.

If you have trouble getting started on a project or on a new goal, try the following exercise.

A BURNING DESIRE FOR SUCCESS

If excuses and delays stop you from making changes in your life, here's a tip that should light a fire under you.

Think of the goal you would really love to get started on, if only . . . Make a list of those "Ifs."

If only I had the time

If only I had the talent

I only I knew the right people

If only there weren't so many demands upon me

Keep going. It's *your* list. What ifs (and buts) are holding you back? What excuses are preventing you from starting on your dream goal?

Just one piece of paper should do. Write those excuses down. Take a day or two. No sense rushing a good list.

When you have a good list of ifs take that piece of paper and burn it. That's right, go somewhere where it's safe to light a fire (not under an automatic sprinkler) and burn your list of excuses. Watch it until it's ashes. Sweep those ashes away.

That's it. No more excuses. They're gone. Burned. Kaput. There's nothing to hold you back from starting on your goal. Go for it!

Consistent success comes about when you trust the training and preparation you have done enough to let it happen. Top athletes know that they can't *make* success happen by "trying harder." Instead, they try to reach their Achievement Zone. That's when success becomes likely.

If you try to exert too much control over your performance, it deteriorates. Thinking about the future or worrying about your performance hurts your chances of doing well. A typist who thinks too much about where the fingers should go will actually type more slowly. Excellent performances are almost automatic, they are so relaxed and natural. Athletes often tell me that they perform at their highest level when they "let go." What they are letting go of is their desire to control the outcome of the performance.

Bad performances are sometimes called choking by fans and athletes. Most people believe that choking is caused by lack of "toughness" under pressure. In fact, choking isn't related to motivation, character, or toughness, but to your ability to stay in the Achievement Zone. Instead of trusting yourself to do well and letting your automatic pilot take over, your conscious self tries to stay in control. Because you have to think about your decisions instead of trusting your judgment, you tend to overanalyze situations and react slowly to changing conditions. It shows when your performance gets messed up.

Psychologist Dr. Roy Baumeister from Case Western Reserve University showed that *thinking about* what you are doing doesn't help skilled performance. People playing a commercial game requiring hand-eye coordination were told to think about their hands while playing. They immediately did worse on the game. In another experiment, the psychologist came up to teenagers playing Pac-Man in a video arcade. Kids who got a good score were asked if they would like to play a free game "for research." They all agreed. The psychologist then said, "I want you to get the best score you possibly can, OK? I can only give you one chance, so make it the best you can do." Under this increased "pressure," the players averaged 25 percent lower than they had scored just moments before. They choked!

The young video game players consciously thought about what they were doing and the results they wanted, *instead of focusing 100 percent of their attention on doing it.* Consistent performers know that they must not give in to this tendency. They trust themselves to perform up to expectations and to make the right decisions.

How do you go about letting go of your desire to control the outcome? Simply trust your preparation for reaching the Achievement Zone. Consistency is the skill of remembering to stick to your plan, even in the most pressure-filled moments of your life.

When you're ready to give it your best shot, remind yourself to stay with your own Consistent approach. You might say something to yourself, such as *OK, this is the moment I've prepared for. I'm ready.*

Let's go for it. Or you could remind yourself in a very simple way to trust your preparation. Many of the athletes I work with simply say to themselves, *Now! Do it!* Trust your game plan for success.

Step 3. Expect the Unexpected

Develop a consistent approach to performance, but don't expect that things will always go smoothly. Tammy was a sprinter I worked with leading up to the Barcelona Olympics. As part of her Consistent preparation for her race, she liked to listen to music for the last half hour before starting. She chose inspirational music such as the theme from *Chariots of Fire* or *Rocky*. This helped fire her up for a big race. But on the day of her Olympic semifinal, she unpacked her bag at the race and realized that she had forgotten her tape! What to do?

Fortunately, we had discussed the possibility of this occurring. "Expect the unexpected" was Tammy's motto. She sat in a corner of the dressing room as she usually did, and instead of listening to her cassette, she closed her eyes and hummed the music to herself. Tammy told me later that this was more effective than her tape could ever have been. She imagined scenes from the movies she was thinking about and was more inspired and focused when her race began than usual. She won in sensational fashion.

The lesson I've learned from many such incidents is to anticipate problems in your quest for success. No matter how well you prepare for a project, speech, or game, something unexpected always happens to knock you off balance. The way to handle this is to make preparation for the unexpected *part of your performance plan.* Think about some "what if?" scenarios and imagine how you would handle them. For example:

- What if you allow some time after your presentation for questions, and no one asks any?

As part of your preparation, write down a few questions that you often hear on the subject. If no one asks a question, say something like "Well, a question I often hear from customers is . . ."

▪ What if your preparation for an exam is excellent but they ask a very tough question right away that upsets your Concentration?

Expect that you will be challenged. As part of your exam-taking plan, think about how you will deal with questions that have you stumped. For example, you might plan to leave them until last, so that you have more confidence after answering all the straightforward questions. You can now spend all your remaining time on the tough ones.

▪ What if your day is fully booked with presentations to new customers and potential clients, and something happens at home that upsets you and distracts you?

This is a tough situation, but with your mind/body skills, you can handle it. First, use Productive Analysis to decide if you should take a day off. If the upsetting situation is serious (for example, your child is running a very high fever), it may be more important to reschedule your clients. If you decide to go ahead with the client contacts, decide when you will take care of the home situation. Tonight? Tomorrow? Now put the situation aside and Concentrate 100 percent on doing a great job for your clients. Stay focused by using performance cues. Keep your energy level high with Energizing thoughts. And if you start to worry about what's happening at home, use your Keeping Cool skills to calm down.

You get the idea. There is an effective way to handle every surprise, every roadblock. If you *expect* that you will have problems in achieving your goals, you won't be surprised and flustered when such problems occur. A dramatic example of the power of being prepared for the unexpected occurred at the Summer Olympic Games in 1992. American Trent Dimas was preparing to begin his rings routine in the men's gymnastics competition when he was delayed. The judges were discussing the correct score of the competitor before him. He had to wait for several minutes, which is highly unusual.

Nine times out of ten, athletes delayed by such an unanticipated event begin to panic. I've seen it many times—the athlete begins to worry about the delay, starts to imagine what might go wrong. They tense up and perform poorly. But instead of getting nervous and distracted by the delay, Trent closed his eyes and rehearsed his routine in his mind. Viewers watching the television coverage could see Trent moving his head as he rehearsed the somersaults and special moves he was about to perform. When the signal finally came for him to begin, he opened his eyes and moved into place. Unexpectedly, he gave the performance of his life and won the gold medal, much to the delight of Americans watching the coverage at home.

Trent and his coach had obviously planned for unexpected emergencies. You can, too. You can't predict every roadblock that you will run into, but you can decide how you will react to roadblocks. A great way to handle these frustrating episodes is to take the time to refocus and decide how you will adapt. Rehearse a refocusing approach (see the skill of Emotional Power) for times when you get upset. Make such refocusing a standard part of your plan for effective preparation. If you don't need it, that's great. You can get on with the process of achieving your goals. But if you do need it, you're fully prepared—as always.

The experiences of Bob Foth, John Bertrand, Tammy, Trent Dimas, and many others show that if you can develop a consistent approach to performance, you're more likely to stay in your Achievement Zone. Legendary football coach Paul "Bear" Bryant once said, "Have a plan for everything. A plan for practice, a plan for the game. I try to have a plan and the guts to stick with it no matter what happens." Even in high-pressure situations, when others find it tough to perform at their peak, you will be able to deliver a winning performance if you stick with your game plan for success. Others will marvel at your remarkable confidence. So plan your work, and work your plan.

SUMMARY

How to Learn Consistency

Step 1 ■
Develop Your Own Plan for Success

Step 2 ■
Stick to Your Plan Under Pressure

Step 3 ■
Expect the Unexpected

From the Comfort Zone to the Achievement Zone

My interest in the Achievement Zone was piqued when I was a teenager playing tennis. In those days I had no explanation for the wonderful game I played during a tense final. The search for answers has taken me halfway around the world and has given me a host of memorable experiences. I've learned about what it takes to achieve success from my research, from sharing ideas with other sport psychologists, and from observing successful people in action. But I have learned the most by working with motivated people who are giving it their all to achieve their best. Their honesty and openness in sharing their struggles with me has given me the greatest learning experiences of my life.

Despite all the knowledge we have accumulated, I believe there is much more to learn. The beauty of the search for the Achievement Zone is that the process of self-discovery is ongoing and fulfilling. You will always be the expert on what it takes for **you** to reach your Achievement Zone. I hope you take the knowledge I have shared with you and use it as a building block for your own accomplishments.

If you wish to succeed, you must discover your **personal** Achievement Zone. Recently I found out how hard it can be to succeed at a higher level. There are times when we get complacent about our accomplishments. We think we're doing our very best, when in fact we are capable of much more. Sometimes it takes a slap in the face to wake us up.

In 1993 I received a terrible slap that caused me to reexamine my life work. My brother Chris, just twenty-two months younger than I, died in a tragic accident in Australia. He was only thirty-three. I returned to Australia for the funeral, but was soon back at work. But I was unhappy and confused. Chris and I had been so close growing up, especially playing sports, and now I couldn't believe that he was gone. It was difficult to accept.

As usual, it was Annemarie, my wife, who got me moving forward again. One evening she sat down next to me and asked why I was so unhappy. I mumbled something about losing Chris, but she persisted. "You know Chris would want you to move on with life, to make things happen. What's holding you back?" As we talked, it slowly dawned on me that I deeply wanted to spend time with my parents and siblings. I had never needed them more, and I suspected they needed me. Haltingly, I made the suggestion to Annemarie: "How would you like to spend some time in Australia with the children?"

I was delighted and amazed when she agreed. Although we were very happy in our jobs, we both hold our families dear. She agreed that the time was right for our children to spend a long period with their grandparents. Now I had a goal to pursue. It was the motivation I needed to take a critical look at my life. When I did, I realized that I had fallen into the Comfort Zone in many areas. Even though I had the greatest sport psychology job in the world, I realized that it was time to seek new challenges. I had become too comfortable in my work—I needed to take some risks in order to get back in the Achievement Zone.

This other kind of zone, the Comfort Zone, has little to do with excellence. This is the zone we stay within because it feels comfortable and safe. Inside its boundaries we take no risks. Athletes often have the experience of moving beyond their Comfort Zone and experiencing a sense of panic. A golfer may suddenly realize that he's on his way to shooting a record round and on the next hole he takes triple bogey. He's back within his Comfort Zone.

As Annemarie and I talked about the idea further, we became excited about the possibilities. We both realized that there were several new goals we could pursue in our careers. The final piece of the puzzle fell into place thanks to one of my athlete clients. As she left one day, my client Becky turned back to me and commented, "You know, it's a shame that you get to work with so few athletes. I mean, how many athletes do you see at the Olympic Training Center? There are thousands of athletes out there who could benefit from sport psychology. You should write a book or something."

I had never thought about it, but Becky's suggestion made perfect sense. Now I had a new passion, something I wanted to do with all my heart. So we quit the security of our jobs and moved to Australia for a year. I saw my parents every day and they got a chance to know their two grandchildren. Annemarie was able to spend time building up our consulting practice. And I wrote this book. We were back in the Achievement Zone, and truly happy. I can honestly say that this has been the most wonderful year of my life, despite the sadness that brought us together. My brother is gone, but his memory lives on with all the family.

I found that the only way out of the Comfort Zone was to challenge myself. Why should I have found this surprising? The athletes I work with tell me this every day. They are winners because they refuse to live in the Comfort Zone. They strive to reach their Achievement Zone. You, too, have all the skills you need to be a consistent winner. All that remains is for you to put these mind/body skills into action in pursuit of your dreams. What can stop you?

As I write my final thoughts, I wonder how to encourage you to take up the quest to reach your own Achievement Zone. And my thoughts turn to my years of working within the Olympic movement. One of the great things about being involved in the Olympics is the inspiration the experience provides. There are many ceremonies and symbols associated with the Games that remind us to strive to be our best. One of those symbols is the Olympic flame, which burns in Olympia, Greece, and every two years is brought to a new Games city by a relay of runners. When you next watch that flame being passed along by the relay runners, in Atlanta, or Nagano, or Sydney, think about your own life quest. Is your life flame burning brightly, or do you need to reinvigorate your pursuit of your life goals?

All I can ask of life is to know that I fulfilled my potential. And in order to reach my potential, I must discover my Achievement Zone. When I do, I feel pride and satisfaction in a job well done. And I hope that I can do one thing more. I hope that I can pass on the torch of hope, just like the Olympic runners, by my example. Many Olympic athletes are nourished by that thought, that they provide inspiration to many by their efforts to achieve greatness. My hope is that you will also find nourishment in the quest to achieve success. What can you achieve if you try with all your skills? What goals can you accomplish at work, at home, and at play when you harness all your talent and energy by using the mind/body skills you've learned? And who can you pass the torch on to? Who will you help to succeed?

My search for the Achievement Zone goes on. I hope yours does, too. If the knowledge I have shared helps you reach your life goals, my happiness will be immense.

Helpful Resources

- For more information about sport psychology, a good place to start is the **Association for the Advancement of Applied Sport Psychology** (AAASP). This is a professional organization for sport psychologists. It publishes educational materials about sport psychology for the general public and interested organizations. A list of Certified Consultants in sport psychology is also available through AAASP.

  For information, contact:

  DALE PEASE
  AAASP Publications Director
  University of Houston
  Department of HHP
  Houston, TX
  77204–5331

- For further information on sport psychologists, contact the **Division of Exercise and Sport Psychology.** This group is part of the American Psychological Association. They provide interested students with information on careers in sport psychology and provide general information on new advances in the field. There are over 1,000 members of this group.

For information, contact:

CHRIS CARR, PH.D.
APA Division 47 Secretary
Ohio State University Athletic Department
The Ohio State University Sports Medicine Center
2050 Kenny Road
Columbus, OH
43221

- There is a home page on the World Wide Web for these and other sport psychology organizations. The address is:
    http://spot.colorado.edu/~aaasp/
Or search the Web using the keyword "sport psychology."

Notes

Introduction

Pages 5–6. The study described here is by Dorsey Edmundson and Sean McCann (1995), "Single subject research in sport psychology: The impact of training on elite athletes' use of mental skills."

Overview. Sport Psychology: The Science of Success

Page 8. The quote from Ingrid Kristiansen is from an article by Kenny Moore in *Sports Illustrated*, July 1986, page 20.

Pages 12–13. I've relied most heavily on two areas of evidence in identifying the eight mind/body skills. The first is a series of psychometric studies of athletes I've undertaken over the past eight years. Initially I collaborated with Michael Mahoney, using his Psychological Skills Inventory for Sport (PSIS). My more recent work has been influenced by the psychometric studies of Lew

Hardy, using the Sport-Related Psychological Skills Questionnaire, and Pat Thomas, using the Golf Performance Survey. Together, and with the help of Jeff Bond, we have constructed the Test of Performance Strategies (TOPS), which allows us to assess how athletes use these skills.

I have also been heavily influenced by the work of sport psychologists who have interviewed elite athletes concerning successful strategies in sport. The experiential and qualitative studies of Terry Orlick, John Partington, Dan Gould, Sue Jackson, and others have greatly enhanced our understanding of what it takes to succeed in sport.

Pages 14–15. The test of mind/body skills is adapted from the Test of Performance Strategies (TOPS), with permission.

The First Skill. Action Focus: Achieve Your Life Goals

Pages 24–26. There is a large body of research on the differences between a result focus and an action focus in sport. A good summary of relevant research can be found in the chapter "The Jekyll/Hyde nature of goals: Reconceptualizing goal setting in sport," by Damon Burton. It can be found in the book *Advances in Sport Psychology* by Thelma Horn, published by Human Kinetics in 1992.

I've also drawn heavily on the work of sport psychology researchers Joan Duda and Diane Gill.

Page 25. A fascinating account of the rise of Wal-Mart is presented in *Sam Walton: The Inside Story of America's Richest Man,* by Vance Trimble, published in 1990 by Signet.

Page 32. The study of weight training was conducted by Howard Hall and Anthony Byrne: "Goal setting in sport: Clarifying recent anomalies," published in the *Journal of Sport and Exercise Psychology,* 1988, volume 10, pages 184–198.

The Second Skill.
Creative Thinking: Use the Power of Your Imagination

Page 63. We published this study in 1985 in the journal *Cognitive Research and Therapy,* volume 9, pages 335–341. It was called "The effects of positive and negative imagery on motor skill performance."

Pages 63–64. I have thoroughly reviewed the evidence for the effects of imagination on performance in a chapter called "Imagery and Mental Practice," written with Doug Jowdy and published in Thelma Horn's book *Advances in Sport Psychology,* 1992, by Human Kinetics, Champaign, Illinois.

Page 66. The quote from Albert Einstein is from the book *Einstein: The Life and Times* by R. W. Clark, published by World in 1971, page 87.

Page 66. William Tancred competed for Great Britain in the discus in the 1968 and 1972 Olympic Games. He threw 51.74 meters in 1968 and 57.24 meters in 1972. We met when he visited the Olympic Training Center in Colorado Springs as part of his Churchill Scholarship.

The Third Skill.
Productive Analysis: Think Like a Winner

Pages 78–80. Readers interested in the differences between verbal styles of thought and imaginal thinking can find an explanation of the "dual code" theory in the book by Alan Paivio *Imagery and Verbal Processes,* published by Holt, Rinehart and Winston in 1971. He calls the two types of human thought the pictorial and the verbal.

Page 82. The study of tennis players was carried out by Judy Van Raalte, Britton Brewer, Patricia Rivera, and Albert Petitpas: "The relationship between observable self-talk and competitive junior tennis players' match performances," published in 1994 in the *Journal of Sport and Exercise Psychology,* volume 16, pages 400–415.

Pages 82–83. The study of what athletes were thinking during performance was carried out by Susan Jackson and Glyn Roberts: "Positive performance states of athletes: Toward a conceptual understanding of peak performance," published in 1992 in the journal *The Sport Psychologist,* volume 6, pages 156–171.

Page 90. A good summary of research relevant to the skill of Productive Analysis can be found in the chapter by Linda Bunker,

Jean Williams, and Nate Zinnser, "Cognitive Techniques for Improving Performance and Building Confidence" in the book *Applied Sport Psychology*, second edition, by Jean Williams, published by Mayfield in 1993.

Page 94. The study of competitive skiers was carried out by Rotella, Gansneder, Ojala and Billing: "Cognitions and coping strategies of elite skiers: An exploratory study of young developing athletes," published in the *Journal of Sport Psychology* in 1980, volume 4, pages 350–354.

Page 97. The research of Ron Smith and Frank Smoll is described in their book *Children and Youth Sport: A Biopsychological Perspective*, published in 1995 by Brown & Benchmark.

The Fourth Skill.

Keeping Cool: Stay Calm in Pressure Situations

Page 124. Centering is described in the book *Attention Control Training* by Robert Nideffer and Roger Sharpe, published in 1978 by Wideview Books, New York.

Page 128. For a clear guide to autogenic training (and for many other relaxation methods), take a look at *The Relaxation and Stress Reduction Workbook* by Martha Davis, Elizabeth Robbins Eshelman, and Matthew McKay. Now in its third edition, it is published by New Harbinger.

Page 133. The so-called catastrophe model of performance anxiety is described by Graham Jones and Lew Hardy in their book *Stress and Performance in Sport*, published in 1990 by Wiley. A good summary of other research relevant to the skill of Keeping Cool is contained in the chapter "The Arousal-Athletic Performance Relationship: Current Status and Future Directions," by Dan Gould and Vikki Krane. It can be found in the book *Advances in Sport Psychology* by Thelma Horn, published by Human Kinetics in 1992.

Page 133. The study of soccer players was carried out by Ian Maynard, Brian Hemmings, and Lawrence Warwick-Evans: "The effects of a somatic intervention strategy on competitive state anxiety and performance in semiprofessional soccer players," published in 1995 in *The Sport Psychologist*, volume 9, pages 51–64.

The Fifth Skill. Concentration: Focus on Performance

Page 144. The study of archers shooting is by Dan Landers, Steve Petruzello, Walter Salazar, Debra Crews, Karla Kubitz, Timothy Gannon, and Myungwoo Han. Called "The influence of electrocortical biofeedback on performance in pre-elite archers," it was published in 1991 in *Medicine and Science in Sport and Exercise*, volume 23, pages 123–128.

Page 144. The study of karate athletes was carried out by David Collins, Graham Powell, and Ian Davies. "An electroencephalographic study of hemispheric processing patterns during karate performance," published in 1990 in the *Journal of Sport and Exercise Psychology*, volume 12, pages 223–234.

Page 144. A good summary of other research relevant to the skill of Concentration is contained in the chapter "Attention and Athletic Performance: An Integrated Approach." It's written by Stephen Boutcher and can be found in the book *Advances in Sport Psychology* by Thelma Horn, published by Human Kinetics in 1992.

Pages 144–145. The theory of flow is described in Mihaly Csikszentmihalyi's book *Flow: The Psychology of Optimal Experience*, published in 1990 by Harper & Row.

Page 146. The beneficial effects of meditation were explored by the Harvard researcher Herbert Benson and described in his book *The Relaxation Response*, published in 1975 by Morrow. An excellent resource is *How to Meditate* by Lawrence LeShan, published in 1974 by Bantam Books.

Page 151. Jack Nicklaus's thoughts on the mental side of golf are reported in the article "My strongest weapon," by Jack Nicklaus and Ken Bowden, published in 1993 in *Golf* magazine, December, page 44–49.

Page 152. The study of elite skiers was carried out by Rotella,

Gansneder, Ojala, and Billing: "Cognitions and coping strategies of elite skiers: An exploratory study of young developing athletes," and was published in the *Journal of Sport Psychology* in 1980, volume 4, pages 350–354.

Page 158. The story of the inventive assembly-line worker is drawn from page 39 of Mihaly Csikszentmihalyi's book *Flow: The Psychology of Optimal Experience*, published in 1990 by Harper & Row.

Page 159. Bruce Abernethy's research is reported in the study "Expertise, visual search and information pick-up in squash," published in 1990 in the journal *Perception,* volume 19, pages 63–77. Similar findings emerged in his study with David Russell, "Expert-Novice differences in an applied selective attention task." This was published in the *Journal of Sport Psychology,* 1987, volume 9, pages 326–345.

Pages 163–164. The quote from the figure skater is from page 168 of a paper by Sue Jackson called "Athletes in flow: A qualitative investigation of flow states in elite figure skaters." It was published in the *Journal of Applied Sport Psychology,* volume 4, pages 161–180. The other quotes are from my research.

The Sixth Skill. Emotional Power:
Respond Effectively to Strong Feelings

Page 170. Nick Price was quoted in an Associated Press article, "Price in lead but not in 'zone,'" in the New York *Daily News,* August 15, 1994, page 93.

Some of the research relevant to the skill of Emotional Power is summarized in a chapter by Chris Madden, "Ways of Coping," which can be found in the book *Sport Psychology: Theory, Applications and Issues* by Tony Morris and Jeff Summers. It was published in 1995 by John Wiley and Sons.

The Seventh Skill.
Energizing: Turn It On When You Really Need It

Pages 191–192. The interview with Billy Mills is from the book *Tales of Gold* by Lewis Carlson and John Fogarty. It was published by

Contemporary Books, Chicago, Illinois, in 1987. The quotes are from pages 350–351.

Pages 194–195. The story of Carl and Marlene was shared with me by my colleague David Campbell from the Center for Creative Leadership in Colorado Springs. He writes about it in his column "Inklings," in the newsletter *Issues and Observations,* 1994, volume 14, pages 9–10.

Page 202. The research of Martin Moore-Ede is found in his book *The Twenty-four Hour Society,* published in 1993 by Random House.

Page 205. The study of candy eaters versus walkers was conducted by Robert Thayer from California State University and reported in an article called "Energy, tiredness, and tension effects of a sugar snack versus moderate exercise." It was published in volume 52 of the *Journal of Personality and Social Psychology* in 1987, pages 119–125.

Page 208. Bob Anderson's book *Stretching* was published in 1980 by Shelter Publications.

Pages 209–210. The exercise intensity rating method is called the Borg Rating of Perceived Exertion (RPE). It is described in detail in an article by G.A.V. Borg, "Perceived exertion: A note on history and methods," published in the journal *Medicine and Science in Sports and Exercise,* 1973, volume 5, pages 90–93.

Page 212. The work of Francis Crick is described in the book *Apprentices of Wonder: Inside the Neural Network Revolution,* by William Allman. It was published by Bantam in 1989.

Page 215. The book *Eating for Peak Performance* (1994), Second Edition, by Rosemary Stanton is published by Allen & Unwin.

Page 217. The book *Weight Loss Through Persistence* is published by New Harbinger Press, 1994. Dan Kirschenbaum is not only a weight-control expert but a fine sport psychologist. He was the U.S. Olympic Committee's sport psychologist at the 1991 Olympic Festival in Los Angeles.

The Eighth Skill. Consistency: Prepare for Success

Page 223. The study of elite golfers was reported in an article by Patrick Cohn, "An exploratory study on peak performance in golf," published in *The Sport Psychologist,* 1991, volume 5, pages 1–14.

Page 225. This research was reported in a series of studies by Debra Crews and Steve Boutcher. The studies are:

"An observational analysis of professional female golfers during tournament play," published in the *Journal of Sport Behavior,* 1987, volume 9, pages 51–58.

"The effects of structured preshot behaviors on beginning golf performance," published in *Perceptual and Motor Skills,* 1986, volume 62, pages 291–294.

"The effect of a preshot routine on a well-learned skill," published in the *International Journal of Sport Psychology,* 1987, volume 18, pages 30–39.

Pages 228–230. I was helped in my development of the intervention I used with Grant by conversations with Dan Kirschenbaum of the Center for Behavioral Medicine–Chicago and Northwestern University Medical School, and with Dave Cook of the University of Kansas.

Page 234. The article describing this research is by Terry Orlick and John Partington, "Mental links to excellence," published in the journal *The Sport Psychologist* in 1988, volume 2, pages 105–130.

Pages 235–237. This story is excerpted from *Born to Win: A Lifelong Struggle to Capture the America's Cup* by John Bertrand and Patrick Robinson. Published in New York by Hearst Marine Books, 1985. The quotes are from pages 53–55.

Page 239. Roy Baumeister described this research with game players in a paper called "Choking under pressure: Self-consciousness and paradoxical effects of incentives on skillful performance," published in the *Journal of Personality and Social Psychology* in 1984, volume 46, pages 610–620.

Acknowledgments

Many people have touched my life and helped in different ways with this project. I know I can't thank them all, but I want to acknowledge some special debts of gratitude.

- Special thanks to my mentors in sport psychology who have guided my work during the various stages of my career. Their example and enthusiasm has always been an inspiration to me. Thank you, Jerry May, Rob Woolfolk, David Feigley, Jack Atthowe, Budd Ferrante, Dan Landers, Dick Suinn, Dan Gould, Charlie Hardy, Deb Feltz, and Bill Morgan.

- My deepest appreciation to all the athletes I've been privileged to work alongside.

- Coaches must have a deep understanding of psychology in order to be successful, and I've been lucky to learn by working with some of the best. I have great respect and admiration for those who have given so much to the Olympic Training Centers over the years. Thank you, Nancy Myrick, Dragomir Cioroslan, Ric Purser, Ron Brandt, Lenny McCaigue,

Craig Griffin, Bob Mitchell, Fred Borden, Mike Larimer, and Kathy Casey.

■ I have so many friends who have made my time with the Olympic movement so memorable. Thanks to you all. A special thanks to the folks in Sport Science and Technology whose hard work on behalf of athletes everywhere is an inspiration, especially Jay T., Sarah, Steve, Tanya, Jeff, Tom, Karla, and Tim. Also, there are many volunteers within the Olympic family who generously give of their time to encourage the spirit of Olympism—they get little recognition, but they deserve our heartfelt thanks.

■ In a field as young as sport psychology there must be trailblazers who show the rest of us the way. My work would not have been possible without the pioneering efforts of Bruce Ogilvie, Dorothy Harris, Jim Loehr, Terry Orlick, and Bob Nideffer, and I salute their hard work and perseverance.

■ I especially want to thank three distinguished scholars from abroad with whom I am fortunate to work: Lew Hardy, a delightful Yorkshireman from the University of Bangor in Wales; Pat Thomas, a keen mind and a dear friend, from Griffith University in Australia; and Jeff Bond, the founding father of applied sport psychology at the Australian Institute of Sport in Canberra. Their work and research has been an inspiration to me.

■ Many sport psychologists have helped throughout my career, and I'm indebted to them. My work has been shaped in so many ways by their writings, teaching, and in discussions with them. Many thanks to them, and especially to: Andy Meyers, Dan Kirschenbaum, Al Petitpas, Steve Danish, Robert McKelvain, Maureen Weiss, Diane Gill, Dave Coppel, Bruce Hale, Dave Yukelson, John Anderson, Ken Ravizza, Charles Garfield, Denis Waitley, Sue Jackson, Jean Williams, Carole Oglesby, Ron Smith, Michael Sachs, Mark Andersen, Bob Weinberg, Hugh Armstrong, Michael Asken, Steve Heyman, Rob Stainback, Dave Cook, Bob Rotella, Tara Scanlan, Frank Gardner, Cal Botterill, Larry Brawley, Linda Bunker, Damon Burton, Richard Cox, Debra Crews, Jim Davis, Rod Dishman, Joan Duda, Rich Fenker, Burt Giges, Dan Begel, Rich Gordin, Wayne Harris, John Heil, Keith Henschen, Andy Jacobs, Marlin Mackenzie, Penny McCullagh, Rick McGuire, James Millhouse, Mimi Murray, Bill Parham, Kay Porter, Jim Reardon, Glyn Roberts, Bob Schleser, John Silva, Wes Sime, Bob Singer, Aynsley Smith, Frank Smoll, Bill Straub, Jim Taylor, Robin Vealey, Betty Wenz,

Jim Whelan, Tommie Lee White, and Len Zaichowsky. I'm lucky to have so many of you as good friends.

■ A special debt of gratitude to the students who have studied this fascinating area with me. Along the way, they have helped many athletes and coaches, and their unwavering commitment to the athletes they serve has been an inspiration. I have learned from them in a myriad of ways. Thanks, Mike Lesser, Susan Walters, Doug Jowdy, Vance Tammen, Mike Greenspan, Shirley Durstchi, Kirsten Peterson, Chris Carr, Bob Swoap, Jerri Gibson, Jean Muerhoff, Suzie Tuffey, Frank Perna, Megan Neyer, Dorsey Edmundson, and Renee Parker. And Alan Budney, Rob Stainback, and the many volunteers who helped out in the crunch.

■ Sincere thanks to Rainer Martens, who pointed me in the right direction when I was thinking about writing this book.

■ This book was typed on a Macintosh Powerbook using Microsoft Word, and I've grown to love that combination.

■ My love and thanks to Mum and Dad for everything. Especially for teaching me many of the mind/body skills at an early age. Thanks to Kieran and Jenny for their love and support. And also to Bob and Rosemarie, whose generosity of spirit is fantastic.

■ I can't express enough thanks to Sean McCann, who is a great friend and a brilliant sport psychologist. One-on-one with athletes, he's the best, and I always discover new things when I'm with him. Also, he was a huge help with this book—a motivator and a kind critic.

■ I learned a great deal about the practical side of writing books and getting them published during this project. Thank you, Mort Janklow, for having the idea and sticking with me. Thanks, Eric Simonoff, for all your help throughout. And thank you, Stacy Creamer. I can't believe the time you've spent editing and revising these pages. Your excellence made all the difference.

■ To my two wonderful sources of energy and inspiration, my children. My love and thanks to Theresa, who would ignore her mother's warnings "not to bother me" and sneak into my study to give me her pretty drawings while I was writing. And love and thanks to Bryan, who was never too busy to indulge me in a quick video game when I needed a break.

■ And most of all, to my wife, Annemarie. She was an inexhaustible fountain of support and encouragement. She read every word many times. She adds meaning to my every moment.

About the Author

SHANE MURPHY is the co-founder of GOLD MEDAL PSYCHOLOGICAL CONSULTANTS, a company devoted to assisting organizations and individuals achieve excellence. From 1987 to 1994 he was the chief sport psychologist for the United States Olympic Committee in Colorado Springs. Gold Medal Psychological Consultants works with small and large companies, not-for-profit and educational organizations, and sport organizations. Workshops and training seminars on the eight mind/body skills for success are available. Consultants also work with individuals who have performance concerns. Other programs include:

- Lectures
- Coaching
- Weekend retreats
- Effective team building
- Parent education workshops
- Custom on-site consultation

For program information or assistance, write to:

GOLD MEDAL PSYCHOLOGICAL CONSULTANTS
500B Monroe Turnpike, Suite 106
Monroe, CT 06468

Or call (203) 459-0515. Send e-mail to TheZoneDoc@aol.com

Dr. Murphy's previous publication is *Sport Psychology Interventions*, published by Human Kinetics, Champaign, Illinois, in 1995. It is a practical book for helping professionals who work with athletes at any level. Dr. Murphy is the editor of the volume, whose chapters are contributed by leading sport psychologists.